THE BRITISH

vs

KENYA'S MAU MAU

"It's a fine book; it should be on history bookshelves in libraries, & should be required reading at least in college history classes."

—Mary Thorne Kelley- Advance copy Reviewer

A Memoir of Family and Community

Also By Wanjirũ Warama

BOOKS

Unexpected America

Entangled in America

Years of Shame (a 3-story novella)

Beyond Conscious Self (a two-story Novelette)

The Colonized and the Scramble for Africa

The Colonized and Kenya's Mau Mau Revolt – Re-titled (The British vs Kenya's Mau Mau)

The British vs Kenya's Mau Mau

The British Colonial Farm

SHORT STORIES

New Beginning: Why Religion Never Appealed to Me Until...

ANTHOLOGY

Why Religion Never Appealed to Me Until... (Personal Essay – San Diego Writers and Editors Guild 2023 Anthology)

THE BRITISH

— vs —

KENYA'S MAU MAU

Wanjirũ Warama

Athomi Books
San Diego, California, USA

Wanjirũwarama.com

United States of America – December 2024

Library of Congress Control Number: 2024924273

ISBN: Paperback: 978-1-954423-10-7

E-book: 978-1-954423-11-4

Cover Design by ebooklaunch.com

Published by Athomi Books
8064 Allison Ave, #684, La Mesa, California, 91942
United States of America

First Edition

DEDICATION

I dedicate this book to the three generations of Kenyans who fought for Kenya's self-determination and independence.

The first generation of men and women who sacrificed life and limb and resisted the British invasion.

The second generation who, as children, witnessed Kenya's invasion and loss of their families and communities' lands. The they grew up, they formed and organized regional and national political associations and campaigned in Kenya and England. They suffered discrimination, harassment, and detentions. At the same time, they hoped and waited for the colonial government to respect their constitution and the rule of law, listen to reason, apply fair land distribution, and stop discrimination and human rights violations

The third generation: Kenya Land and Freedom Army (KLFA) and World War II veterans—who joined forces with KLFA members. Tired of waiting for natives' decades-old activism to soften the hearts of their oppressors and make changes, this generation's warriors abandoned their families, took to the forests, and waged guerrilla warfare against the British colonizers. Without KLFA (popularly known as the Mau Mau) members' impatience, patriotism, and courage, I would be illiterate today.

Map of Kenya and its Neighbors

TABLE OF CONTENTS

THE PEASANT WORKERS

ON THE ROAD AGAIN

Translations

Gĩkũyũ	Kiswahili	English
Gĩkũyũ	Kikuyu	Tribe or language
Mũgĩkũyũ	Mkikuyu	a Kikuyu person
Agĩkũyũ	Wakikuyu	Kikuyu people
Mũthũngũ	mzungu	white man
Mũtũmia mũthũngũ	Bibi Mzungu	A white woman
Athũngũ	wazungu	white people
Ngoi	–	baby carrier
Kĩondo	chondo	woven basket
Ngai	Mungu	God

NOTE: Swahili – popular term; Kiswahili-grammatical term

If ever there were a time for a candle in the darkness, this would be it. Using a spark of hope, kindle the flame of love, ignite the light of peace, and feed the flame of justice.

—Melanie Davis

Author's Note

The nonfiction stories and events throughout this book took place from 1956 to 1959. My community, parents, siblings, and I learned, witnessed, or experienced them except for those incidents I have referenced from historical accounts.

Quotations came from my recollections, reconstruction, and statements by relatives and others, which I have translated from Gĩkũyũ or Kiswahili to English or quoted from reference books.

I use actual names except in a handful of cases where my community and I did not know the individuals' names or the names were hard to pronounce and, in time, faded from collective memories.

It's helpful to remind ourselves that, like the rest of the continent of Africa, the country of Kenya is a complex place with diverse cultures. This book covers only a small part of my family and my Gĩkũyũ community.

The reader should also note that Meru, Embu, Mbeere, and Tharaka, small Bantu tribes and close cousins of the Gĩkũyũ, got sucked into the Mau Mau revolt. Although historical events are included, this book is a family and community memoir that focuses on the Gĩkũyũ peasant farmworkers and Kikuyuland, the epicenter of the Mau Mau activities.

*For legibility, I have avoided using italics as much as possible.

THE PEASANT WORKERS

Chapter 1

THE PEASANT GIRL

I had a happy childhood for a girl born to peasant parents on a colonial farm in Kenya. Despite colonial constraints, for over twenty years, my family had lived in a version of a Gĩkũyũ homestead with no neighbors for at least two miles. Then, the activism that had smoldered in the country since the British invasion reached its zenith in 1952. The Mau Mau freedom fighters took to the forest, and the colonial government declared a state of emergency in the entire country, arrested and detained community leaders, and soon introduced villagization.

They moved Gĩkũyũ people in droves to the *native reserve*, Kikuyuland. The ones landowners hand-picked to remain on the farms, like my family, were clustered into villages.

When the landowner moved my family to the fenced village in mid-1953, we ended up with a smaller homestead than our first one at Kĩrĩma-inĩ.

Like the rest in the village, the new homestead comprised round mud-and-thatch cottages with conical roofs that came in various sizes, built around a courtyard. The granary, woven with vines and built on stilts, and the chicken coop completed the compound.

It nestled behind the village close to a woven chain-link fence about nine to ten feet high, reinforced by long posts and barbed wire. Several rows of slanting barbed wire crowned the top. The fence surrounded the village, leaving a pedestrian entrance to the east.

After living in the fenced village for about a year, I learned that Kamunge—the British landowner who owned or managed the farm—and his family lived one mile eastward, across Tindaress River, in a sprawling farmhouse set on about ten acres.

My parents and other farmworkers did not know his real name or could not pronounce it, so they called him Kamunge or Mūthūngū (white man).

A third of the farm hugged Jumatatu Mountain Range to the north and east, dense with trees of all ages, heights, and thicknesses and enough overgrowth to qualify as a forest. It provided adjacent lands with a temperate climate, perfect for coffee bushes.

The other two-thirds was a savanna with wire grass, shrubs, and weeds, with trees and bushes growing in lonely patches, distances apart or in clusters, broken only by wheat or maize plantations or cow pens.

But for the people's encroachment, the farm was a complete ecosystem. It supported many animals—antelopes, wild pigs, hyenas, monkeys, skunks, rabbits, squirrels, tortoises, snakes, ostriches, wildfowl, and millions and millions of birds and insects.

Before we moved to the fenced village, Kamunge did not object to where his farmworkers lived on the farm as long as they worked for him nine hours a day, six days a week.

After two years in the village and in the middle of the British versus Mau Mau war, people had come to terms with a dusk-to-dawn curfew and a war seemingly with no end on the horizon.

Chapter 2

TROUBLE IN THE HOMELAND

The stand-off between a faction of the natives and the British colonizers that mired Kenya had been long coming. Overt and covert political activism had always been a part of the Agĩkũyũ and other Kenyan communities since the British landed on their shores, invaded, and conquered Kenya, micronation after micronation, at the end of the nineteenth century.

After the British conquerors appropriated the land and zoned the country, they divided their spoils into Crown Lands, White Highlands, and Missionary Lands. They allocated commercial plots in townships to Indians. And relegated the natives to what they termed *native reserves* (Kikuyuland), similar to Navajo, Cherokee, and other native reservations in the United States.

That settled, the conquerors upgraded the country into a British colony in 1920.

Despite the entrenched colonizers, native activists were not deterred or lost hope. Year after year, they continued to campaign against the seizure of their lands, inhumane treatment, skewed laws, violation of their civil and human rights, and colonialism.

Meanwhile, Agĩkũyũ veterans returned home from World War II, and the colonizers discarded them like old boots. On their way out, the veterans got an earful to keep their mouths shut on what they saw or did on the front lines.

Distressed and broken, they rejoined their communities with no jobs or prospects. When they settled into their new reality, the veterans joined the non-pacifists, the self-trained patriots, Kenya Land and Freedom Army (KLFA). The now-stronger group (popularly known as the Mau Mau) elevated their political activism and agitation to a higher military level. They demanded the return of their seized lands and independence and cared nil about the British constitution that the colonizers had imposed on the natives.

The Mau Mau agitation peaked in October 1952 when they took arms and waged guerilla warfare against the British colonizers. The fighters camped in forests around Mt. Kenya, Nyandarua Mountain Range, and other scattered hideouts.

For eight years, every man, woman, and child from the so-called trouble-maker tribe—the Gĩkũyũ—in rags or suits became suspect. They had to be contained and suppressed.

On October 20, 1952, the colonial government arrested and detained 129 prominent Agĩkũyũ political activists without trial. The mainstream group, which had mainly campaigned for independence through democratic means based on the colonial constitution, included Jomo Kenyatta (the man who later became the first president of Kenya), other Gĩkũyũ political activists, and a handful of their non-Gĩkũyũ supporters.

The following day, October 21, the colonial governor, Sir Evelyn Baring, declared a state of emergency in the entire country. This gave the governor a free hand to pass policies and decrees and throw anyone who seemed suspect into detention.

First, to cut communication between the freedom fighters and the rest of the masses, the colonial government rounded up and detained those suspected of supporting and spreading Mau Mau's aspirations, including journalists, publishers, teachers, office workers, and community leaders.

Second, the government needed to contain the Gĩkũyũ population for easier control. However, the colonizers needed the agrarian tribe to produce food for the nation and cash crops for export to England and elsewhere and to support the war effort against the freedom fighters.

So, the colonial government decreed that the private sector, the civil service, and landowners should pick employees they wanted to keep. Those employees needed to be trustworthy, loyal, and untainted by Mau Mau politics.

At Kamunge's farm, where my family lived, as in all the other farms, the chosen Agĩkũyũ male workers had to sign loyalty agreements, agreeing to stick with the farm and defend it during the rebellion.

Then, the officials and the police, in coordination with landowners and other employers, mobilized the whole country, hauled the rest of the Gĩkũyũ farmworkers and employees in processions of canopy-less lorries, and put them in camps to sort out *in* which *native reserve* (Nyeri, Mũrang'a, or Kĩambuu) they or their parents originated. This was called the Exodus.

After officials determined who went where, they corralled the entire Gĩkũyũ tribe into "protected" villages in the native reserve, town neighborhoods, and on colonial farms.

As a final precaution, the government officials screened them to ensure those chosen to remain on the farms did not harbor the slightest streak of self-determination or allegiance to the Mau Mau. The police came at intervals in the middle of the night and hauled groups of men and women away to detention camps. They confined them for at least a week. The officials interrogated and tortured many of them when they denied they had taken the Mau Mau loyalty oath.

The European landowners then clustered their "loyal" employees into secure villages per the government's directive.

Baba was among the employees chosen to remain on the farm. Unless he chose otherwise (a chosen employee could opt to join the Exodus), it meant his two families—first and second—would also stay on the farm.

Staying put was a simple choice for my father. Apart from a brief forced military stint in World War I when he was a young man, Kamunge's farm was his first actual job since he left his home in Nyeri, now part of the so-called native reserve or Kikuyuland, in the latter part of the 1920s.

He had sworn never to return to Nyeri; it reminded him of the colonial turmoil he had undergone as a boy and young man. On the farm, he was answerable to only one man, not subject to the whims of the militant colonial authorities like in Kikuyuland.

Although he would not admit it, Baba identified with the farm and felt a part of it. He started as a field hand and did other odd jobs for about ten years before Kamunge promoted him to *nyabaara*, supervisor, even without knowing how to read and write.

By then, Baba and his family had lived at Kĩrĩma-inĩ, a private homestead, for almost a quarter of a century. He felt settled enough to practice polygamy for ten years before it became too burdensome, and he and his first wife, Kaguyu, called it quits in 1947.

Kaguyu and her grown children could have remained on the farm through Baba despite the divorce. As Gĩkũyũ proverb says, "A woman with a child is never divorced."

But Baba's first family preferred to leave.

Even Waigwa, that family's second son in his late twenties, whom Kamunge had picked to stay behind on his own accord, refused to stay. Not emotionally invested in the farm like Baba, and with news of people his age fighting in the forest, Waigwa preferred to get closer to the action. He hated to remain at

Kamunge's beck and call, "Like *a wife*," he said. Three years later, he regretted that decision when his life hung in the balance.

Mami's birth family did not have a choice. Major Holman, the owner of the farm where they worked, two farms away from Kamunge's farm, had let them go. My grandmother Nyandia left with her husband, Ndurumo, and their adult son, my uncle Eliud "Njoroge" Machira Ndurumo, his wife, a toddler son, and a baby daughter. Ndurumo's two brothers—Thimbara and Mũbĩa and their families—stayed behind at Major Stein's farm, next door to Kamunge's.

Baba's second and much younger family—Mami and us children—remained with him on Kamunge's farm.

Chapter 3

WE THE LUCKY ONES

By 1955, about two years after we moved to the fenced village, the Mau Mau revolt against the British colonizers had reached its pinnacle, and my parents and other villagers—like the rest of the country—were coping with their new reality of a dusk-to-dawn curfew. Besides the regular IDs, the colonial government had decreed that every man from the age of sixteen carry a passbook in which employers noted their permissions. Villagers could leave the farm for necessities only after they received permission from Kamunge.

Young and old shuffled toward him, one at a time, as if approaching a king seated on a throne—shoulders hunched, hat clutched in one hand, and a passbook in the other. Kamunge asked about the purpose of the requested trip and the destination before he gave permission and noted it in the passbook.

A handful of younger employees, sick of having to kowtow before another man, dodged protocol, sneaked to Njeki's Shopping Center or elsewhere, broke curfew, and suffered jail terms if caught.

Boys who looked sixteen, like my brother David—a mere one year younger—worried about passbooks, jail, and other restrictions.

Despite the hassle, however, we were the lucky ones.

Although Kamunge, like any white man, made sure farmworkers followed colonial laws and restrictions, the police did not enter his farm, a private property, to bother the villagers unless he called them. This insulated my parents and my two teenage brothers somewhat, unlike people in Kikuyuland who dealt with or witnessed all manner of atrocities—from searches to murders.

*

Stories trickled down to us by word of mouth or from occasional letters—self-censored in case they fell into the wrong hands—about the upheaval in Kikuyuland. From overhearing my parents and my mother's friends speak, I could tell life had become dire for the people living there.

The war tide had also turned in favor of the colonizers. Besides having bombs and superior weapons, the colonizers extracted valuable information from captured Mau Mau senior members who turned traitors in exchange for their own lives. These traitors, conversant with the inner workings of the Mau Mau, divulged critical information that enabled the colonial government forces to infiltrate the Mau Mau leadership at the highest level.

The colonial forces then set new tragedies in motion. They dropped bombs, planted landmines, and burned forests around Mt. Kenya, Nyandarua Mountain Range, and other Mau Mau strongholds to smoke out the so-called "terrorists."

One traitor snitched on Dedan Kĩmaathi, the Mau Mau leader. The colonial government forces tracked him down and shot him in the leg. They captured him on October 20, 1956.

A plane dropped fliers around Kamunge's farm and elsewhere, showing a shirtless man in handcuffs lying on his back in a hospital bed. Because of Mr. Kĩmaathi's seniority, unlike other Mau Mau members who met with the noose in days or weeks, the colonial government hanged him within four months on February 18, 1957.

No matter the news, rumors, or war anxieties, my family and other farmworkers hunkered down, focused on farm work and their families, and kept on living.

Our homestead had become our best refuge. But as I grew older, I learned that was a mere façade because, although Baba was a good provider, his anger had always simmered like a deep, ripple-less river. He let it out when he occasionally turned violent in his homestead, the only place he could control.

Otherwise, our household ran like any mini-organization with a specific division of labor. Even I, a peasant girl of about eight years, held an important spot in our family.

Chapter 4

DIVISION OF LABOR

As a peasant girl, I was a mini version of my mother, minus her pierced earlobes. Besides playing and running quick errands for my parents, my primary job was babysitting. Up to about age eight and a half, it had never occurred to me I needed an education.

Baba and Mami remained quiet about it. I cannot say for sure, but I doubt they planned to take me to school or, perhaps, they never thought about it. Whatever the case, school had to wait, at least until I did more growing to realize I needed to advocate for myself.

Meanwhile, because it was wartime, we just existed—my family and I. We focused on survival. Now I understand my parents shielded us from the gory details until the news got too close to home. My life revolved around my mother, caring for my little brother while we hung out in our courtyard, where my younger siblings and I spent most of our daytime hours.

On my way to age nine, I was the oldest of the five children still at home and the one in charge of my brother Waweru, who followed Morry, the first one I had babysat since I was six. During the day, except for when I fed Waweru, or he sat, or I played a game, he stayed—asleep or awake—wrapped behind my back in a ngoi, a baby carrier, reinforced with a piece of cloth.

Several children from families Mami approved came to play with us. We jumped rope, played hopscotch and hide-and-seek, and imitated picking coffee cherries on shrubs by Mami's vegetable garden. There was already a distinct separation between boys and girls. When we girls remained at home minding our younger siblings, the boys went goat herding. They hunted, using slingshots, played football with balls they made from rags, "drove" or rolled on tractor trails the toy lorries they constructed from wires or rolled *mĩgara,* bicycle tires, swam in the river, or ganged up on each other.

I longed for late afternoons when Mami returned; I loved it when she was home. About mid-afternoon, I looked at my shadow to assess how long I needed to wait before she returned. (I could tell time by the sun's location and my shadow.) If she delayed, especially if she stopped at our garden on her way home, our entire household faltered but recovered when she appeared at the entrance.

I can still picture my mother hunched over, carrying a bag of produce on her back if she had passed by our garden or a load of firewood with kĩondo bags on top. After she unloaded, she first suckled the littlest of the brood, who was already tired of feeding on substitutes in plastic bottles.

Then Mami started on her evening job of preparing our supper.

We spent our evenings in a series of sameness, each cherished after the day's toil as a goat herder, family mule, or in the fields. Nyũmba, Mami's circular thatched house, the biggest in our courtyard, faced south, while the goats' cottage across the courtyard faced north. Mami sat on one side of the fire pit, and we, her brood, occupied the other two sides, seated on low benches or the dirt floor.

Mami stoked the fire to keep it robust. The fire crackled or threw puffs of smoke that my siblings and I fanned off our faces.

Mami needed as many hands as a mama octopus to attend to all six of us. And that wasn't even counting Simon and David, who were already teenagers and in school. Simon often visited teenage friends somewhere in the village, and David was at boarding school.

Joseph, two years my senior and the family's chief goat herder, led the campsite group as we teased, challenged, and shared gossip while we kept vigil for Mami's cooking.

Joseph spent his days wherever he and other goat herders took their animals to pasture under the hot equatorial sun. He had no lunch unless he foraged for wild fruit during the day. He complained the most about hunger. He asked us to listen to his stomach rumble, and if we disputed his claim of being the hungriest, he wiggled and massaged his midriff for Mami's benefit.

Mami brushed off food complaints with a light-hearted comment to avoid getting distracted or ignored them altogether. She usually cooked a mound of ugali, a dense porridge made from maize meal and eaten with greens, meat stew, or a combination. She first sautéed collard greens—and sometimes the leaves of black-eyed peas, cabbage, managu (which tasted bitter like arugula), or various other greens—with onions, tomatoes, oil, and salt. Then, she prepared ugali. Or she prepared a meal from the mixture of maize and beans or the various peas she had boiled the previous night.

Evenings were an idle period for Baba except during the weeding season when he worked in our garden after work. Before dark, he occasionally minded a sickly goat in the courtyard or checked and pruned the tobacco crops he grew behind the granary. When our maize matured, he guarded it against wild pigs two to three days a week at night until it dried. And every so often, he sneaked out at night to harvest his beehives.

Baba did not bother to get permission to sneak into the woods or our garden after dark. Despite the landowners' long reach, he did not expect Kamunge to call the police to his private property to crouch under bushes, ready to pounce on an occasional lone peasant.

Because my parents followed the Gĩkũyũ custom of separate houses for a husband and wife, Baba sat in his thingira—his private, one-bedroom man-castle, smaller than Mami's nyũmba. It faced west with a view of the whole courtyard. He sat on a three-legged stool, his feet resting on top of his black sandals made from vehicle tires and his hat on his folded knee in case he needed to wear them to go outdoors. His feet seemed too tender to step on dirt like the rest of the family.

He poked and prodded his own fire that Mami or one of my brothers had made for him earlier in the evening. Meanwhile, he thought, pondered, reminisced, and waited for food like the rest of us.

We all waited.

Impatience, hunger, and tea thirst festered. We behaved as if Mami had left a part of herself cooking during the day while she labored in any of Kamunge's plantations.

"Someone can die of thirst in this homestead," Baba called out whenever his shot of caffeine failed to appear on time after he arrived home from work. It never occurred to us we all waited for the one person who had already clocked more than an entire day's work.

But Mami never complained.

She adhered to our family's division of labor. She even took on another job to help Baba revive his tobacco business.

Chapter 5

SIDE HUSTLE

Baba was the second person in his family to work for someone else. (His sister, Aunt Julia, was the first.) He had always worked for himself until he reached a point when he had to look for a job if he wanted to stop the harassment and consequences of being a tax dodger.

Back when he lived in Nyeri, part of the Agĩkũyũ homeland, the colonizers' government required every man to pay a "hut tax" in British shillings and pounds based on the number of houses a man had on his homestead. The aim was to force natives into the new cash economy and paid employment. But, because the men had no cash to pay the taxes, they had no alternative but to leave their communities and look for jobs in labor-starved European farms (or in towns)—the very land that had been taken from them and their communities.

That was how my father ended up—80 miles away from his homeland—at Kamunge's farm in the mid or late-1920s. He later returned, fetched his family—Kaguyu and four children—and brought them to Kamunge's farm.

Baba did whatever Kamunge asked of him. He dug, planted coffee and other crops, picked coffee cherries, hung onto a plow they called a harrow (an iron arm-like piece with a point pulled by two oxen) that dug up the fields, and did other odd jobs. As a mailman, he walked miles to Solai railway station to deliver and pick up mail.

Ten years later, when he proved responsible and trustworthy and did not need supervision, Kamunge appointed Baba as nyabaara, an overseer.

With a secure job, wife, children, goats, and a compound of his own a distance from neighbors, Baba felt settled enough to address his flailing marriage.

Despite bringing forth four more children and losing one of them as a toddler, his marriage to Kaguyu had continued to wither since their long separation. He stepped out of his monogamous marriage and married Nyachuru, daughter of Ndurumo, aka Mami, as his second wife. This changed the dynamics of his turbulent marriage and, from his perspective, stabilized his homestead.

With his homestead running relatively smoothly, Baba started a side business—curing and selling hides and skins. Afterward, he expanded the business when he started growing tobacco.

He ran the two businesses for at least seven years at Kĩrĩmaini, with Mami as his helper.

When we moved to the fenced village in mid-1953, the instability of moving twice within four months sidelined his business. He restarted the businesses after the family adjusted to village life and war restrictions.

He bought hides and skins from the market or the occasional goat he slaughtered for our family. After he dried and treated the skins, he carved them into long straps and the remnants into short ones, which he sold to women at the market or to drop-in customers at home. Women knew not to haggle with Baba. He preferred the haggler to buy on credit if she lived in our village instead of offering a discount on the already low price.

Women used the long straps to tie bundles of firewood or water containers they carried on their backs. They used the shorter straps for kĩondo bags or ngoi (baby carriers). Also, in a twisted way, parents folded those same straps to assault their children in the name of discipline.

Besides his hides business, Baba grew tobacco on a patch of land between our homestead and the towering fence that surrounded our village. He planted, weeded, pruned, harvested, cured, and chopped tobacco leaves into bits. He dried them on gunnysacks spread on one or two wood planks he set behind the granary.

When the tobacco turned crispy, he bundled it into cylinders using dry banana fronds he bought at the market. Each cylinder measured about a foot and a half long and four inches in diameter.

To my brothers' relief, as with hides and skins, Baba shouldered the tobacco production by himself lest the quality suffer.

But he could not do it all.

First, men did not grind tobacco. Second, even if they did, Baba lacked the skill. But from the beginning, back in kĩrĩma-inĩ, he had an able and willing partner in Mami, who had ground millet flour for porridge since she was a young woman. She could whip snuff tobacco to satisfy the fussiest nose.

She used a rectangular stone that weighed close to twenty pounds, elevated at its head—like the one she used to grind millet with—so she could grind downward.

Mami set the stone between nyũmba and the chicken coop so the smell would carry away from the courtyard. She knelt at the head, held her smaller rectangular two-pound grinder, and ground away.

When the tobacco turned into powder, she sprinkled oil, then ground, sprinkled, and ground again until it turned into a fine, dark powder like dark chocolate. It took her about two hours to grind the amount she needed for the market. Like tobacco addicts, Mami sneezed and coughed intermittently throughout the production.

While she ground the snuff, Baba sorted and bundled his straps, ready for the market the following day. They went to the big Bahati market on the Sunday after payday, about a six-mile walk through shortcuts. On the second Sunday, before villagers got too broke to spare shillings and pennies, my parents went to Kabazi Market, four miles over Jumatatu Mountain Range.

The money came in coins we called gathendi (one cent—next to worthless), king'otore (ten cents), gathumuni (fifty cents), and shiringi (100 cents that made one shilling, the most common currency used by the villagers. The shilling is next to worthless today). The banknotes came in fives, tens, twenties, and hundreds. But my parents' retail, like the rest of the sellers, was too small to use paper money; they transacted business in coins. I might have seen a twenty-shilling note in my teen years because of school fees, but I never saw a hundred-shilling note before my early twenties.

At the open-air market, Baba hung his straps over a rod on low posts and spread them lengthwise at the periphery, where people with oversized items sold their wares.

Mami joined the other sellers—all women in those days—at the center of the market. She measured the snuff in two sizes of tiny spoons, depending on a customer's budget. The biggest spoon measured half a teaspoon, and the other about a quarter.

She scooped the snuff into quartered khaki paper or dry banana fronds, folded, and tied each packet with a sisal string. The tiny bundles looked like little brown charms.

To save time during high demand, Mami prepared a heap of charms before customers arrived. If a customer brought his own container, she scooped the snuff into it.

As with his hides and skins, Baba did not allow haggling or loans for tobacco; he hated asking for his money from people with little or none to spare. A man either paid in full or went without. But he could do nothing about an occasional sneaky man who asked to sample the snuff, got enough to satisfy his craving, and afterward had no money to buy.

When my parents returned from the market, Baba headed to thingira and Mami to nyũmba. After Mami unloaded her baskets, she went to thingira carrying the small cloth pouch where she had put shillings from tobacco sales. She emptied the coins on the floor, counted them, and gave them to Baba as bank depositors do. Baba did not recount the money.

He took all the income from tobacco & hides and skins, while Mami kept only the measly few coins from her occasional sales of surplus eggs. She used the money to supplement her plantation wages to buy necessities like our clothes, toiletries, and items we did not grow.

My mother boasted about the potency of her snuff. She claimed consumers bought other sellers' tobacco only after hers ran out. She also bragged about Baba's leather straps, which she claimed were so smooth they never scratched women's skins.

"If he runs out," she said, "they wait for his next supply."

Baba gave her a sidelong look with a hint of a smile but said nothing.

We did not know what our father did with his money or when Kamunge paid him. We only knew when it was payday because Tugen migrant workers who lived outside the village drank alcohol and raised a ruckus while they danced and sang their melodious traditional dance and songs.

It took me a long time to debunk my belief that my father and all men kept surplus cash and did not concern themselves with paydays.

Years later, Mami told us—before Baba had several children in school—he saved most of his wages and business income for about two months before depositing the money at the post office. When he did not get a Saturday off, he asked Kamunge to deposit for him.

He opened his first and only savings account at the General Post Office in Nakuru, our hometown, in 1932—about five years before he and Mami married.

Chapter 6

MONKEY SEE MONKEY DO

My father broke the addict's first rule—he got high on his own supply. Throughout my formative years, I watched him inhale a pinch of snuff tobacco or, occasionally, roll dry, unprocessed bits into a ball and stick it under his left lower lip.

Mami, an incidental participant, sneezed and coughed while she processed the snuff. Afterward, the cough continued until her lungs cleared, only to repeat the circle a week or two later.

A year after she quit the business, she developed severe pain in her ribcage that put her in the hospital for close to a month. The doctor had to pump out slimy liquid twice. Henceforth, she suffered permanent bouts of coughs and sneezes that got triggered by smoke, dust, a laugh, cold weather, or other unidentifiable causes.

But my mother remained ignorant of the cause of her discomfort. Even when she sold tobacco, she could not stand its addictive results. Her face tightened, and her brow wrinkled as she turned away whenever she saw a tobacco addict pinch his nose to eject brown stuff or shoot generous spit to the ground.

She shooed us children away when she ground the tobacco. Sometimes, she concentrated on her work too much to notice me when I hung around close by. If the wind came, it blew snuff into my eyes. They stung worse than the assault from wood smoke. Because of the sting and Mami's coughs, snuff never appealed to me.

But the tobacco bits Baba processed fascinated me. I admired how tenderly he tended to his crops. He carefully prepared a bed for small seedlings, transferred them to his part of the garden, pulled weeds, pruned, cured, cut, dried, and, finally, enjoyed a tiny ball of the product under his lip.

After two years of watching him enjoy his product, my mind developed an urge to copy him, a nudge I could not tame. To satisfy the urge, I first needed supply. Luckily for me, I did not have to steal the bits. No matter how meticulously Baba handled his tobacco, accidents happened, and he left bits strewn about.

I also needed privacy. But in a household littered with children, even on Sundays, privacy came at a premium. Every time Baba prepared his tobacco during the week, that Sunday, a sibling hovered around. I suppressed my urge until the next time.

But one market Sunday mid-morning, I was the only one loitering in the courtyard but for the chickens and possibly the cat. With nothing to occupy myself, the idea of tobacco resurfaced.

This is it! I thought.

I ambled behind the granary. My bare feet stepped gingerly, not to soil the tobacco bits now that they were worth putting in my mouth. I ran my eyes over the ground where my father had packaged his cache two days prior. I spotted generous big and small bits, but before I collected what I needed, I turned my back toward the granary and glanced from side to side. Satisfied no one lurked nearby, I bent and picked up several meaty bits. In case they crumbled, I carefully rolled them, stuck the ball between my lower lip and gum, and then inched away from the crime scene toward a more secure private spot behind the chicken coop.

Baba and the other men left their lumps in place for hours, but without the luxury of time, before a sibling sauntered along, I planned to keep mine for only minutes before I shot a stream of rich, brown spit.

As I write this, the scene replays in my mind where, within seconds, intense bitterness tortures my under lip; to get relief, I swish my mouth twice. My tobacco bump moves, which disturbs its integrity. It crumbles into smaller and smaller bits.

Bitter, frothy juice pools and inflames my mouth.

Heat rushes to my face, which makes me mix up the protocol. Instead of aborting my experiment and emptying my mouth, I tighten my body, fists clenched, and swallow the rich froth in one gulp. It lands on my stomach and jolts me like an eruption. My insides rumble and convulse as my whole body goes aflame. I become dizzy. I plop down. I cannot handle that either. I drop to my side, my head resting on my forearm. Within a short time, I pass out or fall asleep.

Did I go under for one hour? Two hours? I could not tell.

Between the heat from the sun and the ingested tobacco, I woke up sweaty, lethargic, and sick. My body still smoldered, but it did not convulse anymore. I shuffled to the shade under the eaves of nyũmba.

I have no recollection of whether I moved to another spot.

With the tobacco attack and without a bite of food or a sip of water, dehydration wreaked havoc in my body. I remained in ill health by the time the family regrouped. While Mami prepared supper and we sat around the fire, I sat stone quiet, wishing I could lie down.

"You are awfully quiet," Mami said. "Are you sick?"

"No," I said, thankful I had outgrown forehead and chest temperature tests with her backhand. I was then more concerned about her finding out what I had done than how terrible my body and my peeled inner lip felt.

When she refocused on her cooking and my siblings jabbered, I feigned sleepiness and excused myself. None of us ever skipped supper, but with Mami's attention spread thin, my action did not register with her.

Minutes before I dozed off, I vowed never to touch any form of tobacco again; that vow has remained as firm as back then.

Chapter 7

TRAIN THEM YOUNG

At age six, I babysat my brother Morry when Mami took me to her plantation job, where she picked coffee cherries. But when we moved to the village, on higher ground, she determined I could not handle the incline and left me at home. She carried Morry on her back to wherever she worked.

When I turned seven-and-a-half, Mami put Morry on a bottle and left him at home with me. From then on, I minded him six days a week.

The older my siblings and I got, the more Mami piled errands on us.

She sent us to fetch items only a few feet from her, or from the courtyard, or the village—hold the baby, wash the plates, take this to so and so, take this to *thoguo*, and on and on.

She rarely said thoguo, your father. Instead, she referred to Baba as Me-thingira (the ones in thingira). Like my siblings, I got used to it and never gave it a thought. In my teen years, I realized she used the plural term instead of the singular Arĩthingira, but I never thought to ask her why. So far, my later inquiries have yielded no explanation.

Mami hated to borrow things (Baba never did), but once in a long while, if we ran out of salt or tea leaves before she got her weekly pay and sent one of my brothers to Patel's General Store, she sent us—mainly the girls, my sister Tabitha and me—to borrow from one of her three friends.

When we borrowed, it usually took place between friends. But one woman outside Mami's circle of friends borrowed from us, contrary to this protocol. She borrowed everything she needed to make tea by sending each of her children to a different house. She also borrowed items outside the norm, like cooking oil. Whenever the woman sent her child to borrow at our house, Mami gave with her jaws tightened or said we did not have extra.

According to Mami and her friends, the woman lived a disorganized life; she even ran out of seeds during planting season and had to exchange labor with whoever had seeds to spare.

Although I expected my parents to send us on errands, I hated it and pouted when Mami sent me back-to-back as if I were her only child. Like the boys, I kept score and protested, "You haven't sent Joseph." (Now I realize that, like Mami sent us girls, Baba sent boys only; he sent us girls only if the boys were not home.)

"I saw him before I sent you," Mami would say. "You don't complain when I give you food first, do you?"

But I knew she realized her gaffe when she sent a different person on the next errand.

Since I turned eight, Mami sent me to draw water from the hydrant outside the village gate, a block from our homestead. Kamunge had piped in the water from Tindaress River untreated. (I never drank clear, pure water in all my childhood.) At least the thick vegetation had strained off most of the dirt generated by floods, crossings, baths, and clothing washes upstream on the other side of Jumatatu Mountain.

Before plastics came to Solai, like the other children, I fetched water in one of our old gallon cans with stubborn paint trails on the outside that Mami could not clean off. I am unsure where the gallons came from; perhaps they were discards from Kamunge, the only person who could have used paint on the farm.

I loved the freedom of strolling through the village to fetch water.

As I grew older, I sometimes hauled a basin of dirty dishes on my head and washed them by the hydrant. I placed them to drain on the nearby grass as if on a dish rack. Meanwhile, I played and socialized with children or picked up village gossip from women who came to wash theirs. Mami never washed at the hydrant; it wasted too much time, she said.

I especially liked to wash her floral china saucers and cups behind her back. I doubt any other household in the village owned china because every time a woman saw me wash, she eyed the china or made an envious comment. I do not know how I learned that people valued china more than the white-coated or basic-colored enamel plates and mugs we used. Coupled with Baba's glorified overseer job, I believed my family teetered a rung above the others in the village. That thought gave me a whiff of satisfaction.

The cups and saucers came from a set that Baba's youngest sister, Aunt Julia, gave Mami as a marriage gift when she and Baba visited her in Nairobi in 1937.

When they returned home to the farm, pride of ownership was the only value Mami derived from the gift. She stored the china in a wooden trunk in her bedroom. For years, such fancy dishes were unsuitable for our family. Even if they were appropriate, Mami had no cupboard to display china. It is also doubtful she expected her children to grow into people who could use such dishes. Europeans drank from such cups on saucers, not Africans. Mami and Baba, and everybody else in the village, drank from colored enamel mugs—one serving, no budget or time for refills.

But Mami's careful storage could not save the doomed dishes. My every wash ended up with a piece less.

My sister Tabitha must have sneaked to do the special washes, too. By the time Kamunge ordered my family to move again, only six saucers remained. But Mami lacked the energy to fuss; managing a homestead, her garden, children, and a job had trivialized such matters.

Over the years, though, she shared two highlights of their Nairobi trip. The first was their visit to the whites-only Nairobi Racecourse, where Aunt Julia took the newlyweds. Despite the gift of tickets and permission from a prominent white doctor that Aunt Julia worked for, the racecourse gatekeeper shooed her and her visitors off to wait on the side grassy area, away from the gate.

After every white spectator had settled in, before the race started, Aunt Julia approached the gate and presented the tickets to the gatekeepers again. The attendant who had shooed them aside begrudgingly let them in. Of course, they could not venture to the stands, lest it made the colonizers uncomfortable enough to eject them from the racecourse or involve the police. They sat on the grass between the stands and endured hostile stares.

Mami understood about people occupying other people's lands, but she never got a grip on why white people treated other humans so poorly. To her, that was misbehaving like small children. "Why the fuss?" she said years later. "Watching animals gallop? Waste of time and money."

Nevertheless, she enjoyed the trip because she went to Nairobi, the big city, for the first time and received a special gift. And to top it all, Aunt Julia took them to watch a dance at Kaloleni Dance Hall. Mami talked about that dance—dancers' shoes massaging the floor—to her dying day. Baba never mentioned that trip.

*

There were certain chores for boys, such as helping Baba slaughter a goat or accompanying him to harvest one of the six beehives he hung from trees scattered in the woods. Joseph enjoyed these tasks because he liked to get into things, and if Simon could do it, why not him? He never seemed to consider that Simon was four years older than him.

Simon liked the slaughter and the harvest but not other tasks like minding children, cooking, or gardening. Because David, the oldest, had gone to boarding school, and we girls were not old enough to handle "female" chores, Baba and Mami piled on Simon too many adult responsibilities.

My younger brothers—Gĩthũi and Morry—cared little for goat slaughter. As they grew older, they loved honey harvesting because of the novelty of a night out. But, at eight and ten, they were of little help. Baba caved in once and let Gĩthũi tag along. Curious, he closed in to see how a beehive looked inside as Baba sliced out slabs of honeycombs, but he shrieked and backed off into the darkness when he was stung. He proved a nuisance and a distraction.

David was of no help, either. He went along on these outings while on his school holiday. But boarding school had made him soft, happy to stay in the rear, wincing, afraid of the unavoidable occasional stings.

If Kamunge knew about the beehives, he kept it to himself. He and Baba went way back to when Kamunge worked as a struggling young farm manager. According to Baba, he and Kamunge had worked side-by-side on some projects.

On harvest day, Baba covered himself from head to toe in a homemade bee protective suit. It made him look like a bushman astronaut. Simon dressed similarly but did not cover himself as well. They gathered their tools and left at dusk. One tool I recall was a compact roll of twigs measuring about two feet long and three inches in diameter. I understood that Baba lit the roll and smoked the bees to the back of the hive while he dislodged slabs of honey cobs at the front.

Mami cooked in Baba's thingira on such days while she and we children waited for their return.

When they came and unloaded the honeycombs, Baba sorted them into two grades, each in a separate basin. From watching him, I figured that the more caramel-colored and clearer the honey, the sweeter and the higher the grade.

He gave each of us about a three-inch square of honeycomb from the high-grade basin. It must have contained multiple teaspoons of honey.

Honey dripped down my arm at intervals, and I licked it fast. To stop the leak, I bit the edges. It intrigued me when the honey became unpalatable. After I ate half of the square, its sweetness cloyed in my throat and turned into a tangy bitterness. I saved the rest.

Baba did not eat honey. He used it with water, sugar, and mũratina (luffa) to brew beer.

*

When I turned eleven and Tabitha nine, Mami said, "You are old enough to wash your own clothes." My clothes turned out okay, but as for Tabitha's, only she could claim they were clean. She put her clothes in a basin half-full of water, lathered them with soap, kneaded a handful of times, replaced the water once, and hung them. Because of the tropical sun, tiny, soapy bubbles shimmered all over her clothes before they dried.

When Gĩthũi's turn came—the child who shunned chores like a disease—he skipped the soap altogether, dipped his clothes in a basin of water, pressed a few times to submerge them, and with no dry patches left, he pulled the clothes out and hung them.

"My children can now wash their own clothes," Mami bragged to a friend or two.

But I saw her sneak to the fence several times to retrieve and rewash our clothes.

Chapter 8

BEYOND HUNTERS AND GATHERERS

Mami cooked in nyũmba for two years after we moved to the fenced village. She then started cooking supper half the time in thingira to save on firewood.

Because we had no refrigeration, we ate fresh, whole foods that she boiled, stewed, steamed, stir-fried, or roasted. These included maize, regular potatoes (Irish potatoes), sweet potatoes, all sorts of beans, peas, black-eyed peas, njahĩ (white-eyed peas), lima beans, millet, pigeon peas aka Gĩkũyũ peas, various greens, fermented or fresh mixture of maize and millet porridge, and grits.

When we grew old enough to help plant and garden, we munched on raw carrots, tomatoes, sweet potatoes, or chewed maize stalks like sugarcane after Mami pulled out the ears.

I loved grits mixed with beans. But it took enormous labor to produce grits before mills came to Solai. Mami first soaked dry maize kernels overnight. She then put the first bunch in a ndĩrĩ, a wood stump holed on top like a mortar, dug a foot or more into the ground, and about three feet above the ground. She pounded the kernels with a wooden pin that measured three to four feet long. Meanwhile, we children romped in the courtyard or ran errands for her—before Tabitha and I grew old enough to help her pound.

To lighten the labor, sometimes her friends came to help. Two to four women synchronized the pounding like jugglers. They sang and talked as they pounded, which turned the Saturday afternoon festive for the women and us children.

Mami rinsed the now-quartered or smaller bits of kernels and removed the fibrous skin (pericarp), ready for the second pounding. By the fourth round, she had grits and a rinse of thick white liquid. She cooked the grits with beans.

For the liquid, she stirred in millet flour, put it in one or two four-gallon gourds, and stored it to ferment before she cooked the porridge. When she had help, she ended up with three or more gourds. Baba liked the sour porridge, but we children drank it for the first few days and stopped when it became too sour.

When mills came after we moved to our second village in the early 1960s, Mami sent one or two of us children to get maize ground at Major Stein's farm on the other side of Jumatatu Mountain Range, three miles away.

We could have used Kamunge's free mill by his huge storage barn, about fifty yards from his colonial house, but the mill didn't grind grits; it ground maize to flour only.

Mami grew vegetables at our large plot and on the plot next to Baba's tobacco, between the fence and our homestead. Our main vegetables included onions, tomatoes, collards, pumpkin leaves, kahūrūra, black-eyed pea leaves, and cabbage. The wild ones included bitter managu, wild stinging nettles, mushrooms, slimy terere, togotia, and tharageti.

Terere, a fast grower, was ready to eat shortly after the first rains, before the other greens. The few times we ate it, my siblings and I liked it, although we never admitted it because people claimed only the very poor ate it. My family did not think that label applied to us. (Nowadays, I have spotted people growing patches of terere, but that kind isn't as slimy as I remember.)

Mami, like the rest of the women, rarely used spices apart from salt and oil and occasional curry powder. She always used onion, tomatoes, red pepper, and salt for sausage stuffing. Sometimes, she spiced tea with ginger or cinnamon.

We loved our mother's cooking. But her cabbage turned out so bland that even our goats, who sneaked up on us and stole our food when we left it outdoors, could have frowned at it.

To cook cabbage, Mami fried onions in oil. When they browned, she added tomatoes. In a minute, she put in chopped cabbage, added salt, and stirred the mixture a few times. When it started sticking to the pot, instead of reducing the fire by pulling out the firewood, she added water and covered the pot. We ended up with overcooked, soggy cabbage soaked in tasteless liquid. The dish turned out passable when, once in a long while, Mami improved it with beef cubes.

On the same plot by the fence, Mami also grew sweet potatoes (with purple or white skin), which we call Gĩkũyũ potatoes, or simply ngwachĩ. They grew so abundantly that they reared their tips above ground, which tripped us when we walked through the garden.

She also grew pumpkins for their leaves and fruit. One pumpkin grew too big for one person to carry the short distance to our courtyard. Two young men hauled it, balanced on a burlap sack stretcher like a patient. When they put it down, one man claimed the pumpkin weighed at least one hundred pounds. Another said it could win an award.

I gawked at the man in wonder; not gone to school yet, I had never heard of a competition, let alone one for food.

Several people came to marvel at Mami's wonder. She talked and grinned with pride as if she had used a special skill to grow the pumpkin. My dear mother could not have been happier if she had won a prize.

*

We were mostly vegetarians but binged on meat when Baba slaughtered a goat. Or at Christmas time, when Kamunge shot a cow or two and got his workers to slaughter and distribute chunks of meat to his workers. Our only other meat came from an occasional two-pounder of beef Baba bought at Njeki's Shopping Center or when he let Mami slaughter a chicken.

Although she single-handedly cared for the chickens—from eggs to chicks to chickens--Mami controlled only the eggs. Otherwise, Baba had a total say over people and animals in our homestead unless a child became bratty. Then Baba told Mami, "Do you see how your child behaves?"

Mami needed to ask his permission before she slaughtered a chicken. She either felt shy about asking, or her responsibilities distracted her. We, therefore, rarely ate chicken, and when we did, we savored it as a delicacy.

It did not help that Baba called chickens "birds," "bush animals," or "wildlife." These were things he never ate and hence forgot we missed the delicacy.

Fish and pork did not exist in Solai, a state that endures. Tindaress River, the only body of water around, had no fish. Besides, Gĩkũyũ people never ate wildlife that lived on land, let alone animals in lakes and rivers. I ate fish for the first time years later, at the age of twenty.

Pigs were nonexistent, too. When I ate pork as an adult, I never liked its taste. But I loved sausages sold at fast-food joints.

We hated January, February, and half of March when the equatorial sun scorched the land bare. Some families foraged for food during these months, looking for wild greens on riverbanks. Or they ate plain boiled dry maize or grits without beans. During that period, many children suffered from malnutrition. According to Mami, thin, brown hair and potbellies signaled starvation.

Word went around that eating mole meat for a month treated potbelly disease (kwashiorkor) faster than hospital medicine.

I saw no mole "medicine," but Mami said a man in our village trapped moles for his sickly son, and the boy recovered. Meanwhile, everybody remained ignorant—and many still are—that lack of protein caused the disease along with scruffy, ashy bodies and slow or stunted growth. Nowadays, malnutrition may include ballooned bodies because of sugar and carbohydrate overload.

Mami was adamant that her children not suffer from malnutrition. But with limited time to cook wholesome traditional Gĩkũyũ foods, and with our hungry eyes on her, she cooked in a hurry just to fill our stomachs. Other times, the stomachs did not get full when she brought home from the garden only a few vegetables or other foods than we needed.

Ignorance played a part, too: No one learned what comprised a balanced diet—this was something they never had to think about before colonization because they had access to a variety of foods. Now, too many mouths to feed and restrictions on what Africans could grow caused malnutrition.

Although my siblings and I suffered from malnutrition and slow growth, we never fell sick because of it or suffered noticeable hunger signs.

To her credit, Mami remained vigilant as she prepared for those unproductive months, something I saw no other mother in the village do.

During months of plenty, she collected every edible vegetable she could spare and dried it. These included collard greens, pumpkin leaves, black-eyed pea leaves, stinging nettles, and mushrooms.

My siblings and I liked mushrooms because of their chewy texture. They tasted almost like meat, we claimed. But we disliked the other dried vegetables They never got soft or tasty, no matter how Mami spiced them. My brother Joseph nicknamed them kauka (dry). Whenever someone said, "We are eating ugali with kauka," a chorus of moans and groans followed.

I hated kauka as much as Mami's soggy cabbage.

Years later, my mother still celebrated her kauka ingenuity.

For soggy cabbage, she excused herself by saying, "Nobody knew how to cook cabbage well in those days."

Chapter 9

RETAIL PURCHASES

Besides Mami's vegetable-drying ingenuity, Kamunge's son, Kang'oro, took it upon himself to advise Baba on nutrition.

Baba knew Kang'oro since birth. He saw him attend school in Kenya and leave for more schooling in England, a typical practice of British landowners back then. They sent their children to European-only elite primary or high schools in Kenya, such as Prince of Wales (now Nairobi School), and then sent them to England for higher education.

After the young men returned to Kenya, they eased into jobs as military elites, administrators, and landowners. When it came time to marry, the men returned to England to court women who did not frown at life in a new, untamed frontier.

Studying abroad gave the eligible bachelors a bigger pool to choose from instead of relying on the limited number of pioneer daughters, helped keep ties with the homeland, and boosted the European population in Kenya.

Were the young women meekly following along? Hardly. Many women commoners could not resist the idea of native servants waiting on them as if they were royals.

*

Baba lost track of Kang'oro's progress, and we never learned whether he attended college when he left for England.

But in time, as his father became older, Kang'oro assumed in stages the entire farm management. Baba now dealt with Kang'oro, the second generation. The two met at least twice a week when Kang'oro dropped in at job sites or sent for Baba to discuss the needed projects. When the two got familiar with each other, he advised Baba on ways to enhance his family's nutrition.

He told Baba about commercial baby foods and how they freed mothers from the burden of carrying babies around when they worked.

Ignorant of our ways, Kang'oro overlooked (or did not concern himself with) babies who breastfed throughout the day or babysitters like me, who got held back from school.

He also advised my father on the economy of buying household supplies in bulk. Baba had to take Kang'oro's word for it. He knew nothing about domestic affairs or running a household. Although better informed on nutrition than Baba, Kang'oro knew zero on how to run a Gĩkũyũ home. But when he went to Nakuru town, he decided what merchandise our family needed, bought the items, and deducted the cost from Baba's wages at the end of the month.

For starters, Baba came from work carrying two plastic packets of powdered milk and a baby bottle.

To feed Morry, now over a year old, Mami mixed two tablespoons of powdered milk with the unfiltered water Kamunge piped from Tindaress River for his employees' convenience.

Now that she had an alternative way of feeding him, Mami left Morry at home in my care. Three hospital stays soon followed. Morry fought for his life for that entire year before he insisted on using a mug like us older children.

Mami never learned why Morry threw up from both ends of his little body. In those days, doctors never shared with parents what they or their children ailed from. I doubt they connected contamination with the feeding bottles because, during the bottle-feeding campaign, after hospital stays, medics sent mothers home with powdered milk and feeding bottles.

Two years later, my brother Waweru dealt with similar bottles. During one of his hospital visits, with our mother not available, the doctor admitted me, too, at nine years old so I could mind him. During our stay, the nurses and women with sickly children pitied us, ". . . the poor children," they said as if we were orphans. The women reverted to sneaky side glances when they learned the whereabouts of our mother.

Mami lay in another ward, ailing from throbs in her rib cage, the time the doctor pumped out thick liquid on two occasions, and the aftermath led her to develop a chronic cough like a smoker.

When my second and last sister, Wairimu, came along three years after Waweru, my mother had become accustomed to the convenience of powdered milk. Baba soon upgraded it to canned milk called *Similac*. Contamination and Mami's worry about her sick children hung around our household until the children became strong enough to withstand the germs or for Mami to wean them.

*

On another occasion, Baba brought a big, colorful box that he handed to one of us before he entered his thingira. "It's for the baby," he said. "Give it to your mother."

Mami eyed the package; she did not seem to recognize it. Because she was busy with the evening meal, she kept the package until the following day.

The following day, Mami held the baby while she looked at the package. We crowded around her, happy our father could afford such colorful, modern food from the store. Mami squinted while she turned the box this way and that, front and back, eyeing the mysterious images and words. We could not help her; none of us could read.

She opened the box and put a handful of chips in her palm, felt them with her fingers, trying to figure out how to feed dry chips to her toothless baby.

Even if someone could read the English instructions and the baby could eat such food, Mami still would have used the unfiltered water with a touch of brown. We had no milk to speak of except for the imitation—the daily quart Kamunge assigned to each head of household. He had the milk skimmed off its last drop of fat. It resembled light white-colored water we called mathache. Women said it was unfit for babies.

To our delight, Mami doled out fistfuls of the cornflakes to us several times a week until she emptied the box.

Why did Kang'oro make suggestions without knowing about our family's situation?

Like every colonizer, he swam in ignorance about us and our ways. Mami suckled us for two years and fed us protein-rich porridge during our second year. I cannot help thinking it came down to shillings and cents.

If Mami, the overseer's wife, fed her baby from a bottle, she could have worked her plantation job without a baby to slow her. This, Kang'oro may have hoped, would entice other mothers to leave their babies at home.

But why did Baba go along?

His ego swelled when his employer singled him out for such advice. Besides, Baba must have become curious about the healthy foods he heard white people fed their babies and wanted the same for his own children.

Because of the cost, at least back then, the experiment failed to catch on.

*

Next, Baba brought a three-quarter-foot bronze-colored grinder, funnel at the top, spout on the side, and a handle on the opposite side like the one that cranked Kamunge's tractor. Kang'oro explained to Baba how the grinder worked, using the kitchen or pidgin Kiswahili that the colonized and the colonizers communicated in. But he forgot to tell Baba about the baby foods Mami needed to grind. The grinder stayed in thingira like a useless toy.

Then, it found its purpose when someone gave Mami half a pound of dry coffee beans (or perhaps she stole it while she worked at the factory's stretches of drying tables). Coffee was one of the cash crops the colonial government did not allow Africans to grow. If someone got caught with coffee, they got prosecuted for theft and got their salary reduced or lost their job or all three.

Despite that, Mami roasted her windfall in a karai—a wok she cooked ugali in—and used a wooden spatula to turn the beans back and forth until they turned chocolate brown. She cooled them before she fed them into the grinder's funnel. When she cranked the handle, the grinder spouted the darkest coffee I had ever seen. By then, its aroma had spread far and wide; a person could inhale it a block away. Because we children did not drink caffeine, the mere breaths of the enticing aroma sufficed, which was a treat nonetheless. To this day, I enjoy the aroma, not the coffee.

If Mami heard noises outdoors while she enjoyed her brew, she turned her head and perked her ears, fearing Baba might return before the aroma dissipated.

The rich aroma never wafted through our courtyard again. I suppose Mami weighed the pleasure of drinking "free" coffee versus the stress of concealing it. I suspect she buried the rest of the coffee or gave it to a woman whose husband looked the other way about such matters.

Our poor grinder became useless again.

Because Mami could not mention the one-shot grinder's success, she lamented the loss of money and gave up on it. But Baba wanted to try it one more time. He ground his dry tobacco bits with disastrous results. The bits stuck to the roller and clogged the mortar. After a click of his tongue or two, he used a sharp twig to remove the tobacco lumps. There ended the grinder's chance to serve our household.

In time, it disappeared, perhaps to give service elsewhere. I never saw it when we moved to our next village.

Chapter 10

BULK BUYING ETCETERA

Baba and Kang'oro dabbled in bulk purchases on three occasions. The first time my father returned home after work balancing, on his left shoulder, a carton of two dozen foot-long beige bars of soap. Another day, he brought a four-gallon tin of lard and, finally, a similar tin of sugar.

The supplies lasted a long, long time. Meanwhile, I agonized for half a year about Baba letting me attend school and campaigned for it the other half, and we still had not depleted the three items. Without many clothes to wash, soap lasted the longest. Lard must have lasted as long because Mami mainly boiled, steamed, or roasted most of our foods. Sugar lasted the shortest because Baba and Mami, besides an occasional visitor, drank tea twice a day.

Except for the few sips of leftover tea Mami gave us to taste, we children did not drink tea before we grew up and left home. But it was not for health reasons; our parents could not afford it. But even with all that sugar, children not drinking tea was the norm. Instead, Mami gave us mugs of maize flour porridge laced with millet flour with no sugar. Sometimes, she put in mathache milk she had left over. To this day, if I drink (or eat) porridge, I add milk but never sugar.

As I write this, most Kenyan children have become tea addicts. They start with breakfast of tea and bread—with or without margarine for town children—or with ugali, or sweet potatoes, or other carbs for rural children. The tea is laden with caffeine and sugar and drunk at least twice daily. I have seen some of my young relatives get cranky or suffer withdrawal headaches if they skip tea.

A minority of parents, however, still feed their children protein-rich porridge made from several grains that include millet and sorghum. For the financially able, the tea accompanies the adopted Western bountiful diet, which, many times, leaves harmful evidence in its wake. Bacon is not common in Kenya except in Western-style homes and restaurants.

But, back in our time, we children still loved the sweet taste of sugar.

I once stole a fistful from the tin. Although no one caught me, I recall how I regretted it later when Mami experienced an awakening that she credited to Jesus, and I soon learned that stealing would land me on fire for eternity.

I suspect my brothers dipped into the sugar tin several times because they were always more enterprising than us girls. But the stealing stopped or went underground after Mami caught Gīthūi, at age five, with evidence all over his front.

"Have you been eating sugar?" Mami asked him.

"What sugar?" he asked, whipped his right hand to his back, and stood still, wide-eyed.

"You know what sugar."

"I don't know," he said, shaking his head.

Scant granules of sugar stuck to his little cheeks and on his shirt, his fingers still wet with sticky bits of evidence after his licks.

"Don't touch that sugar," Mami said. "If you do, I'll know it just by looking at you."

I do not know whether Gĩthũi dipped into the sugar again, but I heeded Mami's warning and never stole sugar again. Punishment or no punishment, none of us wanted either of our parents to catch us doing something unacceptable. And I believed in Mami's uncanny power to know things.

Because she paid for our clothes and the few household foodstuffs and necessities we did not grow, the bulk purchases helped Mami reallocate her meager income to other family needs.

Otherwise, she focused on having a steady supply of staples year-round.

Besides the kauka (dried) vegetables she fed us during lean times, Mami stored dry maize, still on the cob, and beans, peas, and potato seeds. She mixed the loose grains with ashes so weevils (and the family) would not eat them.

If a potato had several eyes at both ends, Mami cut it into two pieces and applied ashes to the exposed cuts. After she dried the cuts, she ended up with two potato seeds. She stored her seeds in the granary.

Mami also stored cooked food in the granary, which was the safest place to store food. Woven with vines like a basket and resting on stilts about a foot and a half high, with jutting boards from its base where a person could sit, the granary not only provided ample ventilation but also discouraged pests from helping themselves to our food.

*

Surrounded by virgin land, when we children grew old enough to do activities outside our homes, we girls became avid gatherers while boys turned into hunters and gatherers. They hunted or trapped rabbits or nganga (spotted wildfowl) in the woods.

We all helped ourselves to abundant fruits and berries that grew in the wild. These included blackberries, raspberries, ngoe (like cherries), which grew on large trees by the river, nathi (ground cherries), and others. We enjoyed those fruits year in and year out.

These foods are no longer available to a majority of today's children in rural Kenya. With land demand after independence and population increase, people have divided most former colonial farms into small plot settlements with scant trees and limited virgin land.

Chapter 11

THE INVADERS

My siblings and I played in our courtyard under a clear blue sky without a speck of cloud in sight. Then, gradually, the afternoon sun became subdued, covered by a cloud, a sign of imminent rain. Just like I could tell time from the sun's location or the size of my shadow, I could tell when rain loomed.

Instead of rain, however, the dark cloud crept toward the village. But it looked different this time. An ominous, gigantic spacecraft-like mass that increased in size as it got closer. As the oldest child left at home, I alerted my siblings. We stopped our play and gazed in awe, unsure whether we needed to run indoors and hide.

Our racket alerted two neighbors, or they had also noticed the marvel. When we heard their voices, we ran to the little gateless entrance between thingira and nyūmba.

The two women gave historical accounts of how long it had been since they saw a similar phenomenon and the devastation it left behind. We children had never seen or heard of it. I looked forward to the exciting experience. My siblings and I engaged in a back-and-forth, unsure, half-hearted chatter. Meanwhile, without an adult at our homestead, I wondered what to do next.

To my relief, Mami hurried in after another half an hour.

"Am I glad I'm home!" she said.

We followed her indoors, now with unbridled excitement. While she unloaded her bags, she said she had to rush to get away. "I've never seen this since my childhood." She said. "It isn't something to celebrate."

The more she talked, the more we became eager to confirm it for ourselves. We returned outside to keep vigil.

The closer the cloud got, the more we imagined the earth shaking and the more people ventured outdoors, especially women and children. The mass looked denser at the center and darkish grey on the fringes. It soon hugged the ground and the heavens and blocked the sunlight. As it got closer, it hummed and whooshed before the sound turned into a buzz of snaps and cracks.

Within the hour, millions and millions of locusts took over the land. They landed on trees, houses, grass, and every inch of unoccupied space. They landed on each other or flew and hovered in complete disorder. Meanwhile, they devoured every living crop and plant in their path.

The adults returned indoors and stayed put, telling their bygone stories while they worried about the devastation to follow. But we children shrieked and made merry outside.

We arched forward and cupped our arms overhead to shield our heads and faces. The squiggly creatures bumped into us, flapped their wings, kicked their thorny legs, and jostled for space.

I hustled with my toes raised and flailed my arms for balance as I skipped from spot to spot for a place to land my foot. But my every footstep shattered several poor, defenseless little bodies. The locusts swarmed, and we collided. They kicked and scratched my uncovered body parts.

Eventually, we took cover indoors, but we could not contain our excitement. I made two more dashes outdoors. But I became squeamish because of the ruptured bodies under my bare feet, and the bumps and kicks from the wiry legs made the uncovered parts of my body itch. I now waited on the porch and closed the wooden door now and then to block strays from diving indoors.

In their three-day stay, the locusts broke tree limbs, felled trees, devoured gardens, tree leaves, shrubs, and weeds, and turned the land as naked as a desert, but for a layer of brown-greenish manure and the poisonous and unpalatable plants like Baba's tobacco and Kamunge's coffee.

Days after our routines resumed, adults replanted short-cycle plants like beans, peas, and others before the seasonal rains stopped. Without our maize staple, women worried about an imminent famine, something I did not grasp yet.

We children had no clue of the precarious life we led—with no safety net whatsoever. If the rains delayed or failed to come, or the locusts visited us, we ended up with little to eat.

Our parents' only comfort was that the rain came every year as if it had to meet a deadline.

*

After the locusts vacated the land, villagers gossiped that the Tugen (seasonal workers from the otherwise pastoral tribe Kamunge brought to help during the coffee cherry-picking season) had collected sacks of the insects.

I went to fetch water from the hydrant outside the village gate, bubbling with curiosity as I craned my neck toward the cluster of circular cottages. I saw locust carcasses spread outside on two plank beds.

When my family gathered around the fire pit, one of us said, "I would throw up if I had to eat locusts," while my siblings and I disparaged the Tugen's strange eating habits.

Mami snickered as she gave us a side glance, a knowing that implied perhaps she had suffered famine in the past.

"Don't show Ngai your full stomachs," she said.

Why did we need to hide our full stomachs from God? Would he jinx us and turn our stomachs empty?

Chapter 12

DELICIOUS AND REPUGNANT

The year the locusts visited, some families suffered starvation, and many others barely had enough to eat. Women and children foraged for greens on riverbanks more than ever. A man "treated" his two children's swollen stomachs with mole meat. My family ate ugali and distasteful leathery kauka vegetables, and although we did not starve, we suffered from scruffy, ashy skin more than usual.

In another two years, the pests descended on Solai again. Villagers shook their heads in dismay. Like before, employees hunkered down at their jobs, unable to wade through the dense swarms. Others remained stranded wherever the locusts trapped them until the creatures settled for the night. The driver of the bus from Nakuru, unable to see through the windshield, parked the bus, and he and his passengers waited by the roadside. On their way home from the pastures, Simon and Joseph had the hardest time calming the rattled herd. When the locusts settled enough for the goats to return home, the poor animals shot across the courtyard and into their cottage as if a predator chased them.

By morning, the locusts had colonized every inch of dirt, shrubs, and trees.

Because our homestead stood on a higher elevation, we sometimes stood behind the granary to enjoy the sunset or the expanse that stretched to where the sky met the earth. When we looked this time, we marveled at the trees that now resembled miles of small circular brown thatched huts in clusters like villages. The entire farm and beyond felt and looked dreary.

Villagers braced themselves for another famine.

Locusts swarmed and jostled in our courtyard, but we stayed out of their way, indoors or on the porch. The novelty of romping with them had died during their first visit.

"If the Tugen don't die from eating locusts," Mami said, "we can eat them, too."

My siblings and I eyed our mother. But none of us questioned her statement. What could we say? What could I say? I never expected locusts to become edible creatures for my family.

Somehow, we understood our family had regressed to the Tugen level. It never occurred to us—at least not to me—that we did not have to eat locusts while Baba owned goats and chickens. Instead, we embraced Mami's idea, chatty and excited, not about the prospect of eating locusts but the thrill of trapping them.

To trap them, we rushed outside and cleared spaces while we braved their kicks and scratches. Each of us set a cooking pot or an open sack before we rushed back to the doorway to wait for our catch. Relieved to find empty spots, the locusts hopped right in.

I derived great pleasure from running around, stooping, ducking, shrieking, and picking up a container quarter-full of unsuspecting hopping creatures. At the same time, their comrades collided with me before I rushed back indoors.

Mami emptied the live locusts into a big pot of bubbling water on the fire, the way I hear cooks dunk live lobsters. I hated to see that part. It still makes me shudder to imagine a live creature in boiling water. But not all locusts ended in doom. The feisty ones jumped to safety just before they touched the deathly water. We swept them outside with a broom.

Mami let the doomed locusts boil in mildly salted water for about twenty minutes, just enough to preserve them. She spread them out on a sack in one corner of the sitting area to dry while she waited for their kin to leave. Afterward, she sun-dried the locusts and stored the crispy cache in the granary.

The day arrived when our palates faced challenges as never before, a scenario that plays in my mind whenever I recall that period of my family's life.

I watched as Mami gathered her ingredients. She started by stir-frying green onions in oil. She then put in diced tomatoes, a dash of salt, and curry powder. After she turned the mixture back and forth for about a minute, she added water to the pot's half-full mark.

When the stew boiled, she stirred in the crispy locusts, a handful at a time, not to break their dry, brittle bodies. She let the stew simmer, stirring it now and then. If deformed bodies stuck out, she added more water. The enticing aroma wafted through the house and into the courtyard.

It was a mystery to me how Mami determined the stew was ready. She hardly ever tasted food before she served it, but none of us, including Baba, added more salt.

She now set the pot aside while she cooked the main dish of ugali. The three-stone fireplace allowed cooking one dish at a time, except for maybe roasting a maize cob or a potato on the side.

It was easy to tell when ugali was ready; it did not stick to the wooden mwiko (spatula). Mami served our meal on enamel white plates and the locust stew in little white bowls.

Many locusts had lost their legs and wings through boiling, drying, and cooking. When I got my share, I assessed the best way to eat the strange dish of little bodies, the sight of which I hated. I started with a winged locust, which was easier to handle. I clasped the wings between my thumb and index finger. With my other hand's fingers, I yanked off the head. It stayed attached to the tiny elongated digestive system, which I discarded. I then bit the rest of the locust and cast off the wings.

The meat tasted crunchy and delicious. But my mind said repugnant. I imagined chewing a live locust! Yuck! I gagged. But with no history of gagging and spitting out food, I swallowed it to get it out of my mouth.

I looked around to check whether my siblings had problems eating the "delicacy." It was hard to read their faces, all bent over, focused on their meals. I returned to my private ordeal to strategize. Except for what Mami left us for lunch, we ate no snacks. By supper, every cell in my body craved food. I now needed to calm my inner critic and tame my hunger.

I balled a lump of ugali, made a dimple with my thumb, kicked the little dead bodies aside with the back of my fingers, scooped the stew, and shoved the loaded lump into my mouth. I repeated and repeated. It did not override my imagination, but my stomach did not care or fuss. Instead, it calmed down the more I piled in.

Halfway through our meal, with more bodies left than the stew, we found our voices. My siblings and I ate as we jabbered about the unappetizing yet delicious taste and asked whether our family had stooped so low as to become locust eaters.

That stew became the first dish we failed to clean off our plates. Mami got the message and discarded the exotic food without cooking it again. In hindsight, she could have cooked the locusts, strained them out, and fed us a nutritious, protein-laden stew.

Today, I credit her locust dish for my distaste for eating squiggly land or sea creatures.

Baba never got involved with our experiments. We hid such activities from him, or he pretended not to notice despite the aroma that sailed through our homestead.

Locusts never raided Solai again. But in January 2020, they devastated communities in Ethiopia, Somalia, and Northern Kenya.

Chapter 13

ART OF SLAUGHTER

Baba and his goats had a complicated relationship, a love-hate union. Wary of mistaken identity, he branded the plain-coated ones, registering ownership like animals mark their territories. The goats loathed the torturous process. But Baba paid them no attention.

For this task, he used an iron with a head of four squares attached to a foot-and-a-half-long stick. After he heated the iron red-hot, one of my brothers held each goat victim while Baba stuck the iron on the goat's rump. The goat squealed as its fur sizzled and emitted a charcoal-like smell.

But the goats and their kids minded little during inspection check-ups. Baba hugged the legs of the goats or their kids while he opened and inspected their mouths or hooves if he suspected an ailment or discomfort or noticed one limping.

Even expectant mothers welcomed help when they experienced a difficult kidbirth. Although they grunted from the strain, they never bleated, kicked, or struggled when Baba and my brothers played midwives. Under no circumstances did Baba allow us girls to get close. But he could not keep track when he concentrated on saving a life.

I once watched from the side of the granary when, one evening, they aborted a full-term kid to save the mother's life. The kid's head stuck out while its body remained inside its mother, no matter what the "midwives" tried.

On happy days, goats trotted behind Baba if he headed to the manger to serve them rocks of pink salt that they loved to lick. Sometimes, he lounged on his three-legged stool on the porch to assess the health of his herd or admire his children and goats commingle.

A fleeting thought once crossed my mind: Baba cares for his goats more than he cares for us. If he noticed something amiss with one of us, say a limp, he never touched the child. The best he did was tell the sickly, "Tell your mother to check that leg."

Despite all that love and attention, Baba was the lone determiner of the goats' lifespans. At one time or another, each of them was coerced to make the ultimate sacrifice.

Females who took too long to breed or males not endowed to produce quality offspring got their lives cut short in their youth. But a prolific breeder lived a long life without the dangers of slaughter. As soon as its womb retired, however, Baba coerced the poor animal to donate its stringy meats and bones to our family. We whined about eating such tough meat but enjoyed the tasty stew it produced.

Long lived the king of the herd. When several males chased a female, the reigning king, with its head protected by prize-winning horns, head-butted his rivals until he knocked them down one by one, denying the weaklings a chance to procreate.

But age doesn't play favorites; it finally crept in, and a younger, potential king stood its ground. He and the ruling king got into a concussion-head-butt match until one won and claimed the girl. In time, the fights became so fierce that Baba had to break the tie. He bestowed the crown on the younger king, and the older one joined the countdown to slaughter.

The king also headed to slaughter if he became too cocky and head-butted human children. I shrieked and scurried a handful of times in my girlhood when a king charged at me. I ducked behind a heap of firewood, which broke the king's momentum. With just one head thrust, it could have maimed me.

Baba did not stand for that—a sign we mattered to him more than the goats, after all.

That he-goat nourished our bodies before it had sired all the superior offspring it expected to produce.

Sometimes, an animal stayed alive by pure chance. Baba craved meat whenever he drank, just like smokers crave cigarettes when they eat or drink alcohol.

From where he sat on his stool on the porch, he watched the goats roam in the courtyard. He lingered on a goat for a few seconds before his eyes moved on. Then his head stopped, and his eyes zeroed in on his choice. He fingered the animal to my brothers.

While he sharpened the knife, my brothers cut leafy branches we called *mathaakwa* (nowadays, people use banana fronds). They made a bed between our garden and the homestead where my parents did their killings—Mami, the chickens, and Baba, the goats.

After they gathered the tools they needed, my brothers chased and grabbed the doomed goat. The poor animal bleated and disturbed the entire household. Most of its colleagues wandered away, subdued, perhaps relieved it was not their turn. But a few looked on, helpless, frozen in place, heads raised, alert, eyes dilated before they unfroze and joined the others.

Baba and my brothers flipped the goat on its side at the leafy bed. The oldest brother (or sometimes one of Baba's acquaintances) knelt behind the goat and restrained it from its midriff by clasping its fore and hind legs and pinning them down. The goat's head turned in every direction while it hollered.

We were used to goats fussing when Baba branded them, or males fought for females, or when the mothers lost sight of their kids. But when a goat begged for its life, it tortured my psyche as the animal protested to the end.

The end came when Baba clasped its jaws and tilted its head backward. One of my younger brothers thrust a container underneath the goat's neck. Baba sliced the throat a third of the way in and turned it downward toward the container. Blood shot out. As it gushed, he pressed the head backward. Within a minute, the stream turned into a trickle, then to drops before it stopped altogether.

A shoddy, hurried slaughter by an amateur, Baba said, failed to drain the blood completely, which left the meat bloody.

The collected blood went to Mami's house, which was later mixed with stuffing of sausages and the two stomachs.

After they skinned the goat, Baba peeled off rwariũngũ, the lining between the skin and the body that would have made perfect bacon. One brother roasted the piece, and the slaughterers ate it. I thought it was part of the slaughter ritual. Now I understand it was a mere practice, like a cook tasting the food.

To open the belly, Baba slit the carcass from the chest to the groin and pressed both sides wide open. He then methodically removed the insides, careful not to burst the tiny gallbladder attached to the liver and contaminate the meat with its bitter bile. He then cut a slit on two different spots on the liver and checked for parasites. Unlike today, we had no meat inspectors.

One time, Baba declared, "The liver is bad." He then discarded all the insides and instructed my brothers to bury them. We ate the rest of the meat, which Baba approved of because, although his roast meat turned out juicy, he and my brothers roasted it well, with no traces of blood left. We never ate rare or medium-done meats as I now see in Western-style restaurants.

Except for that time, Baba always declared the insides clean. He then put them into two pots. Meats that needed further attention—like intestines and stomach—went into one pot, which someone took to Mami to clean. The ready-to-roast organs—

liver, lungs, and kidneys—went into a different pot for roasting with the other meats.

The carving of the carcass followed.

To his credit, Baba treated his goats with respect, even in death. He carved the various parts of the carcass as carefully as a surgeon would. He never left a single strand attached to an unintended limb. If one of my brothers botched a step, Baba scoffed or asked the wrongdoer, "Do you ever learn?"

Only men slaughtered goats back then. Baba, therefore, expected his sons, as future men, to learn.

"Some men mix the entire slaughter," I heard him say to a man once. "They can even ask their wives to slaughter a goat."

He also expected them to know the names of different meat parts.

I have now learned the pieces total twenty-eight.

For his sons' benefit, Baba named each part as he cut and deposited it in a pile—one for roasting then, or later, and the other for Mami's kitchen.

From hearing Baba name the meat parts or from Mami, I learned the names of about half of them.

Not included in the slaughter ritual, we girls, and the very young, turned into sneaky observers. We stuck our heads out and peered from the side of the granary. Sometimes, Baba became too engrossed and forgot to look. If he turned and saw our heads before or during cutting the goat's neck, he shooed us away.

In time, I noticed he chased only the girls away. But it did not matter anymore. Watching him cut a goat's throat became an ordeal for me. My gullet and food tract broke into tiny spasms, and the throat-cutting felt like my own. Henceforth, I could not stand to watch an animal killed. But I remained front and center, looking forward to the outcome. I liked the buzz around our courtyard, knowing how it would play out in the evening.

Chapter 14

MEAT PARTS

My family had followed the same slaughter routine for so long that we, players and non-players alike, knew what came next. When Baba finished carving the meat, one of my brothers had kindled the fire nearby, which had already turned into glowing charcoal.

They roasted the meat over a contraption of chicken wire grille. Meanwhile, Mami cleaned the innards and drained the large and small intestines. The small intestines were the hardest to clean. She milked them an inch at a time while she progressively pinched the cleaned side until she drained the entire bunch. She later boiled the small intestines and lungs, or Baba roasted them.

Similar to slaughtering and naming meat parts according to Gĩkũyũ tradition, Baba based meat eating on gender.

Girls ate different meat from the boys and women from the men. Fathers shared certain meat with their sons, while mothers shared theirs with their daughters. I noticed men ate the tastier parts, and nobody questioned it. Ribs, hind legs, ngerima (the small stomach), and others belonged to Baba to share with whomever he wanted. Occasionally, pieces of ribs or liver dripped down to us children when Baba shared them with Mami.

Men shared meat with their friends. But Baba had no friends. The few he had had at Kĩrĩma-inĩ moved to Kikuyuland during the Mau Mau exodus. He sometimes invited his two acquaintances.

When neither of the two men was available, he ate very little meat besides the few pieces he ate while dishing it to us.

One time, he craved a man's company so much that he invited a Tugen man—the only time I saw him invite a non-Gĩkũyũ. The man, whom I will call Cherono, brought along his pre-teen son to the chagrin of my young brothers.

Cherono and Baba enjoyed homemade beer while Baba warmed a leg roast and a quarter slab of ribs. The son sat quietly and watched them.

"Oh, you have soup?" Cherono asked after he eyed the pot of oily soup at the top across the fire pit. "Give some to my boy."

"I haven't whipped it yet," Baba said.

"Give it to him," Cherono said. "My family is used to fat."

The boy downed a mug of the oily soup.

When Baba carved the meat, Cherono preferred the fattest chunks; he shared them with his son. Joseph, the same age as Cherono Junior, got so miffed he had to see for himself. He pretended he needed to get an item from thingira and peeked.

"Cherono and son are devouring meat," Joseph said, "as if they haven't eaten in weeks."

Word reached us the following day that Cherono Junior suffered record diarrhea. With his mother left back in Tugen country, minding his younger siblings, he kept his father awake throughout the night. My brothers enjoyed telling and retelling that story.

Mami complained about those invitations. She said Baba should have shared the meat with his own boys because they alone tended to the animals.

As for the women's meat, the foreleg belonged to Mami and her girls—my sister Tabitha and me. We also ate a kidney each. I hated its crunchy texture, its chunkiness, and its bland taste.

My brothers ate the neck and the lungs. Sometimes Tabitha and I exchanged meat with our brothers, thinking theirs was tastier than ours, and vice versa.

I liked the spongy taste of the lungs but not the dense heart meat.

If the slaughter happened early in the day, Mami prepared the stuffing that afternoon. It included stir-fried small chunks of meat seasoned with pepper, onions, tomatoes, and salt.

After the cooked stuffing cooled, Baba and my brothers mixed it with the goat's blood for its congealing properties to bind the mixture together.

Baba then stuffed ihu (the four-chambered goat's stomach) and ngerima (the small stomach) with the mixture while one brother held the opening. They then closed the opening by threading it with a sharpened stick, leaving a five-inch stick stuck out for a handle. Baba stuffed mūtura (the large intestine) by himself and tied the ends with sisal strings. They placed the bundles on a mesh grill over a low fire.

The fatty sausage and small stomach belonged to Baba. He or Mami cut the rest into pieces for us.

When Mami adopted Christian ways, she stopped eating sausages stuffed with the bloody mixture. Baba challenged her about the "foreign religion," and the two even got into a fight. But Mami dug in. Finally, Baba swallowed his pride and started making sausages with a bloodless mixture. Those sausages tasted more flavorful and never upset my stomach.

We ate or made soup from most parts of a goat's meat, except the chunk from the anal area, the lips, and the brains.

A day or two after the slaughter, Baba prepped the head and legs. He thrust a long, pointed stick through the back of the gaping head and out of its mouth and placed it and the four legs on a grill over an open flame. He scraped the head and legs' charred fur as many times as they needed to leave the skin smooth and whitish.

Mami washed the head and legs and boiled them in water for hours. When the meat became tender, she removed it and kept the soup aside for Baba to add herbs and whip it. Baba carved the head and gave Tabitha and me the ears with the chunky, dense, tasty fat at its base. Because of its chewy texture, the fat did not make me gag. It was the only fat I did not mind eating.

Baba dried and saved the skins for his business.

But I'm ahead of myself.

The "general" meat, which Baba and my brothers roasted after the slaughter, the parts that I could not figure out, belonged to our entire household.

After roasting, one of my brothers took the sizzling meat in a white basin to thingira. By then, the aroma engulfed the entire homestead and wafted far beyond. Soon, we congregated in thingira early evening. Baba asked one of us to get him the meat "chair," a low wooden bench.

He ceremoniously cut a chunk of meat and handed it to each child. He put Mami's chunk on a plate and handed it to her. She then asked one of us to hand her the salt.

The rest of us never dared sprinkle salt on our meat in Baba's presence. He claimed it destroyed the meat's natural flavor. But he had trained us to eat salt-less meat, anyway.

The cordiality of us seated around the fire pit, devouring tasty meat, is one of my best memories of growing up in my family.

Chapter 15

DRESSMAKING AND WEAVING

When my family lived away from other people, before we moved to the fenced village, I did not question or concern myself with where my dresses came from or what I wore. But now, in the village, I noticed such matters as I grew older. I realized Mami bought her clothes already made but hand-stitched my sister's and my dresses.

In hindsight, I know this was because she could not afford tailor-made clothes for herself and ready-dyed or printed materials for us. Instead, she hand-stitched ours from cheap cotton calico cloth, a dull, white, coarse material imported from India.

Mami spread a blanket on the floor and laid the material on top of it. She measured our body frames with a sisal string that she used to measure the fabric with. She then folded the material, flattened it with her palms, clicked her scissors back and forth and around the material until pieces of a pattern took shape.

She took a week to a month to complete a dress, depending on how soon either of us needed to wear it. Stitching done, she soaked and dyed the dress in water-colored blue, red, orange, or yellow powder she had bought from the market from women who measured the powder in tiny spoons like tobacco.

Tabitha and I made suggestions, although we had no choice in what color our mother used. But she indulged us by dyeing each dress a different color.

The fit turned out acceptable, although always a size too big—no doubt by design so we could grow into the dresses. I never outgrew a single dress. Sometimes, Mami's design went amiss, and one sleeve ended up longer than the other or a neckline too tight or loose.

Mami ignored the sleeve complaints, but for a tight neckline, she took a razor blade and cut a small slit at the shoulder toward the sleeve. As long as the wearer's head slid through, her ears turned deaf to complaints except for mending the slit if it frayed.

She never concerned herself with how our clothes fit as long as they reached down to our shins. If we sat, knees raised, ankles together, the dresses had to reach our ankles. On the rare occasions we forgot and sat with our legs apart, which Mami and the other women frowned at and called sloppy and unladylike, our dresses needed to drape between our legs down to the floor.

I grew tired of my mother's handiwork when she sewed me an ill-fitting dress—the result of a faulty measurement because she had stopped using a string. As if that did not cause me enough agony, she ran out of dye. She told me to wear the white dress until she bought the dye. No one knew when she would buy it because she had quit Baba's tobacco business by then and went to the market only on occasion.

The wait did not bother me. But I hated the extra wide neck opening that caused the sleeve to hang over my upper arm, leaving my shoulder bare and restricting my hand flexibility. To keep the sleeve in place, I flipped the crook of my elbow at intervals as if I suffered from a nervous tic.

As always, Mami knew the answer to my problem. She took the dress, gathered the excess neck area material, and sewed it tightly. When I tried it, it fit better. But her handiwork left a hideous ball of fabric perched on my left shoulder. When I complained, Mami sewed the ball down, which made the lumpy ball tamer and dense. But no matter how much she tried, she could not eliminate the shoulder bump.

After that, she deemed any further complaints baseless.

I stewed about her cavalier attitude toward my wearing such an ugly dress. I thought about that dress daily when it slid down my body. Because of sitting or playing on dirt, my dress looked light brown when Mami bought the dye. She did not see the point in dyeing it. I had already given up; the undyed dress did not make a difference.

I believed my dress salvation would come only if Baba allowed me to start school; I would then wear a uniform made by a real tailor.

*

Besides dressmaking, Mami was our family's weaver. She wove every kĩondo basket we used, which came in various sizes. We used the smallest ones as depository seed pouches while planting or to carry food. We used the slightly bigger ones the same way and for shopping or carrying small loads; the next bigger size was used for regular shopping and also a suitable size for a gift; next came the workhorse, the tin to a tin-and-a-half-size kĩondo; and finally, the largest—one that Mami had to have, not for its usefulness, but as proof that she was a full-fledged wife in command of her domestic household. Whoever named Gĩkũyũ things decided that type of kĩondo warranted a special name. We called it *nyamikwa*.

If the carrier was strong enough, Nyamikwa could carry three to four tinfuls of coffee cherries, maize, or whatever else. I never grew strong enough to carry a nyamikwa. Even if I dared to try and fill it only a third full, the empty two-thirds would have enveloped my body.

Mami hardly ever carried anything in it, either. If she did, which I never saw her do—though some in the family claimed she did—she filled it only half-full. Nyamikwa was another white elephant, just like that unusable grinder Baba brought home. But no one considered nyamikwa impractical, although it lay around in the granary, or Mami used it as storage.

One could count on one hand the women in the village who owned a nyamikwa; it took enormous labor to make one. It must have taken Mami at least two years to weave that basket.

Mami made the bags with twines she processed from green sisal fronds. She put each frond on a flat, smooth wood stump, placed the blunt part of a machete on top, close to the handle, and stepped on it. She then pulled the frond with the other hand and scraped off the green skin and pulp. She repeated this until smooth, damp, beige fiber remained.

After she amassed a heap of the fiber, she washed and dried it for several days until it was ready for the next stage.

From the dry heap, she separated the fibers she needed to make a twine of the thickness she wanted, then separated those fibers into two, which she rolled over her right thigh. When she neared the end of a fiber, she attached another and resumed rolling, and on and on until she ended up with a heap of twine that she rolled into round balls like knitting yarn.

She then dyed the balls into the various colors she needed—black, green, blue, red, and yellow—leaving several undyed white balls that she used for the base to separate and create the design she wanted.

She began weaving only after she determined she had enough fiber to complete a kīondo. She prided herself on how her kīondos could measure up to the ones woven by the most skilled weavers. Even I could spot a novice weaver by the rippled base, the uneven sides, or the finish of their kīondos.

Chapter 16

FAMILY BIAS

In the Gĩkũyũ nation, parents alternated naming children after their father's and mother's relatives—dead or alive—a tradition that endures. In polygamous families, children from different mothers, named after their father's relatives, ended up with the same names. To avoid confusion, a family added "big" or "little" to the name.

For example, my half-sister from Baba's first family and I were both named Wanjirũ, after our paternal grandmother. Although I did not grow up with them, Baba's first family referred to me as Wanjirũ-little, and in my mother's household, we referred to my half-sister as Wanjirũ-big.

With this kind of naming system, fathers tended to favor children named after their relatives, especially the sons. Although this practice of family bias has now ceased, back in my childhood, some fathers discriminated with impunity against children named after in-laws, especially if the children turned out troublesome. Such fathers assaulted or verbally bullied the children and blamed the despicable abuse on the children's behavior. (A well-behaved child was always safe.)

The children's mothers or other adults may have suspected and remarked on the real reason for the poor treatment, but they never intervened. The Gĩkũyũ community even had a name for children named after their maternal relatives. People called them ithũmba (or gĩthũmba in singular). If visitors felt free in a family, they had no qualms about asking a child's name, and if they did not know after whom the child was named, they would tell the child, "I think you are a gĩthũmba," with no malice.

Whether Baba discriminated against his children is hard for me to say because he applied his insults and putdowns to all. But I still wonder whether he sometimes acted from unconscious bias.

When he practiced polygamy, when our family lived at Kĩrĩma-inĩ, Baba did not allow his daughters to attend school or wear Western dresses. Instead, they dressed like his wives, one step from the olden days.

In the olden days, people made clothes from cured animal skin and dyed them with oil and red ochre. Women wore *mũthuru na nguo ya ngoro*, a skirt and a top, while young girls wore a one-piece dress. At the dawn of the twentieth century, women kept the same designs but started using cloth instead of cured skin.

By the 1930s and 1940s, my half-sisters noted that progressive women, including Baba's sister, Aunt Julia, wore Western-style dresses instead of the traditional design.

One Sunday afternoon, Kaguyu, Baba's first wife, bought her daughter, Wairimũ-big, her very first Western-style dress. At six or seven years old, unaware of Baba's wardrobe restrictions, Wairimũ-big shed her traditional wear, slid the new dress on, and strutted into the courtyard, filled with joy.

Baba was lounging in his thingira, drinking beer with three friends, when he saw his daughter.

"Wa-maitũ, toka," (daughter of my mother, come here Wairimũ-big was named after Baba's sister.), he said;

When Wairimũ-big approached, Baba asked her. "How many times do I have to say I don't want this type of dressing in my homestead?" He grabbed her dress at the hem on both sides and yanked it over her head. Her arms shot up. With her little naked body exposed, she hugged herself and froze in place, a hurt, questioning look fixed on Baba. He crumpled her treasured new dress and threw it into a smoldering fire.

"It's wrong to do that," one man said, shaking his head, "especially to a female child."

"Yes, it's too shameful," the second man agreed.

The third man shook his head without a word.

Baba stayed silent.

The men's reaction caused Wairimũ-big to crystalize her confusion. Angry and dumbfounded that Baba could do such a mean and shameful thing to her, she scurried back to her mother's house, crying.

I doubt the irony of Baba's action dawned on him. He sat wearing his western-style hat, shirt, and knee-length khaki shorts. Even the black sandals he wore were made from old tires instead of the traditional skin.

When Wairimũ-big first told me this story in December 2014, she paused before she added, "We lived a life of terror."

This was not a favoritism incident, but it happened when Baba and Kaguyu were literally at each other's throats. It likely came from another tendency men engaged in, "lumping" their children with their mothers. Or perhaps Baba did not want his women to be that progressive.

*

Six years after Wairimũ-big's embarrassing incident, I was born as the first daughter of Baba's second family. Right out of the womb when the midwife announced, "It's Wanjirũ!" I occupied an important position in the family.

It elated Mami to have a daughter after a line of five boys, two dead as toddlers, and the three alive too energetic to give her peace.

Besides the monotony of giving birth to one gender, she wanted a daughter who could help her with "female" chores.

Hours after my birth, Baba rushed to Patel's General Store, three miles away. He included two baby dresses among the baby items and supplies he bought.

Had he changed his mind about girls wearing Western dresses? Only time would tell.

When I turned a year old, Baba and Kaguyu separated. She, Gathoni, her second daughter, and Wairimũ-big, the last born, moved behind the compound next to her married son's homestead.

A year later, on an errand to Patel's General Store, Wairimũ-big bumped into her brother-in-law, Joel, Wanjirũ-big's husband, outside the store. Joel took her inside and told her to pick a dress.

Baba saw his daughter walk about in the courtyard wearing the new dress.

"Didn't I say no Western dresses in this homestead?"

Wairimũ-big, in her mid-teens, stopped, hands on her hips, elbows winged, back swayed, and defiantly faced Baba. "Wanjirũ-little wears a dress, and she is a girl!"

Baba threw his daughter a long, venomous look, mouth tightened. He never uttered a word against the new style, then or ever after, not even six years later when Mami defied the status quo and updated her wardrobe.

*

My parents did not use words like "I love you" or hug me after I reached the age of three. Like everyone else in the community, I did not need their verbal declaration or to have them hovering over me to know they loved me. I knew it by sensing it.

And my firstborn-girl status protected me from my brothers' pranks.

From age seven, my brother Joseph skipped, jumped, or climbed trees to keep up with David and Simon, four and six years older. They played and got into all kinds of escapades.

Two years older than me, Joseph suffered pranks from the two older brothers but lacked the muscle to pull off a decent one against them. But the urge to prove himself got to him one early morning.

I sat on a small three-legged stool before the fire, waiting for Mami to finish cooking porridge. From the corner of my eye, I saw Joseph enter. He stealthily tiptoed behind me. In a second, I jerked forward and screamed, not from the pain or the warm stream that trickled down my neck and shoulders but from the startle.

Mother whipped around, ready to lunge and scoop me from the fire, the only thing she believed could cause me danger from where I sat. When she saw Joseph, she settled for a holler and a reprimand.

Joseph dashed out, his pee spooked, to finish elsewhere.

Baba rushed from his thingira into the courtyard and talked.

Now that my screams alerted the highest authority in my world, I stopped and listened.

Without asking the reason for my holler, Baba warned my brothers that he would beat them severely if any of them as much as spit on me.

From his warning and emphatic tone, I sensed he favored me among my siblings.

During my childhood and teenage years, when he drank, he called me Maitũ, mother. If he disagreed with someone and became adamant, he swore, "Wanjirũ!" If he uttered the name, swearing in his mother's name, it warned all concerned that he had closed that topic.

I doubt I grasped the effect of his actions then, but whenever he addressed me thus, I felt a buoyancy that I doubt my sister Tabitha, named after our maternal grandmother, ever felt.

Later, when Baba told stories—the ones he told when drunk and the only way we learned about parts of his life—he talked about our clan, Anjirũ. The name derived from Wanjirũ, the firstborn of

Gĩkũyũ and Mũmbi, the Gĩkũyũ nation's primordial parents, equivalent to the Western Adam and Eve.

It boosted my sense of self when I learned my parents not only named me after my paternal grandmother but also after the firstborn of the Gĩkũyũ nation.

Incidentally, as a teenager, I noticed that when Baba swore, he sometimes evoked "Wanjirũ!" and other times "Wanjirũ Mũkũrũ!" the elder Wanjirũ, the one they named me after. This meant he had always sworn with his mother. By then, however, it made no difference to my subconscious.

Mami treated her children like any typical mother. She liked well-behaved children who "listened" to her. But that meant little in that era because, except in rare cases, we obeyed our parents.

However, I enjoyed Mami's favoritism before she got another daughter with whom I could compete for her attention. When I fell ill at three weeks old, instead of home remedies or healers, and under protests from Baba and other well-wishers, she rushed me to Nakuru General Hospital.

The doctor kept mum on what ailed me. But at that tender age, he gave me a shot on my bottom, and thus, I became the first child in my family to use modern medicine as an infant.

Mami never grew tired of telling that story—if nothing else—to show she was progressive even before we moved to the fenced village and before she became a Christian.

Chapter 17

Name Calling

Before we moved to the fenced village, I was unaware of insults and name-calling, or no one used them in my presence. But, as I grew older, I learned name-calling from Baba, the village children, or my siblings and I generated them ourselves.

If any of my brothers annoyed Baba, to cool his anger, he dug his fingernails into the offender's head. Otherwise, he preferred verbal putdowns or insults. He called my brothers kondoo (sheep) or chura ũyũ (you frog!) or asked, "Do you have any sense?"

He never dug his nails or called my sister and me names, except once when he called me a name. But we were fair game for putdowns. I recall how he tightened his lips, snorted, and shook his head as if surprised he had such a stupid daughter. At such times, I never remembered my supposedly special status.

One day, Baba called me a name. He squatted in the courtyard, working on a piece of wood, his pliers and hammer beside him. He sent me to fetch an item. On my return, he looked at what I had brought and squinted. Almost to himself, he said, "Oh, nigga."

Confused, I stood still and waited.

A while back, he had called one of my brothers the same name. Like me, my siblings and I had frozen in place, lost.

In my case, after a pause, Baba gave a clipped syllable-by-syllable restatement of what he wanted.

He likely picked up the "Nigger" epithet from Kang'oro, who may have used it to insult his laborers when they got on his nerves. Baba must have realized the insult did not affect his children; I never heard him utter it again.

Mami never called us names. She preferred to liken someone to someone she thought was "defective."

"Your feet look as dusty as so-and-so's," she said, or

"You beg just like so-and-so," or "You are lazy like...."

She always compared us to a person from another tribe, unaware that her cavalier utterances nurtured and cemented our belief in the superiority of the Gĩkũyũ tribe.

Another type of insult was a spit, which showed the greatest dislike for another person.

The scornful spitter assembled spit in his mouth, made eye contact with the target, and shot the spit to the ground. Sometimes, the spitter jerked his head in front or to the side and produced a spitting sound only, an act that produced similar negative emotions.

Women used milder dismissive insults by turning their heads to the side and producing a snappy spit sound. Men also used the gesture while they gossiped about a person they disliked.

We children did not use the spit method; we wielded our own insults or copied them from older worldly boys. I heard children call each other "fakini." This caused little reaction because few children knew what the word meant.

In my teen years, I learned the word was a mangled version of "fucking."

I preferred sticking out my tongue, mocking, or mimicking my adversary. This made the younger children burst into tears.

Boys and girls dared each other into fights. Only the strong did this, but rarely anyone would take them on unless cheerleaders crowded and jeered until the weakling gave in to shame, acted, and lived to regret it.

In one version, a child spat on the back of their palm, stretched the hand, and goaded another to wipe off the njata, "star." The spectators jeered and dared the opponent. Sometimes, a feisty but weak child called the dare, wiped off the spit, and ran like a sprinter, hoping to get home before the bully caught up.

By pre-teen and early teen years, we girls had added a side-flip of one hip to our insult collection.

Whatever insults children and adults used, calling someone ngui crossed the line. None of us called each other a "dog." I sensed that the insult counted as one sin that doomed the utterer to a lifetime of teeth gnashing. Only incorrigible children used that utmost insult.

Even in adulthood, hearing someone call another a dog grated on my mind. I was not alone. In the 1990s, my oldest brother, David, went to mediate a quarrel between our sister Wairimũ and her partner. During the strained dialogue, she called her partner a dog.

David became stupefied that his baby sister could be so disrespectful to utter such an insult, and in front of him at that. He concluded she must have been in the wrong. To avoid taking sides, he left the two to sort out their differences.

In time, the couple settled the matter by going their separate ways, and Maina, the partner, turned his back on his own son.

Years later, when David told me the story, he still wondered where Wairimũ got the nerve to use such an insult in his presence.

"I did not think Wairimũ could use such language," David said, shaking his head.

I still wonder why the word "dog" as an insult provoked such negative emotions in us. If a child called an adult a dog, as one did in our courtyard, we thought the act downright evil.

Chapter 18

BABA THE COWARD

I first learned that Baba supervised other workers when my mother took me to her job to babysit Morry. When she and I first arrived at the plantation, we found him assigning rows of coffee bushes to pickers as they arrived. He assigned one to Mami. During the day, I heard him speak occasionally as he walked about. At lunchtime, he came to Mami's row to get food she had carried for him in a small kĩondo. She did this when they worked at the same plantation. But, most days, Baba carried his own lunch to wherever his work took him.

Late afternoon, I heard him call the end of the workday. He shooed laggards who trailed behind to grab one more fistful of coffee cherries.

"You got to go now!" Baba said as he walked along the rows of coffee bushes.

People referred to him as nyabaara (or nyapara in Kiswahili), overseer, who supervised people wherever the landowner needed work done, a position he held since before he and Mami married.

As I grew older and understood what the overseer did, I held my father in high esteem despite our family being one of the peasants. I did not expect workers to question his authority, call him names, or dare to challenge him to a fight. But two men did just that.

Wainaina wa Kahũhũ, a much younger and taller man, usually wearing beige shirt sleeves and knee-length khaki shorts, threw the first challenge. It made villagers shake their heads and wag their tongues.

The incident occurred on a weekend when Baba had not brewed beer, which he did once a month. During his dry Sundays, he joined other drunks at whatever alleys to quench his thirst. He started this routine after Mami experienced her Christian awakening and quit his tobacco business, and the two stopped going to the market together. With his tobacco and hides and skins business dead, he had nothing to occupy himself on weekends.

One Sunday, he and Wainaina disagreed. The reason and details for their dispute remained unknown to our household.

We learned of the incident when Baba hurried home. Instead of entering his thingira, he perched himself on a pile of firewood near his porch, rolled the sides of his unbuttoned coat, and rested his arms on his folded left leg, his eyes toward the entrance. Although he never sat there, I thought nothing of it until a minute later.

Wainaina appeared at the four-foot side fence between nyũmba and thingira. He walked right up to the gateless entrance, but instead of entering, he faced our courtyard, draped his arms over the little fence, and started on his boisterous insults.

Baba watched—no reaction—nothing.

"Step out here, you coward!" Wainaina said. "Let's face each other man-to-man!"

He dared not enter our courtyard and turn into a trespasser, the aggressor. According to Gĩkũyũ tradition, a man should not take a fight to another man's homestead. He may have also feared the matter would reach their employer.

Wainaina resorted to insults "like a woman," villagers said later.

"I'll not respect you, fakini dog," he said. "I will never follow or obey your stupid instructions."

Baba kept mum, but his jaw tightened, and his eyes opened wider whenever an insult stung him—a man afraid of his attacker.

Mami emerged from her house and glanced around. Satisfied her children stood at the goats' cottage, a safe distance from the fracas, she said, "Ah! I won't waste my time with drunks," and returned indoors.

Meanwhile, Wainaina ran out of potent insults that could rile Baba to go outside our courtyard. He called in his reinforcements—his two children—a son of about twelve and a daughter of ten. The two quickened their steps from where they watched and joined their father. We could see the boy up to his chest. But his sister had to tiptoe because the little fence where they stood reached her neck.

"Call this coward anything you wish," Wainaina told his children.

They hesitated and fidgeted, their fingers by their mouths.

"Go on," he said. "We'll beat this coward along with his family."

He shot a dry spit on the ground and said, "Coward!"

Energized by their father and a chance to insult an adult without consequences, the two children joined the party.

"Step outside, you coward!" the boy said. "My father will pound you like ugali."

"Weakling!" the girl said. "We'll pound your children too."

The three hurled insults at Baba, each determined to outdo the other.

Wainaina bounced while he thrust his index finger toward Baba.

My siblings and I became stupefied, our play forgotten.

Then, the boy hurled his best insult yet.

"You old dog!"

"Woof! Woof! Woof!" the girl said.

I gasped, along with my siblings.

A child to call an adult a dog! We gawked, mesmerized.

Baba shot his eyes toward us while he fidgeted and struggled to contain himself.

A handful of people trickled in behind the Wainainas and watched. When Wainaina became aware of the cluster of witnesses, he backed off. "Let's leave this stupid coward alone," he said. His children trailed behind him, hurling insults.

For the grand finale, the son dropped his shorts, bent, wiggled his small ashy backside, and mooned Baba.

We heard this part secondhand because, hidden from view, neither Baba nor our group saw the boy. I saw only a woman put her hand over her mouth, eyes wide open. Eager to see the reason for her reaction, my siblings and I rushed to the entrance. We saw the boy hitch his shorts up before he disappeared between the houses.

The onlookers could not wait to retell the story to anyone who came later.

Back in the courtyard, Baba remained seated for a minute before he sought refuge in his thingira.

Embarrassed for him, I became conflicted.

My father looked gaunt and weak, slightly bent, to my young eyes, although he likely started as tall as Wainaina. But people followed what he said.

Before the incident, I believed all he needed was to speak to turn things around. Now, a doubt stuck in my mind. But, still, of all the faults I may have attached to my father, a "coward" featured nowhere.

You just wait, I told myself. Baba will do something. But what, exactly, eluded me. Meanwhile, adults called it blasphemy for children to insult an adult.

I expected the matter to end when people trailed off back to their homes. But the spin continued for days. Whenever a woman heard the story, she shook her head and said,

"Can you believe it?" or

"Things have changed," or

"Wainaina's family will not end well."

Men may have talked about the incident as well, but with the war still going on, it was against the law for three or more Gĩkũyũ men to assemble. Perhaps they talked at work.

Embarrassed because Baba did not or could not fight back, I worried that whenever Mami sent me to get or take something to one of her friends or draw water at the hydrant, someone would mention the incident. It stressed me for a while to have such gossip focused on us, while a tiny voice within me hoped the curse would one day catch up with the Wainaina family.

The curse remained potent despite the general dilution of Agĩkũyũ customs, myths, superstitions, and beliefs. Villagers, old and young, feared the curse of an elder, a parent, or a community condemning them to gloom and doom.

Before the British colonized Kenya, Gĩkũyũ society did not have a police force. People relied on the curse as a major deterrent against crime and lawlessness. Agĩkũyũ believed an older person's or a collective admonition became a perpetual curse that hovered not only over the perpetrator but also his descendants unless they performed an appeasement or cleansing ritual.

Chapter 19

NJAGA THE BULLY

Njaga wa Ndario lived to drink, work his plantation job, and give others a hard time; he did not help his wife in the garden, had no goats to pamper, nothing. A confirmed village drunk (That's what we called alcoholics back then), he wore no sandals, no coat, or hat like the other middle-aged men. Instead, he fitted himself in knee-length shorts and a short-sleeved shirt, a khaki uniform he wore seven days a week.

On weekdays, he went to work and returned home to quietly nurse his depressive state. On weekends, alcohol took over his mind and body. He emerged from his cocoon, strutted, chest puffed, and turned the village's footpaths into his stomping ground.

He strode through the village, boasting of his imaginary conquests or singing his drunken nonsense songs. No heads turned in fear or sympathy when people heard Njaga. People had gotten so used to him that they ignored his blather—unless one was an older man or his family.

People claimed drinking had damaged his brain. The old men he targeted feared him because they could not figure out whether he was a typical drunk or deranged as well. His family was fair game, too. He beat his wife and sons without a care who saw or learned about it.

In one incident, he waved a thick board, at least three inches wide, while he chased Kĩariĩ, his first-born son. When he closed in on the thirteen-year-old, he whacked him on the back. The boy staggered, fell on his knees, rose halfway, scrambled, and ran for his life.

Njaga's behavior had become so notorious that it had reached the neighboring farms, especially Major Stein's farm, where Mami's two paternal uncles lived with their families and widowed mother, Kagendo. Uncle Thimbara stayed alert to any of Njaga's drunken blather on the rare occasion he crossed our village on his way to Njeki's Shopping Center. He loathed crossing paths with Njaga. Thimbara was no slouch himself. But Njaga may have come out ahead if it came down to fist-to-fist.

According to village gossip, which may have been an exaggeration, Njaga acted on impulse; he came by his victims by chance and, without giving reason, went full-throttle without concern for the consequences.

But Thimbara's missteps were deliberate. He singled out victims he could dominate and never spared a snipe, a mean word, or a joke for people he considered weak, ugly, or less intelligent. A born comedian but a bully by choice, his jokes made family members split their sides laughing. But people who fell out of his favor—family or villagers—avoided him like a disease because of those home-hitting jokes. Even his wife was fair game, as I later saw in my teen years when I dropped by his homestead while walking home from school.

"Wanjirū," he called out to me and flicked his chin toward his wife in the way of introduction. "I married a njong'i!" (an ugly woman). Then he asked her, "Aren't you glad I married you?"

She gave him a side eye from where she sat by the fire but never spoke.

Flabbergasted, I did not open my mouth either.

Thimbara had even worked as a home guard.

In the mid-nineteen fifties, at the height of the Mau Mau Revolt, European landowners became terrified of attacks. They appointed home guards to guard their villages at night. Kamunge did not take part. But the manager at Major Stein's farm, next door to Kamunge's farm, recruited Thimbara and Macharia and trained them to shoot. He supplied each man with a long gun to guard against imaginary "terrorists" among the laborers.

"I can shoot you," Thimbara said to intimidate an occasional man, his gun still hung over his shoulder. He never got a single opportunity to pull the trigger.

*

I first met Thimbara one Sunday afternoon; I might have been ten or eleven. He appeared at our doorstep, breathing hard as if a hunter pursued him.

"I'm coming from Njeki's [Shopping Center]," he said.

Mami offered him a bench to sit on while she and he exchanged greetings and other pleasantries about family and the blistering sun.

"You need a break before you tackle Jumatatu [Mountain]," she said.

"I wouldn't pass through the village and not say hello to you and your family."

"I appreciate that," Mami said. "I don't get to see much of my family up there. Are they doing all right?"

"Yes," Thimbara said and paused before he changed the subject. "Is that man okay in the head?"

"Who?" Mami asked and perked her ears before she asked, "Njaga?"

"Uh-huh."

"Drinking is what's wrong with him," she said.

"Are you sure?"

"Of course, I'm sure. That's his weekend routine," Mami said. "If we don't hear him, we'd think he's sick."

We could hear Njaga's drivel at a distance, but we had not paid attention until Thimbara mentioned him. Then I understood Thimbara's heavy breathing and his rush into our courtyard.

He declined the food Mami offered and only drank water. He rested for a while before he said, "I better get going before it gets too late."

By then, Njaga's rants had faded away.

*

Despite the fear Njaga instilled in old men and his wild public displays, he did little harm to others besides his family. He usually lunged, planted his stringy right leg in front of his victim, torched the man with his red marble-like eyes, and thundered, "I'll beat you and feed you to my boys' dogs!"

A weak man walked away in haste.

"Coward! Just like your mother!" Njaga said and marched on, singing.

The worst I heard was that Njaga grabbed a man's arms and shoved him off the footpath. The man collapsed in a heap. With his way clear, Njaga strode on, boasting he would teach a lesson to manner-less old men who blocked his way.

According to eyewitnesses, when the cowering man raised his head, he glanced around. He did not need to be cautious: if he paid attention, he could have heard Njaga's tirades fade as he walked away. Unless sober, he never walked without talking or bellowing a rap-like song.

However, the village rumor mill spun a juicier version of the incident the following day. Word shot from mouth to mouth that Njaga had beaten an old man until he crawled on his hands and knees. Njaga's imaginary fighting prowess boomed.

But one day, the bully met his match.

Chapter 20

THE COWARD VS THE BULLY

I considered Njaga with no judgment whatsoever. He was just a part of our village's ecosystem. This could be because our paths hardly ever crossed. Whenever I heard his bellows, I dismissed them offhand.

The few times our paths crossed, he carried on as if I were not there. I quickly moved out of the way and watched him from afar as I proceeded wherever I was going. One Sunday, however, our encounter did not go as smoothly.

Baba squatted by our neighbor's house next to a public footpath, hammering a nail into a stool he was repairing for the neighbor. In a moment of harmony with our father, my sister Tabitha and I sat close by and watched him work.

Njaga, his entire six-foot-plus frame, appeared at a distance, bellowing.

My first instinct was to skip away to our courtyard. But with Baba close by, I waited it out while my mind speculated—what if Njaga confronted my father? Baba would get humiliated in front of us. I would get embarrassed for him, our family, and myself, as I had when Wainaina and his children insulted him.

Njaga marched on toward us, mouthing off his rap rhythm conquests. He stopped about twenty-five feet from us, pointed at Baba, and lunged forward. On the second lunge, Baba stopped working and laid his hammer aside.

"I can beat any man I want!" Njaga said. "I can beat you right now!" He jabbed his index finger toward Baba.

My father lowered his eyes to the hammer, then fixed his gaze on Njaga.

Worried, I braced myself for the worst. With Wainaina's incident fresh in mind, I wished Baba would retreat to our courtyard and return after Njaga left.

Instead, Baba, still on his haunches, behaved like the strongman who, by then, I knew he was not. Njaga, a younger man, could thrash him with one hand. But Baba had two things going for him—sobriety and a hammer—versus Njaga's drunken bare fists. Still, if it came to a bet, Njaga could disarm Baba and beat him to disability with his own weapon.

"Njaga, I have no quarrel with you," Baba said in a calm, deliberate tone. "Go on wherever you're headed."

"See?" Njaga said, took a boxing stance, and flung several quick jabs into the air. "This is what I do to cowards."

Now, ten feet away, it became even scarier because he towered over us.

I felt the urge to cover my ears and shut my eyes, unwilling to hear or see my father attacked. Yet my eyes remained fixed on the two men.

Baba remained calm while Njaga continued his boasts. "I'm the son of Ndario. I'll crush and clear useless men out of my way."

Baba picked up his hammer.

Oh! My! Is he going to strike first? I wondered.

Instead, he pointed the hammer at Njaga and wiggled it.

"Njaga, I told you I have no quarrel with you," Baba said. "This is the last time I'll warn you."

Njaga stopped, straightened his frame, and settled into slight drunken sways, perhaps surprised Baba was ready to fight back. He pressed his lips together and gazed at Baba with piercing red eyes for a long moment.

Baba gazed back, hammer still clutched in hand.

Without another word, Njaga veered east toward the village gate.

In about fifteen feet, his singing boomed again. He was ready to show his fighting prowess to any man who dared him, he thundered.

Relief washed through me.

That day, I regained confidence in my father. And I noted the power of a weapon.

*

One Saturday evening after supper, not long after that incident, we sat around the fire in Baba's thingira, where Mami now cooked most evenings to save on firewood. Baba embarked on one of his drunken monologues, which my siblings and I liked because those were the only times he shared tidbits of his life with us.

"Don't you ever fear anyone," he said, "no matter how strong the person may seem."

Baba paused for a moment to let his message sink in. We waited, eyes focused on him.

"If a bully is bigger than you," he said, "you have my permission to use a weapon—even if it means cutting them with a panga (machete.)"

"Ah!" Mami said. "Why do you tell children such things?"

"Is what I said not so?"

"It's terrible to tell it to young children."

I feared my mother's interference might cause Baba to clam up. She could not understand. She had not seen Baba and Njaga go at it.

To my relief, Baba ignored Mami's protests.

"When you're short on strength," he said, "you make up with a weapon."

"Just like that," he said as he slashed the air with his open hand to the left and to the right.

A panga remained the most versatile tool in all the village households. In the hierarchy of importance, it beat an axe, a hoe, or even a scythe, and now I had my father's permission to use it as a weapon.

When Baba said strength did not guarantee victory, I trusted his advice. I had seen him drive Njaga away with only a wiggle of a hammer. I now hung onto his every word while an idea took shape in my mind about the bully I dealt with.

Our keen attention to Baba's words must have worried Mami because she revisited the machete story one evening in Baba's absence. She said Baba had suffered much since his boyhood, the reason for his cavalier attitude toward violence. She advised us to ignore his drunken utterances about weapons.

I could not tell how my siblings took our mother's advice, but I dismissed it and stood firm in my conviction about the power of a weapon. My father's tutelage had empowered me; he had permitted me to defend myself.

But I did not realize that to defend myself, I needed more than knowledge, or that I needed access to a weapon when the need arose, or that I needed to understand a weapon could cause grave bodily harm.

Chapter 21

Self Defense

Nobody knew about my struggle. I had not shared with anyone that I had suffered for months at the hands of a bully.

After Baba and Wainaina's altercation, his daughter, Nyokabi, who, along with her brother, had called Baba names, turned me into her own project. But without close contact, she and I had nothing to disagree on as our fathers had. She hated to settle for name-calling and itched to finish what she, her twelve-year-old brother, and her father could not. She now confronted me whenever she got a chance.

Based on how Nyokabi ran her mouth during our fathers' quarrel, the mere sight of her made my heart quake with fear. She became my number one enemy, my only enemy in the twelve years I lived in the village.

One afternoon, Mami sent me to fetch water from the hydrant outside the village gate. After I set the gallon down and turned on the spigot, I saw Nyokabi sauntering in my direction. Fear grabbed me and escalated the closer she got.

"Didn't I tell you I'd beat you when I saw you next?" she asked from about ten feet away.

My fear turned into panic, but instead of an answer, I darted my eyes toward the gate, hoping to see an adult stroll along.

Because I had lived tucked in the backwoods for the first six years of my life and now stayed in our courtyard at the back of the village, I had never learned about fights. My experience was limited to Joseph's claims of how goat herders flexed their stringy muscles, village rumors, and Njaga's antics. I had not even heard or yet seen how Baba beat his sons. My only reference was Nyokabi's occasional threats and insults that she directed at me, which terrified me. Lucky me, she had never escalated them to physical attacks only because she had never cornered me alone.

But now she had her chance.

She pushed me with one hand on the shoulder to provoke me or to work herself up.

"Leave me alone," I said, with a feeble push of arms, and stepped back.

She shoved me again, this time with two hands and harder.

I staggered but steadied myself—no more "leave me alone," no self-defense strategy. I opted for total surrender, which, I supposed, would dilute her need for a full-fledged fight.

She now closed in, shoved, and slapped me on the temple.

It stung. I fell, half from fright. I stayed fallen, my eyes shut, and purely from instinct or fear, I played dead.

What will she do next? Kick me?

If I stirred, she might kick or smack me again and harder.

My water container overflowed, but I never moved a muscle, anxious about what she was doing.

After a few seconds, I heard her skip away.

I waited until the sound of her steps died.

*

Mami required us to stay in our courtyard when she and Baba went to work. She named a handful of families whose children she said could join us. Sometimes, children from other families trailed in. We let the ones we liked join us on condition they left before Mami returned. The children we did not care for left when we told them of Mami's instructions.

We children in that era obeyed adult authority without question. I, therefore, never expected a child to insist on staying if she learned my mother did not want her there.

One afternoon, however, Nyokabi Wainaina, at ten years old, became that one child.

She appeared at the four-foot entrance, her seven-year-old sister in tow. Without hesitation, they entered and marched toward us across the courtyard.

As the oldest of my five siblings who remained at home, I turned and walked toward them. I had no qualms about facing a trespasser in the safety of our home. With the other children around me and my little brother Waweru strapped to my back, I did not expect Nyokabi to confront me. Besides, we children somehow understood people did not force their way into others' courtyards.

"You're not allowed to come to our homestead!" I said.

"Your mother doesn't want us to play?" Nyokabi asked.

"She only said who can come."

Mami had said children from Wainaina's family could not come, but I did not want to tell Nyokabi and agitate her, at least not then.

"Then we can play," she said.

"You can't stay," I said.

She gave me a long, jeering look before she said, "Who'll prevent me?"

"Mami said you can't come," I said, thinking my mother's words would mean something to her.

"You just watch me. I'll play any time I want to."

My gaze froze on her, my mouth slightly agape. Was she serious?

"If you interfere, I'll beat you," she said. "My father will come and beat your father. And my mother will take care of your mother."

My mind jumped to how her father had intimidated mine. My confidence shattered while my mind spun for a rebuttal. None came.

Nyokabi inched in, mocked, and mimicked my voice. Slowly, I backed away to increase the space between us, seething as defeat smothered me. I reached the periphery near the uneven spot between thingira and the goats' cottage. With nowhere else to retreat, I stopped, trapped.

Just then, Baba's words rolled into my mind.

If someone bigger than you assaults you, take whatever is at hand, even if it's a machete.

What shall I do? I have no machete or a hammer to wiggle at her. I agonized.

Nyokabi closed in, her sister trailing right behind her.

… *take whatever is at hand…* my father's words continued.

My mind raced. My eyes swept the ground.

I saw a jagged rock—about two pounds.

I bent and grabbed it with both hands.

With my brother on my back and now a stone in my hands, my stance wobbled as I straightened up. I steadied myself and waited, my right hand bearing most of the weight on my shoulder.

I cannot wiggle the stone like a hammer, but my holding it ought to scare the nutty girl, my mind reasoned.

I expected Nyokabi to spew insults before she turned and marched out.

But, instead, she asked, "You think that will save you?"

She tightened her lips, arms outstretched, fingers curled, and rushed at me.

I flung the rock. She ducked.

The rock landed with a thump.

I gasped, my eyelids fluttering. For a second, I shut my eyes for a split second. My body tightened, horrified, hoping the rock did not land where I thought it did. Then the holler came.

The little sister staggered and fell, dazed.

Blood spattered. She hollered louder.

Nyokabi knelt on one knee to render first aid. As she examined the damage, her mouth kept the insults coming.

The little sister flailed her arms, crying, struggling to get on her feet. Halfway up, she wiped the bloody red trails to clear her face. When she looked at her palm, her eyes opened wide. She yelled and followed it with a series of screeching hollers.

Nyokabi fussed while she kept chanting, "This dog has killed my sister. Why can't you fight someone your own size? Coward!"

No more than fifteen feet from us, the other children abandoned their play and watched, frozen in place. The very young bit their fingers, confused.

I became mute with fear, not because I threw the rock, but because, instead of scaring Nyokabi, I hit her sister. Although the seven-year-old girl copied her sister and strode like a warrior, I felt sorry I hit her. A feeling I doubt I would have had if the rock landed on Nyokabi.

With her potty mouth in full blast, Nyokabi held her howling sister's hand, and the two marched out of the little gate.

Wow! How terrible! I had never seen a person hit another like that. Baba had said we could use a machete, but it did not occur to me the act would produce blood.

If I only held a rock, I had believed, just like when Baba fended off Njaga, Nyokabi would not dare attack me.

With the show over, the children resumed their play, half-heartedly at first, then as vigorously as before.

I kept to myself.

Filled with worry a young girl should never have to face, my mind tumbled. How could I have avoided the tragedy? I asked myself. No practical answer presented itself. I remained depressed while I waited for whatever punishment my parents thought I deserved.

Chapter 22

THE VERDICT

My brother Joseph talked of fistfights among goat herders. Despite his occasional detailed accounts, he never identified the fighters. He tended to embellish his stories and underplay or overplay his participation. Because he did not involve my parents, his stories left me with nothing to compare with my case.

By the time my mother arrived home, worry had worn me out. I could not wait to tell her to ease my mind.

"Did you go outside the courtyard?" Mami asked when I finished.

"No," I said. "We were right there where we play," pointing in the general direction.

"In that case," Mami said, "Nyokabi found you in your homestead."

Mami did not interrogate me or fuss about it. I wonder whether she would have remained that calm if she knew the damage I had caused. I never knew the extent of the damage either, besides my quick peek when the girl scrambled upright and blood dripped. I was too petrified by what I had done to look.

My mother's coolness eased my mind somewhat. But it left me wondering whether she would decide not to worry Baba with childish squabbles. I could not rest easy—until I learned of his reaction—in case she told him.

Free of a child on my back, I returned to the courtyard where we spent most of our daytime hours unless Mami or Baba sent us on errands.

When Baba arrived from work, our evening routine went on as always, with Mami making tea before starting the evening meal. But soon, that changed.

As soon as Baba emptied his mug of tea, Wainaina and his entourage entered our courtyard. My eyes landed on the white bandages that decked the little girl's head across her temple and half her brow like a slanting turban. Mr. Wainaina held her hand while Nyokabi walked to his left, and two men followed behind. The group turned left and entered thingira.

The white turban horrified me.

My worry resumed not only because of the wrong I had done but also because I had caused Wainaina to come to our homestead again. No one expected him to step into our courtyard after he and his children insulted Baba.

I heard talk that he "apologized" when his coworkers talked about the fight and that he blamed his behavior on alcohol. But my family never learned firsthand whether he apologized directly to my father.

I rushed to nyŭmba and told Mami about the visitors. I sat on the floor, morose like a sick child, not sure what would happen next. The suspense tortured me.

After five minutes of worry, Baba called Mami to thingira and said, "Bring Wanjirŭ along."

I trembled at the prospect; my heart raced.

"Tell Baba what happened," I told my mother.

"You have to be there," Mami said. "They can't decide on the case without you."

I followed her, on the verge of trembling.

I had heard of rare adult disagreements besides Kamunge's random rules, orders, and jail. But so far, I had not heard of anyone going before such an impromptu council, the ruling of which was binding. And now they wanted me to attend such a council?

Before the British invaded and colonized Kenya, Gĩkũyũ's supreme governing council ruled and settled serious crimes like murder. But impromptu councils—forms of small claims' court-types—settled minor family or community disputes. The impromptu councils survived despite the invasion and dismantling of Gĩkũyũ legal systems.

Now, I headed before such a council for the first time.

When Mami and I entered, our "visitors" turned their heads and all looked at me.

This scrawny, innocent-looking girl did all that damage? Their eyes seemed to say.

Mami never flinched when she saw the white turban for the first time.

The group sat in a semicircle, Wainaina next to his two daughters.

Mami picked up a stool by the wall and joined in. I sat slightly set back on the floor beside her, with Baba on my right.

"Wanjirū, these men say you hit this girl," Baba said and pointed. "Can you tell us what happened?"

"Y-e-s," I said.

"Leave nothing out."

I had never known Baba to ask a child to explain an incident. He alone decided on the guilt and dished out the punishment. But now, he did not ask why I clobbered the little girl. My fear ebbed somewhat.

As I answered his questions, I told the council about the incident and my previous interactions with Nyokabi. "Nyokabi pushes me around and calls me awful names whenever she sees me," I said. "She knocked me down once."

Hearing this for the first time, Mami turned and threw me a questioning look as she shifted in her seat.

I repeated the story I had told Mami about Nyokabi forcing her way into our courtyard. "I told her Mami said not to come. Then she called me names and said she'll pound me, and her father will pound Baba, and her mother will pound Mami. I got the stone to scare her. She rushed to attack me while I carried Waweru. I threw the rock. She ducked, and the rock hit her sister."

Baba turned toward Nyokabi. "Is what Wanjiru said true? That you and your sister found her in the courtyard?"

Nyokabi did not answer. Instead, she turned to her father over her sister's bandaged head. But without prosecutorial powers in someone else's homestead, Wainaina's jaws remained clenched, eyes fixed ahead. According to the council's rules, he could only present his case through his representatives or ask questions for clarification, but he could not counsel his daughter.

When Nyokabi realized she, and even her father, had to follow the rules, she talked.

"Wanjiru is a coward," she said. "Why did she hit someone who isn't her size?"

She then sat upright, arms crossed tightly over her chest, tight-lipped, her eyes fixed on the opposite wall. She was done.

Her words had come out confident, with a righteous tone that implied her assertion explained it all, and Baba should not bother her with more questions.

My father paused, perhaps taken aback, before he turned to the other council members.

For a moment, my confidence in him wavered. Nyokabi speaks two sentences, and the questions end.

How does she get away with such an awful, brazen attitude?

Why don't adults put her in her place?

I admired her begrudgingly and felt jealous that she could muster such courage.

Baba asked one of Wainaina's representatives to start deliberations. They talked in turns, like jurors. When they finished, Baba summarized the points:

- Nyokabi found Wanjirū at her home.

- She refused to leave when Wanjirū asked her.

- Wanjirū was carrying her brother on her back.

- Nyokabi is ten, one year older than Wanjirū. She had also attacked her before.

After a brief deliberation, the self-defense verdict was unanimous. The little sister, the jurors ruled, just got caught in the middle.

Henceforth, Nyokabi kept clear of our side of the village and never bullied me again.

The entire Wainaina clan moved away within a year, which I heard about a week after they left. I do not know whether the patriarch lost his job or what happened to them. Perhaps the villagers' collective curse got them after all.

Chapter 23

PROTECTOR AND TORMENTOR

I hated violence, verbal or otherwise. I hated that Wainaina and Njaga bullied my father, which I believed diluted his authority and diminished our family's standing in the village. But it had never occurred to me, or, perhaps, to any of my family members, that the biggest bully lived in our own household.

Our provider and protector was the person from whom we needed, occasionally, to protect ourselves.

Baba spoke in a regular tone, albeit soft, and used full sentences when he talked with adults. He spoke the same way to Mami unless—on a rare occasion—she upset him enough to warrant a clipped comment and a mean side glance.

To us children, however, although he never raised his voice, he engaged in one-sided interaction only. This amounted to functional questions, orders, warnings, reprimands, or complaints. He rarely addressed us relaxed unless he was drunk, which we loved because he engaged in monologues and even told us anecdotes about his life or chuckled. Even then, he only chuckled and never enjoyed a full belly laugh.

At all other times, his voice carried a tinge of impatience. And because he spoke softly and never got excited like Mami, he gave instructions only when we were near him. I knew to approach him when I heard him call my name.

If he sent one of us to fetch an item, and we asked for clarification, he asked, "Do you have ears?" before he clarified what he wanted.

It meant I did okay when he took the item I brought without a word.

Many times, I relied on his body language to gauge his mood. As a result, I suppose to my benefit, I became quite intuitive.

*

But my father's poor treatment of us girls paled against the physical violence he inflicted on his sons. My brothers never discussed the beatings. They accepted responsibility when goats went astray or raided people's gardens—which caused most of the beatings—or other offenses that Baba accused them of. We had all internalized that abusive parents were the norm.

My brothers started as goat-herd trainees at about age seven when they accompanied an experienced older sibling to the grasslands. During the training period, the trainer endured Baba's beatings for any goat-related offenses. But as soon as the trainee took over, perhaps at age nine, he received the beatings himself.

Joseph told us how he and other boys avoided parents or an occasional man who itched to dish out discipline in the parents' absence. Joseph longed, he said, for the "good old days" when boys wore pieces of cloth tied over their right shoulders. Shirts, he claimed, were an impediment.

To overcome the obstacle, he tore the seams of both sides of his shirt inches from his armpits. When he ran, the back of his shirt trailed behind and flapped like a flag. If anyone determined to catch him grabbed the back of his shirt, Joseph slipped out and left the chaser holding the shirt.

"That worked every time," Joseph said.

Well, until it didn't. Eventually, he had to return home or go to sleep.

*

...98...

When Mami cooked in thingira, if my brothers suspected they had wronged Baba, they knew not to join us around the fire. If they did, they sat at a distance from him. This made it hard for him to catch them unless he sneaked up on them while they slept.

It sounds insane that a parent would sneak up on his children in the middle of the night or at any other time and assault them. But my own father resorted to this bizarre practice.

I think he had done this with children in his first family over the years. In our own household, his second family, there could have been several, but I'm aware of two incidents, one of which I barely witnessed.

In one incident, which remains blurry, family gossip said my three older brothers—David, Simon, and Joseph—bolted out of their cottage before Baba reached the doorway. Their action denied him the beating he had planned. I do not know what they had done or how it ended. They lived like stray animals for three days. To help them without seeming to, Mami cooked mataha or mūkimo, the food we ate over several days, and stored it in the granary.

One day at dusk, I saw my brothers crouched behind the granary. Simon saw me before he dashed and clambered inside. I rushed back indoors, afraid to associate with wrongdoers. I kept the sighting to myself.

The other incident took place in Baba's thingira.

His thingira comprised a bedroom where he slept. But I cannot say much about it because, somehow, along the way, I had learned I should not enter my father's or brothers' bedrooms.

When Morry and Gĩthũi grew old enough to move out of Mami's house, they needed to move to the boys' cottage. But, besides the age difference between them and my three older brothers, the cottage was too small for all of them. Baba built a plank bed in one corner of the living area in thingira to accommodate my two younger brothers.

Unless Mami cooked in thingira, we, except Baba, spent evenings in nyũmba. When our mother told us stories after supper, the brothers arrived at thingira to find Baba already in bed.

One evening, the two, ages seven and nine, entered thingira already heavy with sleep. The last to enter pushed the door closed but failed to drop the wooden board into the door latch. Then, a corner of a coat that hung behind the door lodged between the doorframe and the jamb.

Hours after midnight, Baba got the urge to relieve himself. On reaching the living area, a wedge of moonlight startled him for a second; then, his nerves settled when he realized nobody had broken into houses in Solai.

My two brothers awoke, panicked and confused. They kicked, shielded their heads, and screamed as a cacophony of leather straps rained on them.

Chapter 24

WACKO DISCIPLINE

Baba's assault on Gĩthũi and Morry woke Mami. She rushed outdoors to confront the danger that threatened her babies. After she got her bearings, she settled back and returned indoors, a helpless mama bear who could not protect her children against the resident danger. Tradition and society had conditioned her to it; she had no option but to endure the pain.

When we sat around the fire in nyũmba the next morning, Mami asked my brothers what they had done to anger Baba without a mention of his loony behavior. It was a man's world, as James Brown sang years later.

That assault did not affect me because it happened while I slept. It joined the non-memorable abuses that I had heard of but never witnessed.

However, I did witness two assaults that traumatized me in ways I did not understand until decades later.

I heard the first incident with my own ears. It took place when David came home from boarding school. He could have been fifteen.

One Sunday, he chose not to attend Sunday church service, which my parents considered part of his school curriculum. Instead, David joined Simon on the goat-herding trail. He returned home mid-afternoon because he was not the main goat herder.

Used to eating lunch at boarding school, he was starving. But instead of lunch, he found our parents set for battle.

Baba called out to David in the goats' cottage. When he entered, he found Mami inside as well. The minute he sensed danger, he dashed to get away. But Baba had already shut and latched the door. Baba, armed with a whip, and Mami, with a leather strap, cornered David in the un-partitioned cottage. They both rained whips on David's body as they followed him like in a merry-go-round.

The whip cracks permeated the walls and reached us children in the courtyard, where we stood about, immobilized.

Whenever my childhood memories resurface, I hear those cracks on David's body or the wall when my parents missed their target or David's deathly hollers as he claimed his teeth were falling out. Meanwhile, my parents "laid down the law" with every lash. I recall Mami's voice asking David whether he wanted to turn into a vagabond.

That made no sense to me. I revered and admired my older brother. He was not like us village people. He dressed like Kang'oro in khaki shorts, a white shirt, and shoes. A helpless, pained confusion settled within me. If he preferred goat herding over church, and my parents had to beat and force him into it, I wanted no part of that place. From then on, the word church has always kindled negative emotions within me.

But David's beating turned out to be a mere warm-up compared to when Baba traumatized the entire household. I experienced my first blackout—an incident I cannot talk or write about without getting emotional, and I doubt I'll ever get over it.

Chapter 25

THE ULTIMATE ASSAULT

Our family sat around the fire in Baba's thingira. We children—Morry, Gîthûi, Tabitha, and I, all of us younger than Joseph—huddled together, frightened, seated on one side of the fire pit, on the dirt floor, or low benches. On the other side, Mami sat on a low stool, holding baby Wawerũ in her lap.

My two older brothers were absent. David was away at boarding school, and Simon was hiding somewhere.

Joseph's outstretched form lay across the fire from us on the third side of the fire pit. His right temple rested on the dirt floor, his face toward the burning fire only about two feet away.

The fire crackled, the only sound save for Baba's occasional self-talk, seated on his haunches or low stool beside Joseph's unconscious form. In his left hand, Baba held a bundle of dried twigs rolled up like a torch.

Many years later, I learned from Simon that it was a piece of mũratina (luffa sponge), one of the ingredients Baba used to brew his beer.

He held the little bundle over the fire. After it blazed, he blew out the flame and brought the smoldering smoky torch close to Joseph's nostrils. He did this several times. He claimed Joseph was feigning unconsciousness, and he, Baba, would prove it.

Joseph did not stir.

Did Baba try to revive him so he could beat him some more? Or did he worry he had killed him? Except for Joseph's prostrate form, my brain has blocked out memories of the beating that led to that frozen scene.

As Baba assaulted Joseph's nostrils, I felt burning sensations over my own nose and face, and my eyes watered.

I shut and opened my eyes several times before I became numb and queasy, and my nine-year-old brain went blank.

I have forgotten whether my next memory comes from the same incident or a different beating. But decades later, Simon assured me it was the same incident.

My memory picks up where my younger siblings and I stand across the courtyard by the boys' cottage, about fifteen feet from the activity. There is a full moon, or perhaps someone is holding our glass lamp.

Baba holds Joseph by his little shoulder. He tries to drag him across the threshold while he slaps him on the head and back.

Joseph wiggles to free himself while he emits exhausted, mournful screams like a snared animal.

We children inch closer to the doorway like crowds gawk at tragedies.

Perhaps Mami has laid baby Wawerũ down somewhere because she is baby-free.

She enters the cottage and stands on one side of the doorway.

I suppose Baba wants Joseph to hush and get in bed.

But because he keeps up his struggles to get free, Baba continues to slap him on his head and upper body.

Mami stands by, her face tight and eyes narrowed while the sides of her mouth twitch. After a minute, she lunges and yanks Joseph free by his armpits.

She throws him onto the bed like a sack of potatoes.

"ũgĩkua ndũkanjũre!" (I don't want to be short-changed in killing you!) she says. "Kira no kome!" (Shut up and sleep!)

A wooden chair by the bed nearly catches Joseph by the spinal cord behind his neck. He misses it by an inch; instead, his shoulder brushes on it.

He produces a piercing scream like an alien creature before he hits the bed with a thud.

That scream still lives in a corner of my brain.

Joseph was eleven years old.

Chapter 26

DYNAMICS OF VILLAGE ASSAULTS

Baba phased out physical assaults as each of the boys went to school, in part because they spent limited time herding the goats, which prompted most beatings. He stopped altogether in my brothers' mid to late teens after they went through rites of passage (circumcision). According to tradition, they had transitioned to adulthood. Although he did not beat them, the teenagers or young men had to put up with Baba's verbal abuse and put-downs.

Beatings for the younger brothers continued with less intensity as Baba grew older.

Today, it surprises me that my father did not maim any of my brothers. But it's clear to me that his abuse traumatized all of us physically, mentally, and psychologically. (It's no less damaging when children witness violence in the family, even if they are not harmed themselves.)

The abuse left scars in all of us that nobody else seems to see or recognize the symptoms that contributed to Baba's actions or connect them to the harshness of the colonial era and the family tragedy he wrestled with throughout his life, especially in his younger years.

If my siblings realized how much Baba's violence, poor treatment, and put-downs had affected us in different ways, they might have avoided the abuse they subsequently dished out to their own families in various forms and at different levels. They might have avoided passing the inherited abuse to their own children. My siblings also did not seem to connect the abuse to alcoholism, insane anger, minimal social mobility, and an aversion to risk-taking. At the same time, they toiled alone with minimal or no professional or personal network.

I shudder whenever my father's two severe assaults (I prefer beatings or assaults to the ambiguous word "abuse," which merely means name-calling in my culture and many others) replay in my mind. Seeing someone poorly treated or a violent TV episode can trigger a reaction where a bit of an electrical shock zaps through my body.

Mami spoke up on village affairs at school parents' meetings, mothered us children, and worked herself to the point of ill health to ensure she and Baba provided for us. But she never stood up to him or attempted to protect her children from his violence. The most she did was get agitated.

If Baba became unreasonable, Mami said, "You know how your father is." Or "Don't worry. I'll talk to him."

Like every wife of that era in Kenya and many of today's, Mami was an accomplice. She supported less severe physical "discipline." We all—including the victims—looked at crimes against children, or, occasionally, against wives, as an integral part of family life. The only comfort is that most beatings were mild. Severe or sadistic ones like Baba's were rare and confined behind closed doors. Njaga, the drunk, was the exception because he never cloaked his assaults.

Although family beatings were a part of our lives, I gathered that most fathers rarely beat their children. Perhaps because many of them owned a handful of goats or none, which caused most of the beatings in our household. I heard rumors that Warũgũ, the head milkman and husband of Wanjeri, Mami's best friend, never as much as slapped any of his children. (Incidentally, the men in Baba's first family never assaulted their wives and children.)

But because beatings took place in the privacy of homes, it became hard to tell which parents were committing borderline assaults from the severely sadistic ones.

We suffered in silence. We never discussed such family secrets publicly and did so sparingly among ourselves. Even in later years, when we lived close to our extended family, we guarded our nuclear family's home secrets.

It would not be a stretch to conclude that, in the fifties and sixties, when I was growing up, a father could have maimed or even killed his own child, and the authorities would not have charged him with a crime.

The practice of violence against children and sometimes spouses, although I hope not as serious, has persisted with my siblings' families and now into the third generation. Occasionally, I hear rumors of a wife being mistreated, and one time, in a drunken stupor, a relative told me he would teach his wife a lesson.

A few years ago, I witnessed my two sisters-in-law talk about discipline. One claimed how, over a decade prior, she had beaten her child until he had a nosebleed. According to her, she stopped when the husband said, "Why do you continue beating him? Don't you think he has repented by now?"

I suffered the agony of hearing that story silently instead of speaking up about bygones and alienating my hosts.

I want to note here that I am writing about the abuses I witnessed or learned about as a child with the benefit of hindsight. Because severe beatings happened only occasionally, we never dwelled on them. Besides, I was unaware of the lifelong damage they caused all of us—a fact I dare say has eluded my relatives.

And it's not just parents—some teachers did and sometimes still beat or physically punish pupils as their predecessors did.

However, Kenyan society gives them a pass unless a pupil gets seriously hurt.

I appreciate that teachers have a demanding job, teaching children from diverse backgrounds who learn and understand at a different pace. But it boggles my mind to learn of a teacher who physically punishes students, especially for failing to understand what they are being taught. Looking at the person in the mirror or the school and home environment may often explain the student's shortcomings.

From observation, most parents and teachers who assault children or assault others in the children's presence are ignorant of the lifelong damage they cause their victims, the young minds the universe has entrusted them with raising, nurturing, and shaping.

Chapter 27

WARAMA WA NJERŨ

One evening, when Baba went honey harvesting, Mami told us about part of his past life. Subsequently, she told us more about it here and there. By my late teens, my siblings and I knew most of his life, at least most of what our mother knew.

I interviewed Mami for a college paper in July 1984 and clarified several points. I learned other details from my brother Simon. Because he did not go away to boarding school, like David, he and my father spent lots of time together throughout Simon's teens and early twenties, especially when they went honey harvesting or guarding our garden against wild pigs.

"Your father is a good man," Mami told us that first evening. "But he has suffered a great deal. Perhaps that's why he doesn't scale back on discipline."

Baba's family came from Agũthi Location, Nyeri County, where his grandfather Njagĩ owned land. But because of the colonial disruption, Baba's parents, Njerũ wa Njagĩ and Wanjirũ, moved to Ragati Location, where Baba was born in about 1892.

His parents named him after his maternal uncle, whom the community had nicknamed "Warama," the one who spins. Based on Gĩkũyũ tradition of alternating naming children after their parents' relatives, Baba's parents must have lost three older sons.

From the start, people started calling the newborn "Warama," just like his uncle.

When Baba was a young boy, he saw the atrocities the British visited on the Gĩkũyũ nation in quashing their uprising. That changed and mapped the trajectory of his young life. He took details of that experience to his grave.

His father, Njerũ, died about 1903 after Baba turned eleven or twelve years old, leaving two sons and a daughter—Baba (Warama), Mwai, and Wairimũ.

To keep the family together, as per Gĩkũyũ custom, Wanjirũ needed to marry her late husband's brother. But Njerũ had no brother to inherit his widow. Instead, Wanjirũ took her children and returned to Agũthi, where she married Mr. Kamamia as his second wife.

Baba refused to call Mr. Kamamia his father. "I have a father, even if he's dead," Baba said to his mother during the move. When his mother insisted, he said, "I can't call another man my father after I saw mine die!"

Baba also refused to join a missionary school where they took in orphaned boys. He said he did not trust the missionaries. He knew his people's ways, he said, and wanted nothing to do with their foreign ways.

Why Baba did not go to his grandparents remains a mystery. Instead, he approached Mr. Kĩhagĩ, his late father's age mate and best friend. Mr. Kĩhagĩ took him in for the next five or six years.

Baba never told us what happened to his father's or grandfather's land.

Decades later, the family speculated that distant relatives may have taken over the land or that it became part of the British-occupied outposts. But no one knew for sure. Baba kept it to himself.

Before the British occupation matured, however, there remained limited non-confiscated community/public lands. While still a teenager, Baba cleared a plot for himself.

Meanwhile, in her second marriage, his mother Wanjirū and her new husband bore a daughter in 1905, whom they named Mūkami (who later became Aunt Julia), after Mr. Kamamia's mother. This was Aunt Julia. In another four years, Wanjirū gave birth to another baby girl.

The poor baby had no chance.

*

Baba walked home from where the bus had dropped him in Karatina, returning from Nairobi, where he had gone to buy the ceremonial white sheet and other supplies for his circumcision rites of passage ceremony. When he reached Ragati River, where people washed clothes and others drew water, he crossed by jumping from one jagged stone to the next. Right in the middle, a teenage boy at the opposite riverbank blurted out, "Warama! Your mother died!"

"What did you say?" Baba asked amidst people's racket and water swooshes.

"I said your mother died!"

Baba's legs buckled, and his rear smacked right into the river. Lost for words, he did not ask when or how she died.

In the following days, he canceled his rites of passage.

It's hard to speculate on the horrors that Baba's teenage siblings—Mwai and Wairimū—underwent after their mother's death. They had to care for their two young half-sisters—Aunt Julia, at six years old, and the baby, barely a year old.

Confused, Aunt Julia had not grasped the gravity of her motherless status yet. It confused her when she saw her father and another man roll her mother into her bedding and take her away, followed by another man with a shovel and other tools.

Aunt Julia sneaked out and followed the men. When they kept the shrouded load down, she hid behind undergrowth and watched. Her father and his friends dug a hole and buried the bundle she knew was her mother.

Later in the afternoon, Mr. & Mrs. Kamweti were walking on a footpath when they heard intermittent wails and whimpers.

Concerned, Mr. Kamweti left his wife by the footpath and followed the sound.

In the middle of brush and trees, he found Aunt Julia lying on a fresh mound of dirt, her temple resting over her little folded arms. "Maitū, Maitū, Maitū" (mother, mother, mother), she called out as she wailed.

*

The widower, Mr. Kamamia, did not want the burden of caring for his stepchildren, Wairimū and Mwai, or his own two young daughters. He abandoned the whole brood. People speculated later that he had longed for a son, perhaps the reason he married Wanjirū because his first wife produced no sons.

Baba set out to take care of his siblings.

Meanwhile, when Mr. and Mrs. Kamweti took Aunt Julia home and assessed the situation, they asked Warama to allow them to take custody of her. They raised her for the next six years.

But no one offered to adopt the baby. Baba now cared for his younger brother and sister and his baby half-sister. He could scavenge for food for the two older siblings while the younger brother babysat the other two, but he needed help with the baby. The children also needed housing because Mr. Kihagi's family, where Baba lived, could not take them all in.

Baba solicited help from anyone who could spare a favor. With the community still in disorder, he was having no luck. Before he gave up, though, Waiyaiya, an old widow with grown children, agreed to accommodate the siblings.

But Baba had no goats for the baby's milk. Even with Waiyaiya's help, he had little hope for his baby half-sister. Despite the struggle, Waiyaiya did the best she could. But the baby could not make it. She needed a mother to live, not a grandmother.

*

Baba went through his rites of passage the following year, 1913, under Kĩhiũ Mwĩrĩ's age group banner. The following year, he built a small house on his own plot. He and his two younger siblings lived there until he later built another house for himself and his bride. Decades later, in 1959, Kaguyu, the bride, was buried on that land. Today, distant relatives still own the land.

Baba never talked of his traumatic childhood or the details of how he and his two younger siblings navigated life from his mother's death until he married.

The one part he repeated many times was how he flopped in the river when he learned of his mother's death and how he postponed his circumcision rites of passage. He also talked about Mr. & Mrs. Kamweti, who took in Aunt Julia, and his adoptive father, Mr. Kĩhagĩ, as if they were our relatives.

And he made cursory comments about his horrific, nearly fatal stint as a member of the British Colonial Service.

Chapter 28

BABA'S BRUSH WITH WWI

Halfway through World War I, Baba and his brother, Mwai, were young men; Mwai barely out of his teens. Rumors of white people fighting in faraway lands reached Kikuyuland and trickled to them. But they never learned who was fighting whom. They went about their business, unconcerned with the foreign conflict. After all, they put up with foreign occupation right there on their own land.

The war reached a point where the British colonizers needed help. Where else could they get it but from the colonized? The colonial government decreed that the military would draft one son per family. This meant, at least in theory, that no family bore the burden of the war more than others.

The British soldiers and their African subordinates descended on the community. Families resisted sending their sons to a war they knew nothing about. Eligible young men hid to avoid the draft while their families claimed no knowledge of their sons' whereabouts. Officials roughed up fathers and threatened them with bodily harm unless they told on their sons. Timid fathers broke their silence. But diehards stood their ground. The officials razed those families' homes.

When destroying homes failed to nudge draft dodgers from their hideouts, the recruiters threatened fathers that unless they produced their sons, they and their families would become homeless because the government would confiscate their lands and livestock, the very bedrock of the Gĩkũyũ economy.

Demoralized, parents watched with helpless anguish as the colonizers whisked their sons away, thousands never to return.

Baba had not bothered to hide. He could not hazard the authorities razing his home. As the older of the two surviving brothers, he had surrendered to his fate. It comforted him that his younger brother, Mwai, would mind their homestead and their teenage sister, Wairimũ. Aunt Julia still lived at Kamweti's.

But Baba and Mwai were in for a shock.

When the recruiters came, they snared both, contrary to the one-son-per-family policy. The two brothers' protests went unheeded. They could have appealed to the authorities but lacked the capacity to do so.

According to the colonial policy, a native family man—a father, a married paternal uncle, or an older married brother—could petition the government for relief. But Baba and Mwai had no such married relatives. And neither of them was married to petition for the other.

Dejected, the two brothers left their teenage sister and joined the herd of other draftees, now members of the British Colonial service.

With minimal instructions, the officials led the draftees to Karatina and onto a train. It remained a mystery where or whom the colonial government wanted them to fight.

Along the way, the authorities dished out duties piecemeal. Recruits trekked inland and carried the British soldiers' luggage and supplies on their backs or shoulders back to the train stations. Before the train departed on its longest journey, the recruits made several trips inland. They changed trains in Nairobi.

Because of walking long distances with heavy luggage, exposure, overcrowding, and poor food, some recruits fell sick. A number of them died before they reached their destination. The officials ordered the dead removed at the next stop. The recruits did not learn until after the war how the government handled the bodies.

When the recruits reached Luo land, which they understood was Kisumu on the shores of Lake Victoria, they camped by the lake to wait for their steamboat. How long? They did not know. Neither did they know where they were headed. But they likely headed to Tanzania (Tanganyika at the time) to beat the Germans who colonized that country.

While the recruits waited, Baba, like many others, fell ill. The doctor diagnosed him with mūkũngũrũ (malaria). But he may have caught another worse disease because, even with quinine treatment, the disease persisted. Baba continued to suffer from vomiting and diarrhea and became so weak that he occasionally convulsed and became delirious. Medics quarantined him with other critically ill patients. When he did not improve, the doctor declared him too weak to weather the ailment. Of no further use to the troops, the doctor discharged him to die elsewhere.

To Baba, it did not matter. Treatment just delayed the inevitable.

When the outbound train came, porters readied him and his tiny knapsack. It contained his discharge papers and an assortment of meager belongings, one of them the government-issued dark green mug from which he drank porridge.

Mwai did not catch any of the myriads of diseases at the camp. Worried about his dying brother and their two sisters back in Nyeri, he would have preferred to accompany his brother home if he could. But it was not his decision to make. Instead, the officials gave him a chance to say goodbye.

Mwai approached his brother, where he lay on a stretcher before they took him to the train station. The brothers stared at each other with helpless, sad eyes.

"Nĩũkũhona," you'll get well, Mwai said. "Thiĩ mũchiĩ na thayũ," go home in peace.

Mwai spoke those words slowly as if he knew they were the last words he would ever speak to his brother.

With much effort, Baba focused his withered, sunken eyes on Mwai. He tried to speak but lacked the strength to respond except for a rogue tear that escaped from the corner of his eye.

My brother is trying to be nice, Baba thought. He and I know it's just a matter of time before I succumb. But he stuck to one wish: to die at home.

They both had seen discharged men die while they waited for the outbound train; their bodies remained behind.

At least he made it onto the train.

When the train arrived in Nairobi, Baba's handlers put him on a train bound for Nyeri. Relieved when he heard "Nyeri," Baba promised himself to hang on until he arrived home. Dying at home remained his wish and focus. He faded away many times, but he always woke up and noted whenever the train click-clacked to a stop.

They took him off the train in Karatina town at the same station where he had boarded the train months before. Even in his weak state, Baba worried about how he would get home. But the government workers had their orders. They delivered him to Karatina Medical Hospital.

Baba wished they had delivered him home. But he could do little besides focus on his mantra—hang on until I return home.

Feeling homesick and alone because nobody he knew knew where he was, he wished he could send a message to his sister.

After a month, the medics had stabilized him. But they did not cure whatever he suffered from. Still, they discharged him, now a mere skeleton.

No one knows how long Baba took to get home or how he got there. But when he arrived, he still had his balled-up knapsack that included the dark green bowl-like mug. That mug stayed in the family for over five decades before it disappeared.

At home, his teenage sister, Wairimũ, guided by neighbors, treated Baba with herbs, roots, and soups.

In two weeks, he could hold a brief conversation. By the end of that month, he had gained weight.

"That's when I knew I would make it," he told his family years later.

When Warama's health returned, he courted Kaguyu Waigwa, an orphaned young woman he had known since her girlhood. They got married about two years later.

*

When the Big War ended in 1918, Baba and his two sisters waited for their brother. Uncle Mwai never returned home or ever heard from again.

That was the norm. Unless a fellow soldier saw a fallen colleague and returned home to tell the deceased's family, the British colonial military never told families what happened to their sons.

It's been reported that over 100,000 Gĩkũyũ young men never returned to their families. They died on the battlefield or from diseases and starvation. This figure does not include other Kenyan African tribes' draftees.

As if the loss were not enough for the people to bear, when the Gĩkũyũ veterans returned home, some of them found their lands confiscated to increase the "white highlands"—prime land set aside for whites only—while the colonial government awarded medals and allocated free land to white veterans.

In Solai and the surrounding areas, except for Kamunge's farm, which later went to a World War II British veteran, every farm belonged to a World War I British major.

STATE OF EMERGENCY

Chapter 29

BABA'S FIRST SON

As our village life hummed along, nobody talked about Baba having had another family before us.

Some bits of news trickled to us from an occasional letter the first family sent to Baba about their suffering. But before age nine, I never concerned myself with what I heard about those strangers. Besides, I could not conceptualize what "suffering" involved.

Through Mami's occasional musings, I gradually learned about Baba's first family and the estrangement between them and him.

Njerũ-big, the second born and the first son, named after Baba's father, occupied the most favored slot in the family's hierarchy. But he never enjoyed that privilege. Friction between him and Baba may have started when he had had enough of Baba's abuse. He was also tired of watching his parents squabble.

But according to gossip, he was not a model son, either. The family claimed he was lazy and unreliable. And despite a later mid-life brush with Christianity, when he adopted the name Peter (although no one used it), Njerũ-big never proved the family's claim wrong.

The father and son relationship took its last breath one Sunday afternoon in early 1945.

Baba and Kaguyu had thrown an intimate party at her house that Sunday. By late afternoon, guests had left save for two men, one of them Njeru-big's mūtiiri (a sponsor during rites of pas-sage, similar to a godparent in Christianity). In their presence, Baba and Kaguyu got into a fight. The two guests eased out and hung out in the courtyard to give the couple privacy to settle their differences.

From his house behind the homestead, Njerū-big heard the scuffle and his mother's torrent of words—then a scream. On the periphery of the courtyard, he rummaged for a good-sized stick. By the time he got one, he breathed and rumbled like a charging bull.

But the two men aborted his mission when they grabbed and restrained him.

"There won't be another fight in this homestead," his mūtiiri said.

Njerū-big kept quiet and tightened his body to contain and control his volcanic anger.

"You hear me?"

Njerū-big grunted.

"Is that a yes?"

"Uh-huh."

Under the grasp of the two men, and perhaps embarrassed the men had witnessed his family's feud, Njerū-big tamed his mur-derous rage.

The men let him loose but remained alert.

With his mission to teach his father a lesson thwarted, Njerū-big turned and strode toward his cottage, changed his mind half-way, and made a right-turn, stick still clutched in hand. By then, he had built his heavy breathing back up.

He headed to the back of the homestead, where young maize plants thrived. Instead of Baba's head and shoulders, the plants became the substitute. With all his might, he swung the wood like a cutlass hundreds of times. He punctuated his swings with shouts, "I'm a grown man! I won't have anyone assault me along-side my mother!"

Njerũ-big's wife, Njoki, six months pregnant, tiptoed to the side of their cottage to watch her husband in action.

He flattened half the garden before he calmed his insane anger.

Njoki quickly retreated indoors.

"I've had enough of Solai," Njerũ-big declared to his wife when he reentered their cottage.

Njoki kept mum, probably wondering what a riotous family she had married into.

"I'll never share a homestead with Baba again," he said. "I'll leave, and I'll never return to Solai."

That evening, he packed his clothes in a wooden box, and early the next morning, he turned his back on Kĩrĩma-inĩ, the homestead he grew up in.

Three months after the birth of their son, Mwangi, named after Baba, Njoki traveled to Nyeri in the company of her brother-in-law, Joel, and sister-in-law, Gathoni, and joined her husband.

Njerũ-big and Njoki divorced during the war, and Njoki kept custody of their son. When the war ebbed, Njerũ-big married Wanjikũ, with whom he had five children I know of, although I met only two, Maina and Mũkami.

I met Njerũ-big for the first and last time in July 1980, when I went to Nyeri to attend a relative's funeral. After the funeral, he and I sat next to each other in Aunt Julia's living room. He looked as old as Baba. He wore tired clothes under a three-quarters-long grey overcoat belted with a twine, unlike the gray great coat Baba wore in the mornings or at occasional night outings, but flung it or hung it with its broad back belt over his left shoulder.

Amid others talking about the departed, Njerũ-big asked about my parents and the rest of the family in Solai.

He died in 2006, in his eighties, without setting foot in Solai again, not even for funerals.

Chapter 30

BABA AND HIS DAUGHTERS

Baba had six daughters, three from each of his two wives. Five of them are still alive; they range in age from the sixties to mid-nineties. He had a reasonable relationship with most of them, especially because he did not work closely with them like he did with his sons.

But he and his first family's youngest daughter, Wairimũ-big, had a tainted relationship.

Father and daughter first knocked heads when Wairimũ-big was a young girl when Baba yanked off her dress and burned it because he did not allow what he called "Christian dresses" in his homestead.

The second time Wairimũ-big and Baba collided was because of his one-of-a-kind he-goat. His friend Mũkuhĩ, envious of the breed, farmed in his goat so it could sire him a pedigree.

With David in school and Joseph barely four years old, Baba lacked another boy to help Simon. He appointed Wairimũ-big as a temporary goat herder—a boy's job—while the friend's goat got used to the herd.

But Simon and Wairimũ-big had no power over fate. From the first day, whenever the herders approached the goat, it gawked at them, ears perked, before it retreated backward.

When they failed to tame the stressed goat, they decided one would look after it while the other minded the herd. This continued for the rest of the week, but the goat never mellowed.

When it came time to go home that Saturday, Simon failed to coax it to join the other goats. Desperate, he rounded it, trying to force it to join the herd. It freaked out and bolted into the woods. Their search yielded nothing before they gave up. They feared they could lose the rest of the herd into the approaching dusk.

A search party that evening could not track the goat, either. After searchers resumed the following morning, they spotted a place with flattened grass and shrubs, blood and bones strewn about, the predator hooves' smudges unidentifiable.

Baba beat the two herders as sadistic human owners beat their runaway captive slaves.

From then on, Wairimū-big did not care one bit about her father. She sassed and called him insulting names when she turned sixteen.

After the onset of war, as a newlywed, she rode on the exodus lorry to the native reserve before she and Baba reconciled.

Before then, three years after Baba became a polygamist, after he and Mami married in 1937, Wanjirū-big, Baba's firstborn, named after his mother, had committed the unthinkable before she married. She broke the unwritten rule that a child cannot directly or indirectly lay hands on a parent. (Nowadays, people seem more progressive; they excuse self-defense.) She had laid her hands on her father.

One Sunday, Kaguyu and Baba held one of their occasional drinking parties in Kaguyu's house, next door to Mami's. Still new to the family, with a young child and not a drinker, Mami did not join the party.

After the visitors left, Mami winnowed beans in a gītarūrū, a round woven tray, in the courtyard near her house, baby David swaddled on her back. She heard hot exchanges coming from

Kaguyu's house. Because that was common after the two drank, Mami ignored it. Then she heard a struggle and grunts and guttural sounds. Concerned, she approached Kaguyu's house.

"I'll choke you today!" came Kaguyu's voice. "You'll never touch me again!"

From the doorway, Mami saw a human heap in the living room, Baba flat on his back, Kaguyu latched on top of him, her hands clutched around his neck. Meanwhile, Wanjirū-big straddled her mother from behind and pressed her shoulders down.

Mami grabbed Wanjirū-big by her shoulders and threw her so hard she hit the wall. Mami then grabbed and tossed Kaguyu aside.

(In later years, when Mami retold the story, in Baba's absence, of course, to imply she was stronger than either the mother or the daughter, she always capped her narration with "I told mother and daughter 'My parents raised me with meat and milk, unlike you who got raised with maize alone.'")

Baba scrambled to his feet as soon as he got freed, steadied himself, and cleared his throat. After stepping over the threshold, he hurried the best he could toward his thingira while he flexed and rubbed his neck, cracking it this way and that.

Wanjirū-big married Joel, who worked one farm away at *Kwa-Ndege*. (Ndege means bird in Kiswahili. It's likely Mr. "Ndege" used to fly a plane, hence the nickname.) During the exodus, she and her husband and their two young daughters and a baby son left before she gathered the courage to apologize to her father for helping her mother try to kill him.

She and her two disgruntled siblings may have expected never to deal with their father again. But when the war intensified in Nyeri and made their lives unbearable, the two sisters wished the one person who could help them would do so.

Chapter 31

EXODUS TO THE NATIVE RESERVE

It is hard to tell whether my father cared much about his out-of-sight first family's adult children. Even if he did, which I bet he did in his own way, he may have preferred not to deal with them. But he cared about his son Waigwa, with whom he exchanged occasional letters.

Named after his maternal grandfather, Kaguyu's father, Waigwa should have been low on my father's favoritism pecking order, but he turned out to be a good, obedient son. Although a grown man with his own family—a wife and three small children—by the time he and his family left during the exodus, not once had he talked back to Baba.

Waigwa had remained the one reliable son Baba could count on, except for the one time he defied Baba when he fell helplessly in love with Njeri Kuria. The two became inseparable, especially over weekends when they walked long distances accompanied by friends to attend dances and even helped organize them.

Despite Baba's complaints that the young woman had a smart mouth and quick, restless feet, ready to "follow" a man to every alleyway, Waigwa married her. After marriage, to Baba's repressed chagrin, now that the young woman was his daughter-in-law, the couple threw a dancing party in Waigwa's thingira right there behind our homestead.

But by the exodus, that was old news. Baba wanted Waigwa to stay on the farm. With my mother's children still young, Baba wanted a responsible adult family male around.

*

I never became interested in Baba's first family, even when I learned of them. To me, my family comprised Baba, Mami, and my siblings, and other claims on Baba were subordinate to ours. I maintained that attitude subtly until well into my adulthood.

But by the time I turned nine, my half-siblings' lives became real when Baba received a telegram from Waigwa.

*

Before the exodus, British farm owners hand-picked the Gīkūyū families they wanted to keep on their farms. The heads of families picked had to sign a loyalty agreement that specified they would stay loyal and defend the farm. In other words, they became indentured servants unless their employer said otherwise.

Most men did not know how to write; they put thumbprints instead of a signature. The few who could write signed and put their thumbprints beside their names.

The officials did not require women to sign. As dependents, they were of no consequence unless it pertained to interrogation and jails. Their husbands, fathers, or sons spoke for them.

Although picked to stay, Waigwa refused to sign. Kamunge, not keen to lose Waigwa's employment, enticed him by promising him that when Baba retired—a time no one knew when—Kamunge would promote him to an overseer. Waigwa did not change his mind. He had likely taken the Mau Mau loyalty oath.

He and some of his family members could not resist the lure of independence and Gīkūyū people getting their lands back from the British after the Mau Mau won the war.

Kamunge asked Baba to persuade his son not to leave. But when Baba tried, Waigwa retorted, "I don't want to remain at Kamunge's beck and call like a wife."

*

During the exodus, the colonial government designated lorry pickups on the Nakuru/Solai Road. As my family learned much later, the authorities told people not to take furniture or animals to the lorry pickups. But no one mentioned clothes or food. Families packed their clothes and cooked enough food for their journey.

Not until the morning of their departure did they learn that, except for changes of clothes, the officials' rules forbade them to carry food or other belongings. People smuggled the little they could, including food for their young.

But, despite his refusal to remain on the farm, Waigwa and his family and their mother, Kaguyu, were in luck. Because of Baba's long tenure on the farm for over twenty-five years, Kamunge said he would give them a ride, and they could carry food. He picked them up from the lorry pick up spot and transported them to the camp in Nakuru town in his Land Rover.

Waigwa and his mother each carried two sacks of maize, beans, and flour. According to Wairimū-big, her mother hid a head of an ax—to install the handle later—inside a mound of ugali.

Fearing theft by officials during body searches, Waigwa left his money behind with Baba so he could send it in installments after Waigwa and his family arrived in Nyeri.

The other family members joined the exodus lorry crowd. This included Wanjirū-big, her husband Joel, and their two daughters and baby son (Wambũi, Wamũyũ, and Mũrigũ); Wairimū-big and her husband, Njoroge Mũchũngũ; and their half-brother Werũ (the bonus son), who, unfortunately for him, left without his bride of one year because her father, Alan, refused to allow her to leave.

Instead of being transported directly to Nyeri as they expected, the driver dumped them at the gate of a camp on the outskirts of

Nakuru town. The officials herded them and hundreds of others into a sprawl of tiny structures built of split bamboo and thatch.

According to Wairimū-big, besides the stench from close-by latrines and the commotion, heavy rain fell on their first day, and raindrops splashed through the shacks' cracks. They slept on the dirt floor, covered with blankets they had brought. Some people slept without cover.

The pit latrines were fenced with bamboo next to the housing structures. People could see through the cracks when their colleagues relieved themselves.

"After two days, nobody complained about it anymore," Wairimū-big said years later.

Meanwhile, authorities interviewed the detainees to determine which of the three districts—Nyeri, Mūrang'a, or Kīambuu—people or their parents originated.

Baba's first family members were in luck. When Kamunge dropped Waigwa, his family, and his mother, he told the authorities not to confiscate the family's food and money. Unknown to the family, Kamunge had talked to Baba the day before.

"I'll see that your family doesn't stay at the camp too long," Kamunge had told Baba.

Kamunge kept his word. The British farmers had such power and confidence in the colonial government that it often took a mere phone call to get their favors met.

That one intervention enabled Baba's family to jump ahead of the line, saving them from a week or weeks in the congested, filthy camp. The officials interviewed and transported them to Nyeri after only four days.

In Nyeri, officials herded them and others t Kīng'ong'o camp for the final interview and record. Wairimū-big reconnected with her husband, Njoroge, before the officials released them.

As my parents learned later, Waigwa's suspicion that he would lose his money was justified. By the time they arrived in Kikuyuland, the people who carried money on their person lost every shilling.

Fortunately for the family, Aunt Julia owned a five-acre plot at Gataka-inĩ, where their brother Njerũ-big, who had disavowed Solai, now lived with his wife and son.

Waigwa and his family moved in with his brother's family. Their mother, Kaguyu, and her two daughters and the children occupied Aunt Julia's two-bedroom L-shaped wooden house. Their half-brother Werũ and Njoroge, their brother-in-law, spent nights in the barn.

Despite the crowded housing, Baba's first family found the basics they needed. They had a garden to grow food and room to rear chickens, goats, and two cows. And best of all, as they soon learned, they lived far from government officials' 24-hour watchful eyes.

The men planned to get jobs and lie low while the colonial government and the Mau Mau fought it out. Afterward, they hoped to get in line early for the land they expected the British to abandon.

That is the legacy of my family—no defenders of the nation. Survival and lying low were their mantra. But that did not mean they could stay on the sidelines unscathed. Along the way, the authorities accused two of them—Werũ and his brother-in-law—of feeding the Mau Mau. The two suffered dearly as they fought the accusations. But not a single whisper confirmed their involvement beyond having taken the Mau Mau loyalty oath back in Solai.

The rest of Baba's first family struggled as well. The burden of varied personalities and the discomfort of living cramped together got to them before the colonizers' long tentacles reached their doorstep.

Within six months, Waigwa and Njerũ-big's wives fell out. Waigwa, tired of his wife's nagging, approached a long-time friend of Baba at Gathũmbĩ, near Karatina.

"Warama's family shouldn't suffer," the man said, "while I have an empty house."

Waigwa moved his family and his mother from Aunt Julia's. They became *ahoi*, landless people who lived as squatters on other people's lands. But the relocation shielded them against turbulence, at least for a period. Waigwa got a job—an essential job—at a cereal factory in Karatina.

Chapter 32

WERŨ–THE BONUS SON

Grownups talked about atrocities in Kikuyuland and about courts condemning innocent people to hang. I did not understand. But from the adults' demeanor and the soft tones they used, I figured the actions were terrible.

We lived under controlled conditions. But after the initial screening two years earlier, when I mourned my mother's one week's absence, the villagers did not suffer torture or murder.

Except for a handful of white farm managers accused of slapping and kicking young African men who became belligerent when ill-treated, most of the colonialists in sleepy Solai used insults or put down or drove curfew breakers and trespassers to the police station. The worst things villagers expected were fines or jail terms when they could not afford the fines. But they worried about their relatives in Kikuyuland.

My parents' concerns became real when Baba received a telegram from Waigwa about Werũ's predicament when he became the first Baba's family member to get snared by the colonial tentacles. Aunt Julia's goat bore some of the blame.

Under normal circumstances, Aunt Julia decided what happened to her goats. But she worked as a nurse in Nairobi when one of her goats fell sick and died. The family dug a grave and buried it within hours. They hoped whatever killed it had not spread to the small herd.

But alas, in two days, another goat suffered similar symptoms. The animal looked listless and refused to join the others or feed. It lay down and curled up, away from activities.

To salvage the goat's meat before the diseased vital organs infected it, the family agreed to slaughter the goat. Werũ, his brother-in-law, Njoroge, and their friend, I'll call Mũraata, helped with the slaughter.

After they skinned the carcass, opened the stomach, and buried the innards in the garden, Werũ and Njoroge did the carving while Mũraata built a fire nearby and kept the grill ready.

Halfway through the meat roasting, the authorities descended on the homestead and accosted the three men.

A small group of home guards and their subordinates questioned Werũ and his colleagues and accused them: "You are the people feeding and supporting the terrorists!"

The men's denials that they had no affiliation with the Mau Mau and their explanation of why they had slaughtered the goat only elicited more abuse.

"Bloody liars! Terrorists!" one home guard said and shoved Werũ when he pleaded.

Even if the officials had accepted the accused's explanation, the men had already broken another law, albeit a lesser one. Their friend Mũraata was not a member of the household. It was against the law for three or more Gĩkũyũ men to assemble.

While the home guards conducted the interrogation, others searched every structure in the homestead.

Although they came up empty, they still decided there was probable cause to arrest the men. The officials left the evidence behind; they had seen the meat connected to the Mau Mau, and their word was enough to convince the court of the men's guilt.

That arrest changed Werũ's life trajectory.

Rumor had it that when officers or home guards went on a hunt, they interrogated their catch, manhandled them, and took them to court. But other times, they did not waste their energy on jails or court proceedings; they dished out the punishment themselves.

Werũ and his companions were fortunate. The officials took them to jail. Even then, their fate depended on the guards and jailors they found. Because of the overwhelming number of arrestees, the stressed jailors sometimes became judges, jurors, and executioners.

In jail, the three joined other condemned men. They suffered indignities and were interrogated, beaten, tortured, and hung upside down. The authorities even forced them to dig graves to bury their unfortunate colleagues.

In one instance, officials huddled Werũ with two men unknown to him. The officials told them to dig their own graves. The two men never uttered a word or pled for mercy. When the graves reached four feet deep, the soldier in charge ordered the prisoners to climb out of the graves together with their tools.

The terror-filled men tripped on themselves as they scrambled out.

"Stand in front of your grave," the soldier ordered, "and face toward me."

The men looked weak; they had trouble standing upright.

Werũ's grave was in the middle.

The officer raised his gun and shot the man to Werũ's right, point-blank.

The body fell outside the grave.

The gunman looked at the body before he sidled toward Werũ. Werũ tightened his body and squeezed his eyes shut. He heard the gun cocked before another shot rang out.

Werũ collapsed to the ground.

"Amka!" Get up! the officer said and kicked Werũ on his side.

"The kick awoke Werũ," Wairimũ-big said. "He realized he was still alive."

When Werũ collected his wits and scrambled to his feet, he saw the second man on the ground. By then, Werũ had peed on himself.

"*Bahati yako leo*," it's your lucky day, the officer said.

The soldier ordered Werũ to bury the two men.

When he tried to lift the first man, the man's arms got entangled, and Werũ fell. Weak from hunger, torture, and terror, he lacked the energy to get the body into the grave.

The officer ordered him to break the arms and roll the bodies in.

Werũ did as ordered.

"Werũ survived only because the soldiers didn't want to dirty their hands," Wairimũ-big told me when I interviewed her on December 8, 2014.

Even after this, Werũ had nothing to confess.

On the court date, instead of the court charging each of the men individually, the court charged the entire group as terrorists and convicted each one of them to hang.

Unknown to Werũ, when he got arrested, Waigwa had sent a telegram through his white supervisor at the cereal factory to Baba, stating Werũ and Njoroge were about to get hanged.

Because workers' telegrams and letters went through their employers, Kamunge had seen Baba's telegram a day earlier. When he received it, he paid attention because it came from the factory's white supervisor. For clarification, he called the supervisor. He then called authorities in Karatina before he gave the telegram to Baba the following day. Because of those two phone calls, Werũ and Njoroge were spared. They never learned what happened to their friend Mũraata or saw him again.

As someone told the family later, one of their neighbors, an informant, had contacted authorities and claimed Werũ and the two men were roasting meat to deliver to the Mau Mau.

According to Wairimũ-big, her husband, Njoroge, did not return to Aunt Julia's homestead. He holed up somewhere before the two reconnected and reconsidered their future together.

But when Werũ arrived home, he shook like a leaf on a windy day. With his overjoyed family underfoot, he stammered as he told them snippets of his ordeal.

He remained indoors, immobilized for days.

But one day, he finally gathered courage and confronted the outdoors. Without a word to anyone, he shuffled and shuffled and disappeared.

His disappearance reverberated through our family up to my adulthood.

Chapter 33

LIFE IN PROTECTED VILLAGES

As if Werũ's disappearance were not enough trouble, the next ordeal befell the entire family.

In mid-1954, a British officer with his African constables and home guards descended on the family and their neighbors in Gataka-inĩ community. The officials marched through homesteads, ordering people out.

On their way out, people scrambled to grab whatever clothes and valuables they could carry. According to Wairimũ-big, people who had more time before the authorities reached their homesteads buried their money and other valuables in their backyards. A woman she knew buried her special dishes.

As soon as each family reached outdoors, constables torched their houses. Amidst the chaos, children got separated from their parents, some never to see each other again. Goats, chickens, and pets ran amok, and many perished in the inferno.

Officials herded the family and their neighbors to Gathũmbĩ, near Karatina, one of the huge, fenced, prison-like guarded villages. The village comprised rows and rows of small identical circular huts built of dirt with conical roofs, sprawled on a swath of land devoid of a speck of plant life, and left un-partitioned for easier impromptu searches. A trench ran along the outside of the prison-like fence.

"I've never entered a concentration camp," Wairimũ-big told me decades later, "but that village could as well have been one."

People learned later that home guards and their cohorts returned to the emptied neighborhoods, now littered with mounds of ashy dead or smoldering fires. They helped themselves to animals that survived. They excavated any freshly dug ground they found in backyards for valuables.

Through whispered rumors, people learned the reason for the chaotic evacuation. The authorities had suspected residents were feeding the Mau Mau.

Such activities were so hush-hush that they never went beyond rumors, and there was likely a leak.

Individuals from some Kikuyuland permanent families—who had taken the Mau Mau loyalty oath—supported the cause, volunteered as conduits or couriers, and delivered food, other supplies, and news to the Mau Mau. But people born or raised elsewhere and transported to Kikuyuland during the exodus were unfamiliar with the logistics and too unsettled to feed their own families, let alone anyone else.

Whatever the case, the colonial government intended to cut the alleged supply chain. The officials rounded up people throughout Kikuyuland and herded and corralled them into the so-called protected villages.

Caroline Elkins, who took ten years to research and write *Imperial Reckoning, The Untold Story of Britain's Gulag in Kenya*, states, and I paraphrase:

In June 1954, the British War Council forced villagization throughout the Gĩkũyũ homelands. By the end of 1955, less than eighteen months after the introduction of the mandatory measure, the government had removed 1,050,899 Gĩkũyũ people from their scattered homesteads throughout Central Province (the native reserve), Kikuyuland, and herded them into 804 villages comprising 230,000 huts.

This number does not include the thousands of other Gĩkũyũ men, women, and youth whom the colonial government held in concentration camps or the Gĩkũyũ living in segregated villages like ours that were scattered across British-occupied farmlands or in townships and towns.

As with the other Gĩkũyũ-owned lands, after the government cleared Gataka-inĩ of its inhabitants, it cordoned off the area. Every so often, women returned to their gardens to fetch food, at least whatever had survived neglect and the official attack. But they could only go in the company of armed guards.

People who did not work essential jobs woke at dawn and rushed to gĩtatĩ (government mandatory work with no pay). And because the colonial government had detained able-bodied men in jails and concentration camps, most gĩtatĩ workers were women and old men. Young and middle-aged men who remained in villages did so to work in factories and other essential businesses.

Home guards and their subordinates supervised people from sunup to sundown at the mandatory work sites. People dug and terraced land, dug trenches around the villages, worked for the home guards' families, or worked wherever the officials ordered them. People could not drink, eat, or even talk when they worked; otherwise, drill-like orders tortured their ears, or whips landed on their backs.

Digging trenches affected people the most. Because guards allowed no rest, diggers fainted from exhaustion, hunger, and dehydration. Years later, Wairimũ-big told me she, in her mid-twenties, saw people collapse and die. Guards ordered fellow workers to dig and bury them in communal graves.

Unlike the laughable half-finished trench behind our village fence in Solai, trenches in Kikuyuland were wide, with spikes at the bottom. It ensured that anyone determined to scale the prison-like fence found the spikes waiting.

A story of a man who gambled his life by scaling the fence went around our village. The following morning, loyalists found him prostrate with spikes through his motionless body. Gĩkũyũ men loyalists occupied home guard posts and commanded an entourage of foot soldiers. These officials ensured there was no contact, real or imagined, between the Mau Mau and the Gĩkũyũ community. They also acted as a buffer between the masses and the colonial government, particularly the white community. The poor villagers got caught between the British Colonial officers with their Gĩkũyũ loyalists on one hand and the Mau Mau freedom fighters on the other.

The Gĩkũyũ puppets also did other grassroots dirty jobs. They contained and managed the villages. The government gave them the authority to starve, mishandle, maim, or kill—heinous crimes that qualified those puppets as murderers and rapists, eligible for criminal conviction if Kenya were not a British police state.

Those powerful men answered to a white man, even more fierce, who managed a major village outpost or a bunch of smaller ones.

Home guards were lethal. "To meet a home guard," Wanjirũ-big, my half-sister, once said, "was like meeting a hungry man-eating wild animal on a hunt."

When the colonial government accused a person or people of being members or sympathizers of the Mau Mau, the puppets punished the villagers en masse. This included denying them a trip to the gardens to fetch food, carrying out whole village inspections, or physical beatings and whippings.

To ensure villagers toed the line, home guards conducted impromptu searches Gestapo-style, night or day.

During those official searches, "they beat people, hauled them to jail, or made others disappear," Wairimũ-big said.

She avoided telling me excruciating personal details or about crimes like rape and other dehumanizing incidents she saw or experienced. Those conditions led to her and her husband's separation. By then, the two had a small girl who remained with her mother.

Whenever I asked Wairimū-big for certain details, she scrunched her face, lips tightened, and hung her head to the side. Besides the pain, I suppose, she feared that if she told me, I might write about that shocking part of her life.

Even telling me what she did, sixty years later, she still got emotional and paused several times to compose herself before she could continue.

Chapter 34

My Two Half-Sisters

Baba's first family saw the colonial government's sanctioned assaults, injustices, and deaths. They starved and lived in panic. But, so far, none of them had seen the Mau Mau in action.

Unlike the soldiers and home guards, however, Mau Mau operatives lacked legal cover or freedom of movement among the masses. Hence, they could not afford the luxury of overt, protracted punishment or torture. They needed to be quick and precise in their operations.

But they did not concern themselves with common people; after all, those were the ones they were fighting for. They focused on the colonialists, the loyalists, and their enablers. The Mau Mau struck under cover of darkness and dished out their form of "justice." Although their punishment came fast, it was no less lethal, as my two half-sisters found out.

"We were like walking corpses," Wanjirū-big said much later. "We just went through the motions."

Living in the fortified village, she and her three young children, Wambūi, Wamūyū, and Mūrigū, along with her sister Wairimū-big, with a baby girl of her own, Wanjirū-big became overwhelmed. With their ex-husbands focused on survival, the women had also become husbandless.

Wanjirũ-big's husband, Joel, had gone AWOL or got himself arrested. He could not handle a family. Wairimũ-big and her husband, Njoroge, had agreed to separate; he could not protect or take care of himself, let alone a family. After his close date with the noose, life terrified him.

Now, besides the turmoil they wallowed in, my two half-sisters and their children had nothing to eat.

One day, the two older children took a bowl outdoors and foraged for stray grains. They took a fistful to their mother to cook. The two women worried the famished children would starve to death.

Their mother, Kaguyu, who still lived with her son Waigwa's family outside the fortified village, occasionally pilfered small amounts of food from her son's family and smuggled it to her daughters. But her son, with his meager wages, could not adequately feed his household, let alone provide extras for his sisters and their children.

Kaguyu could not stand to watch her children and grandchildren starve. She sought help from her male cousin, who lived outside the village on his own land and who she understood had connections. If her daughters lived outside the village, they could forage for food because the home guards would not watch them as closely.

But her cousin did not have enough room for the family. He asked his grown, unmarried son whether he could help. Because Karanja, the son, lived alone, he agreed. He petitioned the home guards to let the two sisters and their children move in with him.

After the sisters moved in, whispers trickled down to them that Karanja was a home guard informant. But wherever he went to work, he left in the mornings and returned late afternoons. And, except to visit a friend now and then, he displayed no suspicious behavior.

Before the month was out, officials claimed plants in people's gardens provided cover for the Mau Mau. They ordered owners to clear their gardens of any plant high enough to conceal a squatting person. Only creeping plants like sweet potatoes remained. But Karanja's and loyalists' gardens remained intact, sticking out like oases in a savanna.

The sisters waited, worried home guards would drop in and snare their benefactor for defying their orders. But not a single knock on their door or a raid took place.

But others, who had their eyes on Karanja, got their suspicions confirmed.

One day, Wanjirũ-big and her sister left the children at home and joined the guard-herded group in their garden. The two sisters pulled weeds and gathered sweet potatoes in the allotted time.

At home late afternoon, Wanjirũ-big delayed cooking to save on firewood and ensure Karanja found the food warm. To quiet the children's complaints of hunger, she peeled a medium-sized sweet potato for them to chew.

At dusk, Wanjirũ-big prepared the sweet potatoes for boiling while her sister kindled the fire. Soon, Karanja arrived from work, tired and thirsty.

"It's been a hard day," he said. "Can we have tea before you cook?"

After tea, Karanja excused himself and lay on top of the covers of his bed that he had set in the living area, which he had curtained off for privacy.

The rest sat around the fire pit while the sweet potatoes steamed. They heard an insistent round of raps on the door. Panic set in. The home guards have come, they thought! But they soon noticed the difference. Home guards knocked and mouthed off their authority. This time, the knockers did not.

When one of them eased the door latch, it flew open.

The sisters gasped.

They faced *Matenjagwo* (the ones who never shave)—four-armed, stern-looking men in military fatigues and the unmistakable dreadlocks and piercing, hardened eyes.

"Where is the owner of the house?"

Terrified, the two women's mouths failed them. Instead, like robots, they and their children's heads turned toward the curtained bed.

Two of the men strode toward the bed and yanked open the curtain.

They grabbed Karanja, one on each side, and dragged him with his toes barely touching the ground.

The first blow landed at the threshold.

Karanja squealed—a waste of his breath.

The group vanished into the night.

In the morning, early risers found Karanja's bloody body dumped near the home guards' outpost, a warning to future informants and snitches.

When Mr. Cousin, Karanja's father, learned of his son's death, distraught, he marched straight to his now-late son's house. He wanted answers.

The traumatized sisters told him what happened.

Cousin next paid a visit to Chief Kagīmbī's office. He repeated the story to the chief.

"The sisters witnessed my son's abduction and possibly his murder," Cousin said. "Chief, you need to interrogate them in case they know more."

"There is no need to sacrifice the women," the Chief said.

Cousin insisted; he and the Chief knew each other well.

After a brief back-and-forth exchange, the Chief pulled his rank and said, "I don't want to hear about this matter again."

Cousin left, his face tightened, slightly shaking his head.

Why did the Chief protect the witnesses?

Cousin confirmed later that the Chief said if he reported the sisters to the authorities, they would interrogate them and label them Mau Mau collaborators.

The Chief was one of those officials who kept their heads down, did a balancing act between the various groups, and remained neutral. He knew the sisters from the fortified village, and from their demeanor and the pitiful way they looked, he did not believe they could be collaborators.

Unbeknownst to the sisters, Cousin was an informant just like his son. In months, another handful of *Matenjagwo* visited his homestead and closed that chapter as well.

*

Despite the two sisters' poor relationship with their father, they considered sending him a distress letter. But without them knowing how to read and write, it meant asking their brother Waigwa to write for them. If Waigwa was on excellent terms with Baba and had not asked for help, what chance did they have?

In time, however, Wanjirū-big saw another gruesome episode that left no doubt that she and her sister needed to leave Nyeri before tragedy befell them.

She visited her friend's family one evening. When she and the family sat around the fire, waiting for food, a small group of the stern men in dreadlocks entered. The family gasped, sat straighter, and, from the littlest to the oldest, gawked at their visitors, awaiting the verdict.

Two Mau Mau men approached the man of the house.

"Sit back!" one of them said to the rest of the family as he swung his arm and pointed to the side.

The family scrambled and cowered next to the wall.

The stern men slashed the man from limb to limb. Job done, they cleared the fire, dug a grave in the fire pit, buried the body parts, and flattened the dirt.

They told the family to resume cooking and left.

Chapter 35

THE MAU MAU TRIGGER

What fueled the Mau Mau? What made them sacrifice their lives and families and become that determined and committed? What drove them to such lengths? The reason that made Bildad Kaggia (a lifelong fighter for Kenyans' freedom and dignity) state, "Our struggle demanded great sacrifice, perseverance, discipline, firmness, ... and unity of will." [Maina wa Kĩnyattĩ (2008-113).]

The reason went back generations, from when the British invaded and conquered Kenya. After their defeat, Gĩkũyũ men (and women and other tribes) had not lain back and meekly submitted to their oppressors. As Maina wa Kĩnyattĩ eloquently stated in Agĩkũyũ: 1890–1965, three generations fought for Kenya's independence.

The first generation comprised people who saw Kenya's invasion and led or supported the uprisings against the invaders. These included leaders like Waiyaki wa Hinga, Gakere wa Ngunju, Koitalel, Mwangeka, and many, many others. But their weapons and tactics were no match for the British.

The invaders crushed each micro-nation one by one from the Indian Ocean to Lake Victoria, the lake so named after Queen Victoria by British explorer John Hanning Speke in 1850. (The Agĩkũyũ knew the Lake as Iria rĩa Rũĩgĩ.) Even after independence, it still bears that name. I guess that because Lake Victoria spreads over Kenya, Uganda, and Tanzania, the three countries—if they have ever addressed the issue at all—have never agreed on a name to replace the colonial title.

The invaders overpowered the natives through better weaponry, bogus treaties the invaders signed but never intended to keep, reinforcement from England, and cooperation from several traitorous local leaders like Masaku and Mumia. (Both men's names are now commemorated in Kenya's history as Machakos County and Mumias Town, respectively.) These traitors turned on their people for the colonialists' recognition, approval, and administrative job posts.

The second generation, which included my father, watched the invasion as children. They came of age at the beginning and middle of World War I. The colonial government forcibly hauled thousands of them to war, including my father and his brother Mwai. They worked as porters and did other menial support duties. The British military did not allow or train them to use guns, except in rare cases.

The men who did not get drafted took over the activism of the earlier generation. They included Harry Thuku, Kang'ethe, Jesse Kariuki, James Beautah, Jomo Kenyatta, Mbiyũ wa Koinange, Mũthoni wa Nyanjirũ, Mũindi wa Mbĩingũ, and others.

This second generation did not attempt to use spears, shields, bows, and arrows, which had proved no match for the British guns. They resorted to legal campaigns. But from the ill-treatment they received from the British, they understood the colonizers cared little about native laws. The generation now campaigned based on the colonial constitution. They mistakenly believed the British would somewhat respect their own laws, listen to reason, and leave Kenya. Or, at the very least, would manage Kenya more equitably. The activists seemed not to realize that the British thought of them merely as a sub-human race, good for nothing more than serving their oppressors.

This second generation plowed ahead and started political parties. These included the East African Association, Gĩkũyũ Central Association, and the Kenya African Union (KAU) chaired by Jomo Kenyatta.

Over the years, men and women members and their supporters organized and agitated against the colonial government through newsletters, labor unions, and overt and covert meetings. They appointed representatives to negotiate through official channels in Kenya and England.

In 1931, KAU sent Jomo Kenyatta to the colonial office in England to deliver a memorandum of natives' complaints about their confiscated lands and abuse of power and to request fairer land distribution, better treatment, and observance of basic human rights for the natives. The colonial office in London rebuffed him.

Kenyatta stayed in London for fifteen years, married one of the colonizers' daughters, and fathered a son.

One of his highlights was his association with other African political luminaries, who included Julius Nyerere of Tanzania, Kwame Nkrumah of Ghana, Sékou Touré of Guinea, and others. He returned to Kenya in 1946 (his British wife and bi-racial son remained in England) and resumed the Kenya African Union chairmanship.

Kenyatta brought little to show for his protracted campaign in London. But he had gained an academic education in anthropology and economics, polished oratory skills from addressing groups at Hyde Park, and a clearer political worldview and associations. He and the other activists in his camp still believed Kenya should gain independence through democratic means based on equity, social justice, and human rights. They continued with their political campaigns.

However, a group of their younger members—the children of the second generation—disagreed with the legal means premise.

They declared the natives needed to train themselves and use forceful revolutionary means to eject the intruders.

The splinter group founded a covert association, which trained young men in the art of armed revolution and groomed them to fight for Kenya's independence. In time, they formed the Kenya Land and Freedom Army (KLFA) party.

Meanwhile, World War II had begun.

Similar to World War I, the colonial government drafted another wave of thousands of young African men. But this time, instead of forcibly hauling them, the officials promised them lucrative jobs in government or loans to start businesses after the war ended.

A segment of the men had reached grade eight in school and passed the Kenya African Primary Education national exam (a higher standard of education than many of today's Kenyan high school diplomas), but they lacked the money to attend high school. Others had reached grade eight but failed the exam, and many others had reached grade four and aged out. These men now saw an opportunity to help better themselves.

Unlike in World War I, when the colonial masters confined Africans to menial jobs only, Britain needed more skilled fighters for World War II. They trained the colonized in weaponry and the art of war. Although the British military housed the African soldiers in sub-standard living quarters, segregated them from the Europeans, and fed them poorer diets, during combat, the races fought side by side.

The African soldiers saw white men kill other white men. The commanders also ordered the Africans to do likewise. It gave the novices a valuable new political perspective.

Marginalized and discriminated against while on active duty, the young African men started covert meetings. Cooped up in segregated quarters, in a homogeneous group, they could organize without concern for loyalists, snitches, or gossipers. They discussed the state of colonial Kenya and the strategies needed to change its course. However, they could get clarity for future action only after they returned home and saw how they fit in and how the colonial government treated them.

After the war ended in 1945, the veterans returned home with valuable warfare skills and articulated political awareness. The colonial government paid each of them a month's salary, allowed them to keep their military uniforms, and issued them insignias bearing the image of King George VI. The officials instructed the veterans to wear the supposedly prestigious insignias so their communities would respect them for fighting for the Crown.

Aware of the political agitation and tension in the country, the colonial officials warned the veterans not to indulge in politics or spread propaganda about the war they had fought or the colonial government. If they did so, the officials warned them, the police would arrest them, and the government would treat them as they had the German and the Italian enemies on the front lines.

Then, the government discarded those veterans, jobless and landless. They returned "home," crippled physically, psychologically, or both.

Distraught and broken, the African veterans could not reconcile what they suffered in the white people's war that they had no stake in and the oppression they returned to at home.

Many veterans, mainly from Kĩambuu, the areas surrounding Nairobi, found their families' lands seized and their families evicted. They now had to seek accommodations with relatives and friends in towns or villages.

In contrast, the colonial government awarded medals, land, and seed money (to resettle and run their new farms and businesses) to European veterans (even the German and Italian war prisoners) or employed them in government departments.

The African veterans weighed their options: nurse their bitterness while they struggled to make a living, roll over and watch life pass them by, get disillusioned and turn to criminality, or pull themselves together and think about the ideas they had kicked around during their barracks' covert meetings.

With time on their hands, the young men looked around. They learned of and approached the KAU splinter group that had formed the Kenya Land and Freedom Army (KLFA). The revolutionary group needed more skilled fighters, especially ones trained by the enemy. And the Gĩkũyũ veterans liked the warm reception they received from KLFA and what they heard from its members. They joined forces with the splinter group.

The World War II veterans and the home-trained KLFA (later popularly known as the Mau Mau) members became the third generation to take a decisive stand to fight for Kenya's independence.

In October 1952, they took up arms, entered the forest, and waged guerilla warfare against the British colonial government. Hence, most Mau Mau leaders in the forest were former World War II veterans.

Chapter 36

WAIGWA

So far, none of Baba's first family members had died. Well, Werũ had disappeared, a likely death—based on the conditions they lived under in the native reserve—but the family did not count that as such.

The family's hopes of independence and the natives getting their lands back now seemed like one arduous fantasy. They had gambled but won a nightmare instead.

Rumors swirled in our village that the British wanted to reduce Gĩkũyũ tribe's population or wipe it out altogether, thereby eliminating another future threat. Another rumor claimed the British had offered the tribe independence. The independence would cover Central Province, the native reserve comprising the current three counties (Kĩambuu, Mũrang'a, and Nyeri). If this had happened, it meant a tiny land-locked "country" (smaller than the American State of Connecticut) like what the South African apartheid regime assigned to Transkei and three other homelands in the 1970s. Those like us who lived outside that congested native reserve—about a third of the tribe—would have become peasant foreign workers in their own country.

The British made the offer to Jomo Kenyatta and his KAU group. Although the determined members had sacrificed a big part of their lives in pursuit of Kenya's independence, the colonial government saw them as a more malleable political faction since they campaigned and petitioned for independence through legal means. To their credit, Kenyatta's group refused the offer.

The colonial government had detained those leaders (and subsequently thousands of others) in October 1952. They now toiled in arid Lodwar and Lokitaung detention camps in northern Kenya.

Unlike the rest of the Gĩkũyũ masses, Baba's family had the choice to stay on the farm. But they had opted to join the exodus instead. They now resolved to hunker down, stay neutral, come out alive, and return to Solai. Or, as Waigwa had put it when his spirits rode high, return to the farm and "be at Kamunge's beck-and-call like a wife."

So far, Waigwa had fared better than his siblings. Thanks to his family and Njeru-big's family's disagreement, he had ducked the goat-slaughter arrest and the Gataka-inĩ sweep and inferno. He still worked at a cereal factory in Karatina.

For a year, every time a home guard or a soldier stopped him, he produced his government ID and a passbook. They always found his papers in order. He had ensured that, determined to ride out the war without a blemish. He also kept his own company and hurried home when the factory let employees out.

But his luck ran out when he met with a patrol group of young non-commissioned British officers (NCOs), who people called Johnnies, most of them barely out of their teens. As demanded, Waigwa handed over his passbook and ID. The soldier who checked his papers found them in order. But before he returned them to Waigwa, another Johnnie interrupted.

"These papers help criminals circumvent the law," he said.

Unconcerned, Waigwa waited. They could search him again if they wanted. His pockets held nothing besides the travel papers, now in one of the soldier's hands.

"Yes. You need to search these bloody monkeys better!" another soldier shouted.

Waigwa's heart sank. His body tensed. What was next? He had done nothing wrong, he reminded himself.

The Johnnie who did not want his type of laws circumvented, started his own search. He found nothing in one side pocket. On the second side, he flipped his arm up with a bullet wedged between his thumb and forefingers.

"Look what I found!"

The soldiers wasted little time declaring Waigwa a Mau Mau collaborator planted at the factory. They cuffed him and loaded him on one of those hideous, sturdy, olive-green military lorries that Johnnies traveled in.

Waigwa joined a handful of other detainees seated on the flatbed while the Johnnies sat on benches along the periphery.

At the police station, jailors interrogated and tortured Waigwa with sleep deprivation, starvation, and beatings. They asked him where he tossed the gun and the rest of the ammunition. His claim that he had never touched a gun in his life earned him further indignities.

The first time he appeared before a magistrate, nothing happened except a mention of his case before they remanded him. At home, Waigwa's family gave up on him, worried that he had disappeared like others who went to work and never returned home.

On Waigwa's second or third court date, the magistrate sentenced him to death along with other so-called terrorists.

At that court hearing, one of the accused's relatives recognized Waigwa. He alerted his family when he returned home. The family was happy that he was in jail, not dead as they had feared. But with no male to take up the issue, Njeri, the wife, did not know how to seek help from her husband's white supervisor. Instead, she got a family acquaintance to help her message Baba. When the telegram arrived, Baba and Mami feared the government had already hanged Waigwa.

During that period, in the mid-fifties, because of the pressure of war and jail congestion, authorities often hung the condemned only a few days after their convictions. But Waigwa remained stuck on death row—a lucky break, my parents thought, before they learned of external forces at play.

With no word from the outside, Waigwa anguished about his situation. Every morning, he wondered whether this was the day of the noose. He worried about his wife and young children, but when he imagined them as a poor widow and orphans, that was his limit; he surrendered and made peace with the world. He wondered how a person or a group of people could wield absolute power of life and death over another group.

If a home guard, the police, or a soldier accused individuals or groups—no matter how flimsy the evidence—a court relied on that accusation as if it were DNA.

Many accused lost hope after conviction because the government never investigated most cases. Swamped by the sheer number of accused Gĩkũyũ men, investigators could not cope. Others just looked the other way. What was one more "bloody African" life?

Appeals by non-Gĩkũyũ African public defenders gave a ray of hope to the accused. But the caseload wore the lawyers down. Other help came from non-Gĩkũyũ African (and occasionally Indian) pro bono lawyers, who, although they got sidelined and insulted by the white officials, had the right of movement and were determined to help.

Waigwa resigned himself from life and waited for his date with the noose.

"It is only Ngai who can intervene," Mami said when Baba received the telegram from Kamunge's cook.

Baba did not wait for God; his employer seemed a better alternative.

Instead of helping, Kamunge went into a dramatic rant about how crime had marred Kenya. "The government needs to root out this evil," Kamunge said, "or this beautiful country will return to the dark ages."

When Baba reminded Kamunge of Waigwa's unblemished record since he was a young boy, Kamunge had more to say.

"If the court found Waigwa guilty," he said, "he needs to pay for his misdeed like other criminals. The government can't waver in these troubled times."

Chapter 37

THE COLONIAL PECKING ORDER

Kamunge harbored no ill will when he told my father, with a son about to be hung, that "the government can't waver in these troubled times."

Based on the colonial culture, he was duty-bound to back the government because he, like every European in Kenya, was an honorary officer of the colonial government. These honorees and their helpers fell into several categories:

First came the British farmers, the landowners, the so-called settlers like Kamunge, born in England, and now middle-aged or old men, peddlers of rags-to-riches stories. They owned estates in Kenya like titled royals back in England. They could not fit into the societies they came from. They would have a great deal to lose if Kenya became independent.

Next came their Kenyan-born sons, whose veins the essence of Kenyan colonial culture coursed through. They knew the country as well as they knew their fathers' plantations. The young men attended premier European-only schools, trained in various sports, handled guns like soldiers, and sport-hunted since childhood. They could traverse the Kenyan woodland like native animal trackers. Unlike their parents, these men grew up in comfort and faced no limitations. Kenya was their home, and they were determined to defend it.

During the war, these Kenyan-born, well-trained white men occupied police and military top and middle positions. They became a menace to the Mau Mau and anyone who stood in the colonial government's way.

Then came young Johnnies shipped from England. They came to help the crown in settling the so-called "minor dispute" with the natives. To the young men, their tours of duty were an adventure—help subdue these wild natives and return home—without attachments.

The politicians and other government officials—custodians of the British colony, answerable to the colonial office in England—were determined to keep their jobs, country-club lifestyles, and their white community happy and protected. These men focused on putting the Mau Mau monster in a chokehold, no matter how many natives they trampled on to carry out their mission.

European wives and daughters stayed on the sidelines of the Mau Mau fray. Although they might have erroneously claimed innocence, they were full-fledged accomplices. They supported the patriarchy—husbands, sons, fathers, or brothers—and enjoyed comfortable homes run by native domestic servants, some of them recruited as young boys.

(Few white women wrestled with farm management and the natives unless they got widowed. Karen Blixen [Isak Dinesen] was an exception—she also employed young boys. She has an area in Nairobi named after her, and her former farmhouse is a museum known only to tourists and workers. She seems to have earned a positive name outside Kenya through her writing and contacts, especially after the movie *Out of Africa* came out in 1985. Despite her tenacity, however, she could not hang onto her coffee farm. She left Kenya in 1931.

Although I lived in Nairobi for fifteen years, I never heard of her before the movie came out.

Finally came the Africans who did the colonizers' bidding: Kenya African Rifles (KAR), home guards, the chiefs, and other native subordinates who were in it for themselves and their families. Those at the bottom rung needed jobs and safety. Besides earning a living, the ones above them bet on the winning side.

But there is a Gĩkũyũ idiom that says, mũteng'erio na mũteng'erania gũtirĩ ũtahũmaga. The chaser and the chased both end up tired or with labored breaths.

The colonizers, "the chasers," were also bound to get tired.

Chapter 38

THE INVESTIGATION

Rampant complaints of atrocities against the Gĩkũyũ masses, abuse, and disregard for legal, due process coursed through the colonial government system from top to rank and file. The complaints festered until their sting reached across the ocean. The Colonial Office in London, averse to bad press, aired their concerns through letters to the colonial authorities in Kenya. Emphatic denials followed, claiming "unfounded accusations."

When the complaints continued, the London office sent officials to offices in Kenya to monitor their fellow colonial representatives and report back. These envoys were based in Nairobi, away from the so-called "African locations" and the front lines. The envoys learned about the natives' grievances secondhand through the entrenched colonial culture.

Although they were supposed to improve management and dilute the hardcore colonial culture in Kenya, the officials had no guts to call their countrymen on anything. They sent benign and non-committal reports to the Colonial Office in London. Meanwhile, they lay low to finish their contracts without a blemish on their records and return home to their own jobs. Or they came up with bogus excuses to cut short their work contracts.

Nonetheless, the complaints continued, more amplified as they became widespread, and the masses continued to suffer.

Tired of the appalling publicity, the London Colonial Office sent an investigator. When the man arrived in Kenya, the colonized expected little from him besides following in the footsteps of the earlier emissaries. And the colonizers expected yet another nosy softie without the stomach to deal with the supposedly "marauding" natives.

The man proved them all wrong.

As an upright civil servant, he believed in the might of the British Crown and its alleged fairness model. He ignored the colonial culture of brushing aside or ignoring crimes committed by white people. The man interviewed the colonizers and the colonized, as he would have back in England. Visiting conflict centers like Nyeri gave him the gist of how things worked. Next, he retrieved a sample of files of men already gone to the gallows and others in transition.

Waigwa's file was among them.

In time, the investigator visited him on death row.

Waigwa gave him the names of the factory where he had worked and his former supervisor and told the investigator how the Johnnies arrested him while he walked home from work.

"I grew up in Solai on Kamunge's farm," Waigwa added, "and I'm a father of four young children."

According to Kamunge's account, the investigator telephoned him after speaking to the factory supervisor. Both white men compared notes and confirmed Waigwa's story.

"If the court finds Waigwa innocent and sets him free," Kamunge told the investigator, "I will go to Nyeri and get him myself."

The next day, Kamunge drove to the plantation where Baba worked and told him about the phone call.

At home, that flicker of hope eased my parents' anguish, although Baba remained disappointed in Kamunge for refusing to intervene before Waigwa got convicted.

They now wondered whether the investigator's findings would convince the court to revisit Waigwa's case.

"I expect little from such investigations," Baba told Mami.

"At least Waigwa is still alive," she said. "All we can do is wait. Ngai will reveal the truth."

They waited.

In the next letter from Kikuyuland, Waigwa's family confirmed he was still on death row, but a home guard and a white man in a suit had visited them. The suited man claimed he was an officer of the court. He asked them questions. Except for basic answers, the family said little else. They feared the man might twist their words and manufacture a wrong against them.

After another stretch of time, Baba arrived home and asked for Simon twice within an hour. It turned out he had received another letter.

At least he did not have to ask an outsider to read for him; Simon had cut that pipeline to village gossip and pity when a man read for Baba and then spread the news. Simon had reached grade four and could now read.

The letter gave cursory news, which Mami shared with us children. I later picked up other bits from family accounts.

*

A death row jailer had gone to fetch Waigwa.

Just as well, Waigwa thought, better get it over with.

To Waigwa's surprise, instead of the guards taking him to the building where men and a few women entered and never returned, they took him to court.

"Waigwa son of Warama?" the white magistrate called out when Waigwa's turn came.

The constable who guarded Waigwa pulled his sleeve up. He maneuvered to stand.

The magistrate flipped through pages in a file folder. He reached a page, made a note, and signed.

"Wewe Waigwa kijana ya Warama?" Are you Waigwa son of Warama? the magistrate asked.

"Ndio, Afande," Yes, sir, Waigwa said.

(Afande is a concoction of "A fine day, Sir" that junior white officers gave when older or senior white men said, "A fine day...?" in greeting. The Africans mistook the phrase for something similar to "Sir.")

"You are free to go."

Waigwa gazed at the magistrate, not sure he heard him right.

"Uma ũthĩ; nĩwarekio!" Get out and leave; you have been released, the guard said.

Waigwa shuffled in a daze.

"Thĩ wabichi woe maratathi maku." Go to the office and get your papers.

When Waigwa received his dismissal and travel papers, he sat and leaned against a nearby wall to rest and regroup. It took him the rest of the day to drag his gawky, emaciated frame back to where his family lived.

When his wife and children saw him, they forgot their turmoil and hunger and gawked at the walking skeleton. They soon recovered from their shock and welcomed him home.

"Ngai directed that investigator," Mami said when she learned of the ruling.

The family later learned scant details about the investigation. One was that the investigator had questioned the frivolous or unsubstantiated evidence of many other death-row cases, including Waigwa's. He had also wondered why Waigwa carried only one bullet and no other Mau Mau paraphernalia like a gun, a machete, or a knife.

The investigation had concluded the bullet that nearly cost Waigwa his life came from one of the Johnnies.

Chapter 39

EXTERNAL FORCES AT PLAY

Why did Waigwa and others escape the noose? Did the investigator persuade the colonial government to reconsider their evil ways?

Hardly.

The colonial officials in Kenya stuck to their official line: "These reports (or atrocities) are unfounded." Or "We are making efforts to look into the matter."

But those officials overlooked the Englishmen in their midst, the envoys from the Colonial Office in England, their consciences intact, their contract terms too short to get stuck on a colonial lifestyle or acclimate to the art of oppression and dominance. Several of them found the atrocities and the colonial officials' attitudes toward natives so repugnant they resigned and returned home before their contracts ended.

Over time, the mistreatment and carnage they had witnessed in Kenya grated on the men's minds so much that, to ease their consciences, they sent anonymous letters or leaked snippets to London newspapers.

So, no matter how much the colonialists in Kenya tried to contain the "little Mau Mau monster," leaks continued.

By the end of 1955, the brutality and atrocities directed at the Gĩkũyũ tribe stung beyond the Colonial Office in London. The Kenya colony's turmoil became a regular feature in London newspapers, the recipients of leaks from unnamed "credible sources." It grated on civil society's conscience and reached the halls of the British Parliament.

Members like Barbara Castle of the Labour Party and others kept on the subject no matter how much the Colonial Office refuted the claims. According to *Imperial Reckoning, The Untold Story of Britain's Gulag in Kenya* by Caroline Elkins, Castle traveled to Kenya for a first-hand account. Then:

> Castle made her party's very public declaration
> of war against the Conservative government on
> the front page of the Tribune. The headline read
> "Labour to fight Kenya Thugs," but the thugs
> in this case were not the Mau Mau insurgents;
> they were the leaders of the British colonial
> government and their men on the spot.

Waigwa's condemnation coincided with the time when the colonial government in Kenya needed to prove that its officers followed the law. Hangings slowed for people lucky enough to appear before the court. But "unofficial" violence continued to rage under the radar: shooting "suspects" under cover of darkness, random people labeled suspicious, and tortured to the point of death or castrated without witnesses.

Chapter 40

FAMILY LEFT ON THE FARM

Baba's two families endured varied experiences during the war. The first family's women would have preferred to stay on the farm. But they had no choice. Their men, although among the chosen, opted to leave the farm and join the exodus to Kikuyu-land. They and their families paid dearly for it.

My half-sister Gathoni, married for only two years then, was the only member of Baba's first family whose husband chose to stay. They lived two farms away from Kamunge's farm. Before Gathoni's birth family left, her mother walked there to bid her and her family farewell.

Gathoni and her family went through experiences much like ours, Baba's second family. In mid-1953, the police took her to the screening camp, either the one my parents went to or a similar one. Gathoni, a new mother, was nursing a two-week-old baby.

On arrival at the camp, her group joined others from different farms. The officials shooed them like a herd of animals into a huge storage shed that contained cement, building blocks, and cows' hay. She found a corner to sit in, worrying her baby could get squashed, a tidbit she told me decades later. Among other structures, the camp had mud and thatch cottages where authorities housed women with young children.

The following day, Christian loyalists read to them verses from the Bible, which they punctuated with singing. They sang

Christian songs about the impermanence and suffering in this world and that the downtrodden and the righteous will inherit opulence in the afterlife.

The detainees who knew the songs happily joined in to beat boredom, distract themselves, or because they believed whatever the officials dished out.

Meanwhile, each individual had to go before a group of three Gĩkũyũ men who sat under a shed in a semi-circle. Close by, Gathoni saw two pits; one contained millions and millions of *thuraku*, the deadly safari ants, and the other had a live python.

"Declare your oath," was the first question from the interrogators.

If a person denied they had taken an oath, the interrogators chastised them and rained slaps on them. "What kind of mũGĩkũyũ are you?" they asked. "Does that mean you don't care about independence or your stolen lands?"

When people became adamant that they had not taken the oath and the slaps did not soften them, they advanced to the next stage. The interrogators threw them into the python's pit. Fear alone convinced many to confess, even if they lied about it. But a few hard cores held on. They ended up in the deadly safari ants' pit or suffered more debilitating torture in private.

Except for the few Mau Mau supporters who fell through the cracks during the government exodus, most who remained on farms were simple people with no "lofty" ideas besides earning a living and raising their families. But to avoid mistreatment, many lied that they had taken the oath. The interrogators were conversant with the Mau Mau oath protocol, but they went along and pretended to get convinced.

During the confessions, they asked people to declare the type of oaths they had taken, the oath giver, and where the ceremony occurred. The interrogators then conducted a mini verbal cleansing session—similar to taking another oath—to disavow and cleanse the oath. That supposedly released the confessors from the burden of the oath, which, from then on, would not affect them if they broke their vows.

Gathoni told me the few details on September 14, 2022, in the third person, as if she were a mere observer.

*

The colonialists had taken my parents for screening like all the rest—the worst time of my seven years of life. I woke up one morning and found Mami gone. Instead, Simon, at thirteen, sat in her seat, cooking porridge. Except for that one image, I remember nothing else besides the abandonment worry that plagued me for the entire week Mami was gone.

She suffered little, but Baba, who had gone with the first group, suffered punishment because he refused to lie. When he returned home after eight days, he holed up in his thingira and missed work for three days, the only time I saw him miss work.

He never disclosed what he suffered.

Of minimal note, but perhaps worth mentioning, when Solai and neighboring farms' landowners recruited home guards for their villages, rumors reached our homestead that Kamunge wanted to recruit Baba as our village's home guard. He planned to train Baba to shoot a gun and give him one.

My heart swelled with pride when I learned of the "special" appointment, unaware of what a home guard's post involved.

But nothing happened in our village that could have made Kamunge, his family, and his cohorts uncomfortable or fearful enough to warrant a home guard. Perhaps this is the reason our family never heard of the matter again.

Years later, we learned that being a home guard was far from the honorable appointment I thought as a child; the label bound a family to a generational legacy equivalent to a slaveholder or a member of the Nazis.

Chapter 41

ROOMMATES

After Waigwa's court acquittal, my parents hoped Kamunge would get him and his family, as he had told the investigator. A ride in the back of a jeep or Land Rover driven by a white person was the quickest way for the family to leave Nyeri without official hassle. My parents said they would believe it only if it happened.

But could Kamunge surprise them again?

Five and a half years earlier, he had surprised my parents and others when he drove Waigwa's family and his mother to the Nakuru camp during the exodus and asked the officials to process their trip to Kikuyuland without much delay.

But that was the only time Kamunge had driven one of his employees or any member of their families anywhere, even to the hospital, no matter how sick they were. And yet he promised to drive to Nyeri, eighty miles away, to get a former employee who had abandoned the farm?

As the family expected, Kamunge did not keep his promise. But he did the next best thing. He petitioned the government to allow the family to leave. In the petition, which may have comprised a telegram or a phone call, he confirmed Waigwa would find a job waiting when he returned to the farm.

Baba could have petitioned for his son. But for one of the colonized to get such approval meant a long delay, as if he and his family were immigrants or were refugees from a foreign country.

When Baba got confirmation of the travel date, he sought transportation from Mr. Patel, another man he had known since his financially struggling days in the late 1920s. My brother Simon rode on Mr. Patel's lorry when it delivered cargo to the Solai train station. After the drop-off, the driver was instructed to pick up the Waigwas.

Waigwa, his wife, Njeri, and their now-four children occupied a quarter of the lorry. Except for the additional child, they returned scrawnier and with less than what they left with five and a half years earlier. The family was the first to return from Kikuyuland to Kamunge's farm.

The lorry driver dropped them off at the Patel General Store, three miles from our village. He had no instructions to go out of his way.

Simon led the group into our courtyard. Waigwa wore clean but well-worn grayish trousers, a beige shirt, a wrinkled jacket, and a hat. Except for the old black shoes he wore instead of homemade sandals, he resembled a younger version of Baba. But at about thirty-one, he looked like an old man to my young eyes.

His wife, Njeri, followed behind in a washed-out turquoise dress, a beige sweater, and a multi-colored headscarf with the knot tied at the back. She looked like a typical village woman except for her old rubber shoes. I noticed a prominent black mole on the side of her nose. Their four children looked just like us: scruffy, barefoot village children.

In rural areas in those days, and many years later, a father wore shoes, mainly homemade sandals or occasionally store-bought ones. If a younger, progressive family had shillings to spare, the mother bought rubber shoes that she wore on Sundays or an occasional trip. Children walked barefoot except for a few who passed grade four standardized national exams and went to boarding school. But before 1960, my brother David and Simon Mbûrû, grandson to Mama Alan, our free village masseuse, were the only two boys on Kamunge's farm who had passed the exam and attended a boarding school.

Waigwa slept in Baba's thingira, and Njeri and their children doubled up with us in nyûmba. They planned to live with us while they waited for Kamunge to allocate Waigwa a plot to build their homestead. Waigwa had found a job waiting for him as Kamunge had promised, meaning he just joined the other farm workers.

When they lived with us, none of the family members mentioned the harrowing five and a half years they had spent in Nyeri, and we never asked them.

We waited and waited and waited for Kamunge to give them a plot to build on or say something. Mami echoed Baba, saying that Kamunge probably had a good reason for the delay. But, as usual, Kamunge never mentioned reasons or changes that affected us villagers until he got ready to issue orders.

Meanwhile, Mami cooked for both families. She served food in twos or threes, according to our ages, so no one could accuse her of favoring her own children. She sent two plates to thingira for Baba and Waigwa.

Besides serving us on the same plates, Mami gave my siblings and me more chores or sent us to do more errands than she did the two Waigwa older children. I complained without pointing a finger, but Mami paid me no attention.

With our household's population doubled, my mother overworked and simmered on the inside. She spoke up after the Waigwas' newness wore off. She complained—to no one in particular and in Njeri's absence—about Njeri doing a chore only when told. I once overheard her tell her friend. "Njeri waits for food like a man or a visitor. She does nothing around the house unless I ask her."

But Mami never assigned Njeri a permanent chore or spelled out what she wanted Njeri to help with.

In the evenings, Njeri sat opposite Mami, on one side of the fire pit, with her back to the wall. She looked docile and said little unless she had to or stoked the fire—the same woman Baba claimed had restless, quick feet and a smart mouth before she married his son.

I would not have noticed Njeri never took the initiative if I had never overheard Mami complain. In hindsight, I think this may have been hard to do because Mami acted so capable.

Although I did not concern myself with our kinship, I liked it when the Waigwas lived with us. They were our first house guests since my maternal grandmother visited and spent one night about six years prior. It felt special to tell village children we had a family staying with us. I also enjoyed having my half-niece, four months older than me, to play with.

I liked Njeri, too. An avid storyteller, the likes of which I had never seen, she told us mesmerizing ogre stories that writers today would drool over.

I asked her to tell me stories—a single one even, I said—when I started drafting THE COLONIZED *and the Scramble for Africa*—the first book of this series—but she claimed she had forgotten them.

Chapter 42

STORYTELLER

In the evenings, before the Waigwas came, Mami washed her face, arms, and legs and stepped on pieces of firewood. While she waited for her legs to dry, she occasionally told us a story. It was a relaxed time for us with our mother, hunger satisfied, and no chores. Only when the Waigwas came did I realize Mami's stories were substandard, or perhaps it was because it had been too long since she learned them.

My mother grew up on a colonial farm in Nanyuki and at Major Holman's (Horoma's) farm in the Great Rift Valley, away from Kikuyuland, where people told mythical stories or the tribe's history.

Once the Waigwas arrived, she never hung around in the evenings. When she completed her evening chores, she did her washing ritual and soon left for bed. She also took the kerosene lantern and left us at the mercy of the now-half-burned fire. We did not dare replenish the firewood because of her occasional caution. "Don't stay up all night and use all my dry firewood."

As soon as Mami left, Njeri livened. She sat straighter, moved about on her seat, talked, and assumed the position of the only adult in the room. We pressed her for a story right away.

She asked us to solve riddles as a warm-up. Mami had never given us riddles; instead, she used an occasional metaphor or simile as a caution.

Initially, none of my siblings and I solved a single riddle. Her two older children, Mũmbi, my age, and Mũthee, two years younger, solved most of them. After she solved the riddles her children got stuck on, she started on her evening's feature story. Our favorite stories were about marimũ (or irimũ in singular)—ogres. I recall one story about one irimũ with a second mouth behind his neck where flies buzzed. He could change into whatever form he wanted, depending on his needs. This ranged from a midget, an old man, an animal, or a tall, muscular, handsome man that young women drooled over.

In one story, an unknown smooth-talker and an eye-pleaser from an unfamiliar ridge attended an event. He was called "Monjo." His dancing charmed the community's young women so much that they almost swooned as they ogled him with admiration. He stayed long enough to profess love to one of them. He married Nyakondo before her parents met his parents to perform the customary marriage rituals. The couple soon left.

Monjo and Nyakondo lived in a secluded homestead with no close neighbors. It comprised the typical mud and thatch circular thingira for Monjo and a similar, bigger house for Nyakondo. Monjo forbade Nyakondo from entering his thingira. The two spent time together in nyũmba, contrary to Kikuyu tradition, where a couple lived in thingira until the wife became a mother.

Without children or anyone to talk to, Nyakondo felt lonely when Monjo left for his daily prowls.

She also worried about Monjo's standing as a husband because he had no goats. (Land and goats' ownership were the hallmark of a Gĩkũyũ man.) And he had not introduced her to friends or close neighbors. But he treated her well, and the two never exchanged unkind words. Monjo brought her fruits, berries, roasted meat, and whatever else she needed every time he returned home.

She convinced herself she had married an excellent hunter. What did a little deviation from tradition matter? He was a good provider and paid attention to her when he returned, she reasoned.

When she became pregnant, Monjo became extra attentive. He felt her stomach and even massaged her feet—another untraditional behavior, but it felt good.

When she gave birth, to her horror, her new wonder baby boy came out as a monster. He had the signature ogre front and back mouths.

The stories Njeri told us implied the folly of taking things at face value. They discouraged us from doing the wrong things while they pushed us toward more cooperation and good morals.

She told one story per evening unless it was too short, and we begged for another. But our pleas fell on deaf ears. Sometimes, she told such a long story that she stopped to check on her listeners before the fire died. She squinted and looked across the fire pit. If she noticed nods or a little one stretched on the floor, she cut the story short amid our protests. She always finished it the next evening.

Although we begged Njeri to finish a story, I already felt afraid when an ogre image stuck in my mind. With the fire pit full of ashes and smoldering charcoal (the best time to cover the charcoal with the ashes for the morning kindling), we could only see seated silhouettes. I jumped in fear of any light brush from my neighbor's leg or hand.

In bed, before sleep overcame my fear, I imagined a double-mouthed ogre lurking in the shadows in a nook or under our bed, waiting to snatch me. Along the way, I developed an aversion to darkness, little bushes, or barriers, always fearing an unidentifiable creature would pop out and grab me.

SCHOOL

Chapter 43

FAMILY'S EDUCATION

By the 1930s, Baba regretted that he refused to attend school when missionaries busied themselves with religious conversions, a period he could have had free education.

"The men in my age group who attended school," he told Mami in the 1940s, "now lead better lives than me. They can afford to educate their children."

He had done what he could despite his lack of formal education. He had opened a savings account at the post office in Nakuru Town in 1932. From the mid-thirties, he sent his sons from his first marriage to the one-room elementary school at Ndege's farm, Kwa-Ndege Primary School, on the other side of Jumatatu Mountain. My brother David joined the same school in 1950.

The distance—a third of it up the mountain—covered about six miles from Kĩrĩma-inĩ, my family's first homestead. Jacob Rũrĩrĩ acted as the headmaster, teacher, clerk, and whatever else the school needed to run well.

The school went up to grade four, the level of education the colonialists deemed adequate for an African male to do basic record-keeping, read the Christian Bible, or become a competent servant.

My half-sister, Gathoni, born in 1930, desperately wanted to attend school in the 1940s. Whether Baba learned of this, I could not tell. He did not send any of his three daughters from his first marriage to school. He either did not think they needed an education or, like other fathers, he believed educating girls wasted money. In a patriarchal society, daughters married, worked, bore children for their husbands, and benefited their families.

I once ventured a redeeming excuse for my father when a thought struck me that he did not register Gathoni for school because he hated to have her walk the long distance. But, based on his history, I regretfully must conclude my generous excuse was baseless.

*

When Baba and Kaguyu, his first wife, lived in Nyeri as a young couple, before they moved to Kamunge's farm in the late-1920s, his youngest sister, Aunt Julia, had joined four other girls—termed "mambere" (the first)—the first girls to attend school in Nyeri District (now Nyeri County).

Tūmūtūmū Mission School, where the girls joined as boarders, became famous for teaching not only Christianity but also writing, reading, and arithmetic to orphaned girls and those who were allowed to attend by their progressive fathers. That first group of five girls included two orphans—Aunt Julia and another girl.

As an orphan, Aunt Julia grew up at the home of Mr. and Mrs. Kamweti, who rescued her when they found her wailing next to her mother's fresh grave. But now that her brother, Baba (Warama), was married, Aunt Julia went to their household when the school closed for the holidays.

Happy that he could now support his young sister, Baba did not expect her to return to the Mission. But she insisted. To discipline her, he rummaged for a weapon. He grabbed a termite-infested wooden stick and whacked her with it several times. In the melee, Aunt Julia dashed off.

Baba pursued her. Despite his much longer strides and need to keep appearances, he did not catch the determined, budding teenager before she reached the missionary enclave.

Out of breath, Baba reached the front yard, where an attendant worked on the grounds.

"Did you see a girl come this way?" Baba asked the man. "Is she in trouble?"

"She's my sister; I want to take her home."

"What did she do?" the man asked. "She shot into that building like an arrow."

Baba did not answer him. He quickened his steps to the Mission's building, yards away, and stood by the doorway.

"Your father felt embarrassed," Mami said years later, "to enter an all-women's residence."

*

When we lived at Kĩrĩma-inĩ, I knew David went somewhere during the day. Where? I did not know. After a year in our fenced village, when I was age seven, he went away to boarding school. I did not concern myself or discover what he did there until a year later.

We played in our courtyard when I was eight, and one girl sparked my curiosity.

"My father registered me for school," she said.

"You'll go to school?" I asked, somewhat surprised. A girl going to school was new and sounded revolutionary to me.

"Yes, my Baba said I'm old enough."

With those few words, the girl planted a seed in me. It mattered little that I knew nothing about what children did in school. The seed latched on.

She looks my size, and she plans to go to school? I asked myself. All I do is babysit.

Sometime later, we played house behind our granary, picking seeds from shrubs mimicking coffee cherry pickers.

A different girl looked up at the sun and then at her shadow. "It's time to go to school," she said.

"You go to school?" I asked.

"Yes," she said. "Your Baba doesn't want to take you?"

"I don't know," I said.

It had never occurred to me I needed an education. My two older brothers went to school, but that was their issue, not mine. But after the two girls mentioned school, new thoughts clouded my mind. If girls can attend school, then I should go too. But how can I do that? I babysit all the time.

Enough of those school thoughts, and I turned into a rebel, a low-key rebel. I did not concern myself with who would babysit my little brother if I went to school.

Not that I knew or wondered about my age. Like others in the village, my parents never remembered their children's birthdays. Without the ability to read and write, they never recorded them. And with hordes of children, days, months, and years merged. But Mami remembered David's birthday. Well, not the year, but the actual day. She knew he was born on Christmas Day, a day she could never forget.

Christmas was the only public holiday in Kenya, the day every peasant—besides domestic workers—stayed off work and celebrated. On Christmas Eve, my siblings and I cut wildflowers and stuck them along the front of nyūmba's thatch. A small group of Christians sang carols at Christians' homesteads—they never came to ours.

For celebrations, Kamunge shot a cow or two, had his workers slaughter them, and distributed chunks of beef to each permanent male employee based on family size. Villagers wore new clothes. (unless they couldn't afford them, which became a subject of pity), Christians went to church, men drank themselves silly, and Tugen migrant workers held their largest dances and competed with dancers from other farms.

Like other mothers, Mami cooked the then-rare chapatti, a flatbread we ate once a year with a stew of potatoes, beef, and cabbage.

So, Mami could not forget that David was born on such a day, a day she was too engaged to care for anything else. Much later, thanks to Aunt Julia, who, without children of her own, kept a tab on her brother's children. Through associating with her, David learned of his actual birthday—December 25, 1938.

Afterward, Mother birthed a child every two years, she had said. Later, when my siblings and I got curious about our ages, we counted the number of older siblings, even the dead ones, starting with David's birth date.

When the school bug bit me, without knowing my age, I used the school's measure. To start school, teachers required children to reach overhead with their right arm and touch their left ear. If a child's fingertips could not touch the ear, they had to reapply the following year.

I knew that would not be my problem because I tested myself, and my hand reached to my earlobe. In our family, only Gĩthũi needed the ear test. He had the good fortune of being born after two girls—Tabitha and me—and he was too young to take over goat herding. Baba sent him to school at seven, a benefit that sustained him for the next sixteen years in school without interruption. He escaped goat herding except in a supporting role on weekends. For the rest of us, years of goat herding or babysitting ensured we were more than qualified to start school.

As I agonized about attending school, I thought about sharing my desire with Mami. But I knew she could not register me or afford school fees—that was Baba's responsibility, part of their division of labor. No children in my family attended school unless Baba approved, registered them, and paid school fees.

"The neck never overtakes the head," my mother said when such matters arose.

I knew Baba was the Head and Mami the Neck, but asking the Head would have taken monumental courage. So, I approached the Neck.

"Your father will decide on that," Mami said when I told her I wanted to attend school.

Of course, I knew that.

In hindsight, I wonder how I expected Baba to learn of my need. Perhaps I expected Mami to act as my intermediary. But it took me by surprise when she did, and so fast, and later still, by her unorthodox style.

"I told your father," Mami said in about a week.

"What did he say?"

"He didn't say much; he said, 'Oh!'"

Although the answer did not satisfy me, I wasn't disturbed because Baba had not said "No." I hoped he would grant me my wish. We were used to waiting for him to decide, as he and the other men waited for Kamunge's permission, instructions, or orders. And, just like Kamunge, Baba waited until the last minute.

His delay in letting our family know his decisions had never affected me before, but this was my issue. So, I worried, not daring to expect a positive outcome, and later get disappointed.

But from then on, whenever my mind became idle, it gravitated toward school. I always hoped Baba would say I had reached school age.

In mid-December, he took Joseph—two years my senior—to Njeki's Shopping Center. When they returned, Joseph described their trip with all the excitement and embellishment he could muster. He said a tailor took his measurements and would make him a one-of-a-kind school uniform. That confirmed Baba had registered only him for school.

Afterward, I envied my brother for his elitist attitude toward us, the non-school children, as he called us. While he waited for the opening day in January, he strutted around the house, calling himself a schoolboy even before he stepped into a classroom.

I became more apprehensive as Christmas Day approached. The idea of not attending school until a year later gnawed at me.

I started searching for reasons Baba stayed quiet about my school issue.

I heard Mami and other women complain about the rising cost of education. It used to be sixteen shillings per year, they said. But the school had raised it to twenty-two shillings. I marveled at the teachers' powers. In my little mind, they could raise school fees to any figure they wanted.

Perhaps, besides David and Simon, Baba could afford to pay school fees for only one more child. I feared fees might rise too high for him to afford my school fees, and I might end up a permanent babysitter.

Worry about lack of money latched onto me at nine. And it never let go.

Chapter 44

LUCK OF THE DRAW

The school opened in early January. What year? I did not know. And I bet my parents didn't either. But I knew it was January because Tindaress Primary School opened a week or two after Christmas. Two years later, I learned the year was 1956.

Joseph cleaned himself and wore his new khaki uniform. I eyed him with envy and kept out of his way as he fussed, looking for a comb he did not need. Mami had clipped his hair an eighth of an inch from his scalp. In my mind, he now belonged to an exclusive group. Seeing his preparations also wiped out any flicker of hope I had of starting school that year.

Sadness filled my heart, not like the sadness of abandonment that I had wallowed in at seven years old when the colonizers took Mami and others for interrogation, but a sadness of help-lessness. Even without knowing Baba's history regarding girls' education, I still wondered whether he lacked money or perhaps did not want me, as a girl, to get an education.

I struggled with the idea that it would take me an entire year before I got another chance.

How I envied Joseph for starting school. Blinded by my plight, it never occurred to me that at two years older than me, he needed to start school first.

As I soon learned, Mami was already tired of her children delaying to start school. She blamed it on Baba's goats. She had little to do with them since he stopped building an enclosure in nyũmba to fatten two or three goats at a time. She had fed and watered the animals all by herself. Now, her interaction with them was occasionally when she fed them scraps of food or a few fistfuls of maize kernels as a treat.

Otherwise, I had caught her turning an evil eye toward the goats; her lips tightened before she went about her business. I had also heard her wish harm to the goats. "These goats!" she had said, or "These goats have enslaved my children." Then, her gaze on the romping animals, she clicked her tongue and shook her head. Of course, she did all this in Baba's absence.

I paid no attention to her protests. After all, I did not herd goats. But I paid attention when she lost her cool, unable to contain her anger when Simon's life trajectory changed course.

On a day that Mami worked only a half day, she walked from the granary, holding a small sack of potatoes she intended to peel and cook for our lunch. When she reached the center of the courtyard, Simon appeared at the small entrance between nyũmba and thingira.

"What's wrong?" Mami asked.

"The headmaster sent me home."

"Because of school fees?"

"No."

"What did you do?"

"I did nothing," Simon said. "He said I'm too old to repeat."

"Oh! No!" Mami said as she whipped the sack of potatoes up high and hurled it to the ground with all her might. "I'll never be happy until these animals are dead and gone! That's the only time my children will have peace and get an education!"

We, the stay-at-home children, froze. Simon did the same. When he recovered, he headed indoors to the boys' cottage without a word. Mami straightened and paused for seconds, her face blank, then she bent and collected her potatoes, a bunch of them already cracked or smashed.

If I had developed enough thinking capacity, I would have wondered why my mother did not protest about her two children, whom I babysat and who kept me from going to school.

*

Although I had not considered it before Mami's outburst, Baba's goats caused turmoil in our household. It led to Baba's brutality toward my brothers and their starting school late.

When a herder got into escapades and forgot his charges, the goats strayed. Occasionally, they got lost in the woods or caused havoc in a person's garden. If that happened, Baba beat the young herder as if he were an enemy combatant.

As for education, to start school, each brother had to wait until a younger sibling grew old enough to replace him as a goat herder. For Simon, Mwai, who followed him (named after the uncle who died in World War 1), died at two years old. By the time Joseph came along, four years had gone by, and Simon could not start school until he turned eleven.

After four years of schooling, like many of his classmates from our village, he failed the standardized national entrance exam to advance to grade five. The Ministry of Education policy deemed him and about 95% of his classmates too old to repeat. This provided a fresh crop of laborers for the British farmers.

After his schooling ended, Simon worked part-time for Kamunge and herded goats the other time. He arranged with another herder to watch the herd while he worked.

Now, at sixteen, the authorities required him to get a passbook (travel booklet) and an ID and to pay taxes.

As for Joseph, he had the misfortune of being followed by two sisters—Tabitha and me—babysitters, not goatherders. He had to wait for another boy to take over goat-herding before he could go to school. The next boy, Gĩthũi, was six years his junior, too young to have undergone a herding apprenticeship.

Just like Simon, Joseph started school at eleven years old.

Chapter 45

MOST VALUABLE TRADE

Whenever the schoolboy returned home, he embellished every bit of his day's experience. A natural comedian, Joseph told stories of how his class sang A E I O U and ABCs and about his fellow pupils and teachers. He even made disciplinary ruler tap punishment sound exciting.

"It's wise to let home children know what goes on in the world," he said.

The more stories my brother told, the more frustrated and envious of him I became. I paid attention to his A-E-I-O-U's recital. When they started learning to write, we flocked around Joseph, and he showed us how to write letters and numbers.

Because boys wore shorts, he sat with his knees folded, which left enough of his right thigh uncovered for him to use as a blackboard. He used his index fingernail or a blunt wood splinter to scratch. When I copied what he wrote on my thigh, I ended up with meaningless scrawls that did not resemble knowledge.

No matter how much I desired to learn, my father was the key to my education dilemma. If he had realized where my constant thoughts about school would take me, he might have said something beforehand to ease my mind.

My thoughts trailed to what he and Mami did for me.

My mother cooked, sewed, and washed my clothes, treated me if I fell sick, and took care of every part of my life. But Baba,

I thought, did nothing for me. (With no concept of homelessness, I left out shelter.) Well, he gave me meat when he slaughtered a goat and honey when he harvested his beehives, which I loved. I concluded it was about time he added schooling to the little he gave me.

My singular focus on school and the cost involved triggered an idea of a trade—my first ever. I thought the sacrifice was so big that my father would be impressed and register me in school without further discussion.

But I did not know what to do with my idea. It flipped and grated on my mind for an entire week before I could not hold it anymore. I had to share it with someone.

While we sat around the fire one evening after supper, I blurted out, "I wish Baba would stop giving me meat for a year and instead take me to school."

"Are you joking?" Joseph asked and chuckled.

My younger siblings turned toward me with momentary disinterest and resumed their chatter.

But Mami gave me a long look. She knew how my siblings and I loved meat, especially those roasted chunks Baba served each of us when we sat around the fire in his thingira.

"You must want to attend school very much," she said.

My head made a series of quick nods before I added, "Yes."

It was September, the last school term of the year. I had thought and talked about going to school since Joseph started in January. But it was the first time I came up with a solution. In my naïve mind, I thought that would lighten Baba's cost of education burden. It never dawned on me that the trade meant little to him besides showing him how motivated I was. Except for my brothers' labor and his management, and the cost of the pink salt rocks he bought for the goats, which lasted for years, it cost him little to breed his goats.

Whatever the case, that was my trade—a chunk of meat for school.

Mami eyed me with sympathy, perhaps reflecting on her own life, but it was wasted sympathy because I expected nothing from her. After all, registering a child in school, buying school uniforms and supplies, and paying school fees were a father's responsibility.

To this day, I wonder how I expected my father to learn of my offer. I am not even sure I expected Mami to tell him. But thanks to mothers like mine, I soon learned Mami had her own style of getting her husband to do things while letting him think it was his own idea.

*

My father slaughtered a goat yet again. We assembled in thingira around the fire, him seated on his three-legged stool, the meat wooden board and carving knife in wait. One of my brothers came from the roasting pit outside and set next to him an enamel white basin half-full of sizzling meat.

All eyes focused on Baba while he carved chunks of meat. He could not cut and distribute his offerings fast enough to satisfy my salivating mouth.

He gave a chunk to each child, starting with the youngest. When my turn came, he stretched out his hand, my chunk clutched in his fingers. I waited, alert, my eyes focused, and my mouth ready. But as I started extending my hand, my mother's voice erupted. I gasped softly and froze.

"I doubt Wanjirũ wants the meat," she said.

"What?" Baba said as he whipped his head toward her, a questioning scowl and doubt on his face. He knew his children were little carnivores.

"Well, I'm just repeating what she said," Mami said, shrugging her shoulders. "She said not to give her meat for a year, and instead, you take her to school."

My eyes shifted to her and pleaded, my body in internal fits. Oh, Mother, please, please, not now. I want this meat.

Baba turned his face slowly toward me, pulled back his loaded arm, and rested the elbow on his knee, his brow furrowed. He looked at me as if considering a suitable response to a challenge.

My eyes shifted from Mami to the dirt floor. I raised my eyebrows now and then, like a sneaky thief, to assess Baba's reaction. I had forgotten my eager mouth, my hand back in my lap, overwhelmed by Baba's singular focus on me.

Everyone got quiet. Even my little siblings, who seconds ago savored their meat and swished their mouths this way, and that stopped. They now watched Baba. We all watched him and waited for his judgment.

"Is it true you want to attend school instead of eating meat?" he asked.

I held my breath and nodded, hesitant at first and then vigorously.

"If that's how much you want to attend school," he said, "you can eat meat and go to school as well."

He handed me my chunk of meat.

I exhaled, my mouth tightly closed, euphoria coursing through my body as I extended my hand.

Chapter 46

THE SCHOOL WAIT

Did my father give in to my trade out of shame that his little girl implied he could not afford both meat and school fees? I will never know. Whatever the reason, with his one pronouncement, I could as well have called myself a schoolgirl.

That evening, I went to bed as the happiest girl ever. I dreamed of walking toward a girl in a blue school uniform and a group of other schoolchildren ahead of her.

"It's time to go to school," the girl told me. I followed her. She broke into a run to reach the other children. I woke up before I caught up with her.

The next day, with my goal accomplished, I felt a vacuum, a vacuum I had nothing to fill with. Now, I needed to sit back and wait. But as days rolled by, the sole settler of our school agreement remained closed-lipped.

Although every cell in my body knew Baba would keep his promise, impatience preyed on me. Why didn't he say something, anything, about registering me in school? I could not remind him; I had no such courage. Even if I did, my family privileges did not include the right to badger my father. Mami, yes! But definitely not my father. Even if I had that right, I could not risk it in case he changed his mind in protest.

I waited for a long, long time. At my age, even a month's suspense seemed an eternity. I recalled how I had harped on Mami about school before the idea of a trade dawned on me. But what else could I ask of her after she did her part? I now left her in peace and suffered alone in silence.

Could Baba change his mind? The question nagged me now and then.

But I knew the answer.

In my nine-plus years, Baba had never gone back on his word. So, I knew he would not change his mind. Besides, although my siblings and I were still too young to appreciate and articulate it, we were Baba's second family, his old-age children. Age had softened him and robbed him of a chance of a third family.

Months prior, I had quit asking Joseph what he had learned in school because, after A-E-I-O-U, his class had started learning how to write words like Baba and Mama. It frustrated me when I could not figure out how A-E-I-O-U morphed into words I knew.

Now that I would soon attend school, I tried to condition my mind to learn. I tried to decode Mami's Gĩkũyũ Bible. She had bought it, or someone had gifted it to her so her children could read to her when they learned how.

I sat on the jutting boards of our granary and flipped the pages of that Bible one by one, just for the experience. Sometimes, I brought the open book close to my face and lingered on each page as if I were reading, but it could have been upside down. More than once, a sibling mocked me:

"You do not know how to read!"

Or another would say,

"Wanjirũ holds the Bible as if she knows how to read."

The mocking did not deter me.

Baba passed by once and gave me a quick side glance. It pleased me when he caught me in the act. Whether that nudged him is hard to tell, but he soon broke his silence.

When he arrived from work the following week, he found my younger siblings and me in the courtyard. Instead of getting in his thingira to unload the usual gray coat that he slung over his left shoulder, he stopped.

"Wanjirū," he called to me.

I rushed the few steps to where he stood. He gave me the kĩondo basket he carried his lunch in that morning before he said, "Your mother will take you to Njeki's to get your uniform on Saturday."

Ecstatic, I half-skipped to nyũmba to drop the kĩondo, wishing Mami could take me to Njeki's Shopping Center right away.

"Baba said you'll take me to Njeki's for uniform."

"We'll go on Saturday," Mami said.

I bubbled with excitement at the prospect of wearing a dress made by a real tailor. Before then, Mami stitched my dresses except those she bought off the rack for Christmas.

That Saturday, Mami and I walked the four miles to Njeki's Shopping Center. We found the tailor busy pedaling a black Singer treadle sewing machine set out on a shop's veranda. He offered us a bench where customers waited while he finished the stitching he was working on. Each minute of our wait tested my patience. Mami bought me a bottle of orange Fanta soda as a treat and to keep me occupied.

When the tailor put his sewing aside, he took my measurements and told Mami to return in two weeks.

The uniform reveal was a gorgeous blue pinafore with white sleeves and a collar. It fit me well, unlike the dresses Mami stitched—always a size larger so Tabitha and I could grow into them. With our slow growth, we never quite did.

Mami kept the uniform in her trunk in her bedroom, where she stored clean and important clothes. At least once a week, I sneaked in and peeked at my prized outfit. I could not hurry January fast enough.

When school opening day finally arrived, neat and uniformed, I joined other fresh grade-one beginners and walked the two miles to Tindaress Primary School.

Although I did not know my age, I was ten years and three months old.

Chapter 47

TINDARESS PRIMARY SCHOOL

I lack the words to describe the joy that bubbled in my heart that Monday afternoon, my first day of school, in my new uniform, as I walked with other children on a tractor trail through the savanna.

Our small group reached the Nakuru–Solai Road, where we turned left, and, in a little while, the top of the school building came into view.

A year earlier, our bus had driven by the school when my little brother Waweru̅ fell sick, and, with Mami already sick in the hospital herself, Baba and I took him to the same hospital—Nakuru General Hospital—twenty miles away.

Now, up close, the school building looked larger and better, although nothing like the stone and cement buildings I saw in town.

Tindaress Primary School, the only one for miles, came in one elongated, mud-walled, thatch-roofed, rectangular building divided into three classrooms. Grade four, the senior class, occupied the classroom by the single entrance, and grade three used the middle room. Both classrooms had one small wooden window facing west, and pupils sat two to a desk.

The first and second-grade pupils shared the oversized room with two windows in the rear, where they sat on long benches.

We also used the room for Sunday school, and the adults held their church service.

Right at the back, where the roof tapered off, there was a tiny, windowless, walled-off corridor that hugged the wall, a glorified teachers' office where they stored books and supplies. It could barely hold two adults.

The one entrance with an aisle straight to the back divided the classrooms into two sections. If grade one and two pupils needed to go outside, they had to hush not to disturb the classes in session. And in case of an emergency, the windows were too small for an adult to step on a bench and crawl through.

About 100 feet behind the school building stood three one-room cottages built similarly, where the teachers lived. Set back to the east, between the school and teachers' quarters, were two pit toilets—one for males and the other for females.

People claimed grade-one pupils attended in the afternoons so they did not have to wake up too early. But it's likely it was because they used the same classroom grade two used in the mornings.

The style and condition of the building did not cross my mind. I knew no other school to compare it with, and I focused on finally getting to school.

*

The government has since rebuilt the Tindaress Primary School with stone blocks and corrugated iron sheets and renamed it Jamhuri Primary School. Next to it stands Patel High School, named after Mr. Patel of Patel General Store, its benefactor.

Mr. Patel and his family had been long-term residents of Solai. He had run the only liquor and general store for miles. When Solai Center (Njeki's Shopping Center) broke ground thirty years later, he had already socked away piles of money. Even then, the Center was no competition. It only boomed with activity on Sundays because of the market. Besides the market, there was a clinic headed by a medic not too proud to accept chicken or produce as payment, a convenience store, a tailor, a canteen that sold tea and scones and cupcakes, and a bar licensed to sell beer and *busaa* traditional brew that undercut the home brewers.

Because of the long distance, unless people lived in the adjacent farms, most people went to the shopping center only during the market day on Sundays or weekdays to visit the clinic. Otherwise, they shopped at Patel's General Store.

*

Back then, while Agĩkũyũ and other activists wrangled about their stolen lands, self-determination, and independence, they focused only on European colonizers, the colony's "first-class" citizens. Meanwhile, the Indians, brought as laborers from India by the colonizers at the close of the nineteenth century to help build the Kenya–Uganda railway, were now designated as "second-class" citizens in Kenya, a class several notches above the natives. Having toiled in a colony in India and learned how oppression worked, they carried on their lives in Kenya without interference or distraction and rendered themselves indispensable.

When the colonizers zoned the country, they designated the land as White Highlands—temperate climate lands for whites only—Crown Lands, missionary lands, residential and commercial plots in towns and townships, and native reserves. They allocated to Indians all those commercial plots in towns and strategic spots throughout the country so they could handle Kenya's retail economy and everyday needs, which the colonizers did not want to get involved in.

From then on, the Indians built and ran a country-wide business monopoly that covered manufacturing, distribution, and retail. They educated their children only in town-based schools that mirrored the European schools (Mr. Patel had his employee drive his children to and from Nakuru Town to attend school). They maintained their close-knit family units with their temples, treated their white customers as nobles, and mistreated their African workers and customers as the "lowest caste," whom they saw as good only for serving higher castes.

*

Today, I am glad I remained ignorant of the disparity between our school and the schools Indian and European children attended. Those children, especially the European children, learned in surroundings of serene, lush compounds **attended** by yardmen and cleaners. Pupils did various sports, including horseback riding, and learned target shooting. While our boys hunted using homemade traps, the European boys hunted with real guns.

I doubt my classmates and I would have dwelt on it, though. We never interacted with Indians unless someone went to buy an item at their stores. And, of course, we never interacted with white people except for an occasional sighting of our parents' employer from afar, when he drove alone or with his wife in a Land Rover, or later on when he came to pay coffee cherry pickers during coffee season.

I knew whites enjoyed privileges so lofty that it never occurred to me to wonder what those privileges involved, let alone dream about them. I was too young to connect the many restrictions on our parents and their powerlessness to oppression. Our condition, therefore, never bothered me on a conscious level because every family I knew led a peasant life like ours.

All I wanted was a room with a blackboard, a teacher, an exercise book, and a desk, seated next to other children, learning how to read and write.

Chapter 48

READING AND WRITING

From the first day, our teacher taught and spoke to us in Kiswahili. (Kiswahili is the linguistic term—because every name of a language in Kiswahili starts with the prefix "Ki." But Swahili is the popular term.) But we pupils spoke in Gĩkũyũ to each other inside or outside our classroom. Before I entered school, it never dawned on me that I spoke two languages. I must have picked up Kiswahili around age seven after we moved to the village.

Our teacher first gave us guidelines and rules to follow, which included standing when a teacher arrived at the beginning of each lesson. He then roll-called us and confirmed our registrations. When he called names, he required pupils to stand, say their names, and the names of the farms from which they came. Except for saying the names of the farms, we had to follow the same routine when we answered questions.

He then took us through the drill.

"Habari njioni [alasiri] watoto!" Good afternoon, children.

"Tuko salama mwalimu!" We are well, teacher.

"Keti chini watoto!" Sit down, children.

The teacher said we would learn to read, write, and do arithmetic. I could not wait to start!

He counted from one to ten and asked us to count after him. After three rounds of the drill, he asked each of us to stand and count. Half the children did it, but the rest could not or were too shy to speak in front of strangers.

When my turn came, I stood and started my count. I sensed the teacher's gaze pierce through me, and the other children gawked. My nerves frayed, and my heart raced while my neck struggled to support my head. But I kept on counting while my voice trailed lower and lower. Although it did not dawn on me then, my performance should have pleased me because I had never needed to count in sequence before, let alone in Kiswahili.

The classroom protocol and introductions took so long that by the time we finished the counting session, the teacher announced the end of class and sent us home.

We sprang up to get out, but he said to make one line. He walked behind us and shushed us when we whispered to each other, and others rushed to get out first. We calmed somewhat but still simmered with excitement as we walked in a single file along the corridor across the two higher classrooms, eager to share our day's experiences.

When we reached outside, before we gravitated toward children from our respective villages, we commingled and declared in high-pitched, excited voices to total strangers how well we did.

*

I looked forward to learning how to write when I reported to class the following day. But after the teacher did the roll call, he took us through a repeat counting session. He then arranged us into three groups.

The first group comprised the youngest children, whom the teacher said needed to strengthen their hand coordination. They used their index fingers to practice writing on a patch of loose dirt set for that purpose at the side of the school building. They progressed to the next group when their coordination stabilized.

The second group received slates, miniature blackboards with wood frames that measured about eight square inches, on which pupils wrote with white chalk. If their chalk ran out, they used pieces of rock with sharp edges; the teacher did not object. Sometimes, pupils used rocks with sharp edges to save on their chalk because they could press hard without the rock breaking as chalk often did. But if they pressed too hard, the slate broke, and their parents had to buy replacements.

The third and final group of older children, which included me, used exercise books and pencils. During our writing lesson, the teacher supplied each of us with a half-ruled exercise book, a half-pencil, and an eraser. And in the arithmetic lesson, he gave each of us a square half of an exercise book. I believe the books and pencils came in halves to stretch supplies.

Before the writing practice, we first started learning ABCs. The teacher sounded a letter and then wrote it on the blackboard. To my disappointment, we wrote nothing before the day ended. Things changed on the third day. We started practicing writing ABCs and numbers.

We recited letters of the alphabet in chorus. But writing them proved a challenge. No matter how hard I concentrated, sometimes holding my pencil so tightly my fist shook, my letters and numbers came out crooked.

Two pupils dealt with a "unique" challenge. They used their left hands, but the teacher said they had to use their right. One boy looked confused while the teacher helped him to hold his pencil. The two now focused on the change, which added to their writing struggle.

As if writing crooked letters was not enough, while I focused on getting them right, the teacher introduced capital letters. He wrote each lowercase letter alongside its capital. The letters looked so different! How could they mean the same? I wondered. How would they make words? I could not wait to get to the reading lesson to learn.

Meanwhile, before we learned how to read, the teacher asked us to solve riddles, and he read stories to us. He also required each of us to go in front of the class and tell a story.

We told stories using faltering voices while we fidgeted, our heads tilted and fingers near our mouths to ward off shyness, determined to finish before we fell apart. We giggled at our missteps without judgment from other pupils or reprimands from the teacher. He chuckled and filled in the gaps of our simple riddles or repetitive, disjointed anecdotes about the cunning hare, the slow tortoise, or the ogres.

The lesson turned out robust, enjoyed by all, and the most fun lesson I have ever immersed myself in.

Within a month, we learned consonants and vowels and how to combine them. We sang A-E-I-O-U, which in Kiswahili sounds as:

A as in apple

E as in egg

I as in eat

O as in on

U as in oops

Gĩkũyũ has two more vowels—ĩ as in aim; ũ as in old. Because we learned in Kiswahili, I had to learn those two on my own. The vowels are okay while writing by hand, but they have always been challenging because they do not appear on keyboards.

We learned to say the letters in chorus and individually. We then learned how to combine consonants with vowels to make various sounds. The teacher started us with familiar words, which he broke into syllables: ba-ba, ma-ma, da-da, ka-ka, nya-nya, ba-bu—Father, mother, sister, brother, grandmother, grandfather...

By the end of the first term, I could read the picture/storybook the teacher distributed during the reading lesson, the book he passed along from one pupil to the next.

At home, I practiced reading simple words in the Gĩkũyũ Bible, the only book I saw written in Gĩkũyũ before my adulthood. Eager to learn how to read, and without access to another book, I matched letters and sounded words as we did in our Kiswahili lesson.

Reading proved easier than writing. When I joined a consonant with any vowel, the sound it produced remained the same no matter in which word the combination appeared. That enabled me to read a word even if I did not know its meaning.

Later, when we learned to write, the teacher added a drawing lesson and issued us a plain half-exercise book. I wonder how much value resulted from the drawing lesson because I only remember drawing a "girl" or a "boy" with stick arms and legs or images of a box and a mug.

At the end of each lesson, the teacher collected our exercise books and stored them in the tiny office at the back for safekeeping until the next lesson.

Chapter 49

ARITHMETIC PUZZLE

We learned arithmetic the same way we learned the alphabet. After we mustered counting one to ten, it seemed magical when the teacher showed us how to combine the numbers to get whatever other larger numbers we wanted.

We practiced writing the numbers in the exercise book squares. It took much effort to fit numbers into the squares without encroaching on lines. Other than that, arithmetic turned out easy until it confused me.

Next, the teacher started us with simple additions and subtractions. I gawked at the blackboard as he cracked the door wider and wider into a secret world of arithmetic where he manipulated numbers that produced different numbers. He did it so methodically that I could follow every calculation of the drop-down arithmetic.

However, one afternoon, I became confused when he introduced a unique arithmetic style, different from the vertical one he had taught us. He wrote numbers vertically, like he always did, then wrote them horizontally. It fascinated me when both methods produced the same answers.

Occasionally, I peeked at my neighbors to gauge how well they coped. But, bent over their papers, I could not assess whether they were having difficulties like me until the teacher started walking along the benches, checking each pupil's progress, and making positive or negative comments. He chastised the ones who got their answers wrong.

Day in and day out, frustration and confusion piled on me. I focused on the blackboard while the teacher solved the problems. But I missed a step every time. I then jumbled the horizontal numbers and mixed them with equal and plus signs. The vertical section rescued me; otherwise, I would have scored zero on each arithmetic test we did daily after each lesson. It did not console me when I learned half the class scored less than me.

One day, however, the power of focus and repetition got me out of my misery when every piece of the puzzle fell into place.

As usual, the teacher strolled along the rows of benches, checking each pupil's answers. When he checked mine, I tensed when he crossed my horizontal arithmetic section in red ink.

"You don't know how to do this type of arithmetic," he charged. "You copied from your neighbor, didn't you?"

"Hapana Mwalimu" (No teacher), I said feebly. "Nilifanya mwenyewe" (I did it myself).

"Nyamaza!" Shut up!

I gasped softly and did as told. The teacher moved on to the next pupil. When he later solved the problems on the blackboard, I became elated when my answers turned out correct.

To teachers, like to my parents and other adults, it did not matter if the child told the truth. If a teacher disagreed, denying or arguing wasted energy. It prolonged the verbal putdowns or escalated to a slap or a ruler swat to the head.

By age seven, before I went to school, I already understood that victims fared best if they hushed and ignored adults' big or mini-insanities. And we definitely never indulged in that Western routine of "grin and bear it." In Kenya, grinning meant insolence, deserving a quick whack. But, because children did not grin when adults reprimanded them at home or in school, I can only speculate on what the adults' reaction might have been.

At the cost of my communication skills, at that early stage, I had perfected the art of muted defiance, which I continued using up to adulthood. It was the easiest way to sidestep an accuser.

But to be fair to the teacher who taught us in grades one and two, he never whacked us beyond perhaps a tap on the head, which I do not even remember. But he could use forceful words to show his assertions were final.

But his "shut up" retort mattered little; my relief at discovering how to solve horizontally written arithmetic diluted the hurt. Afterward, I solved all or most of my arithmetic problems.

By the end of grade one, I felt great about my schoolgirl status. I could write better than most pupils at my level, read a picture book, and do arithmetic.

*

In grade two, I started going to school in the mornings and looked forward to the activities my brother Joseph had hyped. "Mornings are when things happen," he had said or implied throughout the previous year.

At eight a.m. sharp, the timekeeper rang the bell. We hurried from wherever we hung out in the schoolyard. We made three lines in front of the school. Grade two at the front, grade three in the middle, and grade four—the senior class—at the rear.

The master on duty appeared with a stick in hand that he occasionally, and almost unconsciously, tapped lightly on his left palm, his eyes scanning the assembled pupils.

"Hamjambo asubuhi wanafunzi," Good morning, pupils, he said.

"Hatujambo Mwalimu," Good morning, teacher.

"The national anthem!"

What does it mean? I asked myself. How did Joseph forget to tell me this part? I now waited and perked my ears, eager to learn.

A teenage boy from the senior class rushed to the front. Somebody whispered, "Prefect." The teenager readied himself while the rest followed suit. Coarse khaki uniforms rustled as pupils straightened, feet together, backs erect.

I did the same.

The prefect started singing, and the rest joined in.

GOD SAVE THE QUEEN
God save the gracious Queen
Long live our noble Queen
God Save the Queen!
Send her victorious,
Happy and glorious,
Long to reign over us
God Save the Queen!

While my fellow pupils sang…Long live the Queen…to reign over us, the Mau Mau members were dying in record numbers, fighting the British to end the queen's rule over us.

In contrast to the prefect, who bellowed out, the rest sang in a subdued, funeral-like tone. The teacher stood solemn but did not sing.

I remained stoic, wondering what the words meant. At one time, I angled my eyes sideways and watched how my fellow class two pupils fared. They wore serious faces, opened their mouths, and moved their lips or kept them sealed. When we later compared notes during our morning break, we recognized only one word—queen. I did not know what it meant. Even if I knew it was a woman's title, the highest term I knew for a white woman was Memsahib, Kamunge's daughter-in-law.

My classmates and I did not know a single word of the English language, and yet our school, like the rest of Kenya, expected us to sing the British National Anthem without learning it first.

But every morning, without fail, five days a week, we stood to attention with solemn faces and hummed along as we mimicked the fourth graders who knew limited African-accented English words.

After the national anthem, the master on duty made announcements. He then walked along each line of pupils, inspecting our clothes, hair, and fingernails. If he determined a pupil was not presentable, he sent the pupil to the front for caning after the inspection.

Teachers did not check below the knees. By then, our shoeless feet had covered a few miles on dirt roads or dew-laden footpaths.

Besides the swats for lateness, teachers ordered pupils who had shaggy, dirty, or lice-infested hair to have their hair shaven by the next school day.

But my grade-two teacher, who also taught grade one, went further and shamed pupils in front of the entire assembly. He kept a pair of scissors for this purpose. Whenever he identified hair culprits, he sent them to the front. He then shaved a cross through each culprit's hair down to the scalp—one line from brow to nape and another from ear to ear.

One day, he became too enthusiastic about shaving and turned me into a surrogate culprit, which caused a rift in my family.

Chapter 50

TEACHER'S OVERREACH

During my school campaign, Waigwa and his family were still languishing in Nyeri, the native reserve. When he and his wife, Njeri, and their four children returned to Solai and moved in with us, I had completed grade one.

Their firstborn, Mũmbi, four months older than me, joined a class ahead of me. Her brother, Mũthee, two years younger, joined me in grade two.

Despite our congested living conditions, we, the household's schoolchildren, shared things and stories, played, and walked to school together without strife.

One time, however, Mũthee caused one of my unpleasant memories of Tindaress Primary School, all because of homework.

Our teacher required us to memorize arithmetic tables printed on the back cover of our exercise books. He started us with the lowest multiplication, 2 x 2, and built it up to 12 x 12. Reciting the tables became our ritual before each arithmetic lesson.

To ensure we learned the answers instead of memorizing them, the teacher randomly picked us to recite any number he spat out, like an auctioneer taking bids. He required pupils to stand and finish giving answers by the second they got on their feet. Otherwise, one received a ruler rap on the head for being too slow.

On Fridays, the teacher gave us homework to memorize one row of the tables. He gave us non-writing homework and only on weekends. Having a similar background to ours, I suppose he understood that weekday homework posed a problem for us after dark. Evenings were when families assembled around fires, talked about their day's activities, and told stories while mothers cooked. The glass or tin can open-flame lanterns most families used were not bright enough for reading or writing.

I practiced my timetables before dusk, seated at my favorite place on the jutting boards of our granary. I also practiced in my mind while I did my chores. If I forgot an answer, I dashed to where I kept my exercise book, flipped it to the table printed on the back cover, and checked the answer.

One Friday, instead of a multiplication table homework he gave us, the teacher gave us simple arithmetic problems to solve. During that Monday's arithmetic lesson, he asked Mûthee to produce his homework. Mûthee stood, his head hung, eyes to the ground. I felt sorry for him because it meant he did not do his homework.

But I should have felt sorry for myself because, to my surprise and chagrin, the teacher did what a person in authority should never do to a child. Because I was two years older than Mûthee, the teacher said I should have reminded Mûthee to do his homework. With that declaration, the teacher put me in charge of Mûthee's homework.

Besides getting upset, it confused me because my parents never knew I had homework unless they saw me do it. It was common knowledge that we were responsible for doing what the teacher asked of us unless we wanted to join the farm's labor force. To our teacher, that did not matter. Besides putting me in charge, he punished me instead of Mûthee.

He called me to the front and, right there in front of the class, shaved my hair, a trail from forehead to nape and another from ear to ear.

Droplets escaped from my eyes during the shave. I seethed the rest of the lesson and kept it up after our class let out.

On our way home, my fellow schoolmates said the cross looked terrible. I hated that people who saw me thought I had lice in my hair or had broken a school rule.

When Mami returned home late afternoon and saw my new hairdo, she asked what I had done to bring that on myself. When she learned of the reason, she became an unhappy mother. But she had no way of making amends on my behalf. So, she retreated into her crazy state, the simmering anger she regressed to when her targets were out of her reach, whether it was the teacher, indirect targets like Njeri and Mūthee, or a person she did not want to mess with, such as my father.

"No child should ever get punished because of another's mistake!" Mami said.

That statement put me at ease; my burden shifted to Mami. I left her to sort the matter while I rejoined the others in the courtyard for our evening play.

Soon, Mami appeared from nyūmba, scissors in one hand and a low bench in the other. She proceeded to the grassy patch by the side of the granary.

"Wanjirū, come here," she said.

She clicked and clicked her scissors until every clump of hair disappeared from my head.

"Brush the hair off," Mami said.

After I brushed off the hundreds of hair clippings, I ran my hands over my head. With my ordeal behind me and now clean-shaven, I looked like every child in the village after a shave and felt fine.

But not Mami; she still retained an unsettled fight in her. One would have thought the teacher had cut her hair, too. Later, when the family regrouped, she snorted now and then as she assembled ingredients for her evening cooking. She fetched items she needed, sending none of us, choosing to do it all.

Njeri, Mũthee's mother, did not say a word.

In hindsight, it now makes sense that Njeri stayed mum and aloof, whether in that case or about doing house chores. She and Mami were two self-confident women, both quick in their ways, Baba would have said. Njeri may have chosen to keep a low profile to avoid conflict with her stepmother-in-law.

As for Mũthee, I think he failed to do his homework because he did not understand Kiswahili well yet and lacked the courage to ask me to help him. It was the first term since his family arrived from Kikuyuland, where children learned in Gĩkũyũ for the first four years of their schooling.

*

Despite the hair episode, attending school in the morning gave me a sense of belonging, a part of the whole. I went each morning eager to learn.

During the reading lesson, the teacher distributed books. He often had only one copy for himself and another for the entire class. After a pupil read a paragraph, they passed the book to the next pupil.

Even without enough books to go around or to read at home, all of us could read by the time we finished grade two.

Despite their abusive tendencies, which they shared with the larger society, those teachers gave their time and undivided attention to whatever they taught us, without interference by a school inspector who came only once a year, if that. Those teachers never held side jobs or businesses; they never reported to class late, with a hangover, or missed a single day—a claim I cannot make about many modern-day Kenyan teachers.

Chapter 51

COLONIZERS' UNINTENDED CONSEQUENCES

As I relished my life in elementary school, it never occurred to me until decades later that, besides Baba letting me go to school and having committed teachers, my education became possible only because of the sacrifice of a horde of political activists, and especially the Mau Mau freedom fighters.

Unknown to us, at the time, the colonial government started villagization to contain the Gĩkũyũ tribe. As a result, Mr. Kamunge, the landowner and my parents' employer, moved my family and others to the fenced village, less than a mile from his colonial house, where he could keep an eye on us.

Although my parents and other adult villagers suffered restrictions and other hardships, the move, in the long run, changed many children's lives for the better, including mine.

With the concentration of people in villages, Kamunge and the neighboring British farmers may have wondered what to do with young children—not old enough to work on the farms yet—loitering around unsupervised while their parents worked in the fields. It made sense for them to start a community school.

Kamunge and four farmers from the adjacent farms agreed that one of them would sell or donate a plot of land to build a school. The landowner we called Kwa-ũndarĩ , whose farm was centrally located, sold or donated about two acres to build the school. Rumors claimed he donated the land, but I have no information that confirms this. It's likely the government bought the land from him.

The other farmers donated materials like timber and grass thatch that their laborers cut from their respective farms. Parents with school-age children helped build the school, while the Ministry of Education provided instruction materials and teachers.

Besides school fees, our parents paid into a yearly building fund (similar to homeowner's association fees) to maintain the school. Teachers likely used that money to buy school supplies because pupils did all the sweeping and gardening work, and their parents did repairs.

Today, I thank the Mau Mau warriors—and political activists and their supporters—who left their families and took to the forests to fight for the freedom of their fellow citizens.

Without their activism and sacrifice, my family would have remained isolated at our first homestead in Kĩrĩ ma-inĩ. Baba would not have sent me six miles away to the one-room boy's school—even if the school agreed to admit a girl—at Ndege's farm on the other side of Jumatatu Mountain. It's also likely that Kenya would have taken another decade or two of political strife, campaigns, and negotiations to attain its independence.

If that had happened, like other youngsters whose fathers lacked school fees or foresight, I imagine today I might be an elderly woman with no formal education, still living in Solai, scraping a subsistence existence, growing my food in a small plot, with a horde of grown children and grandchildren.

It is such a contradiction that the British imported formal education to Kenya, for which I'm forever grateful, but Mau Mau freedom fighters had to fight and die by the thousands for me and many of my contemporaries to get that education.

BECOMING A CHRISTIAN

Chapter 52

WORSHIP

By age six, when my family still lived at Kĩrĩma-inĩ, I had heard about my people's primordial parents, Gĩkũyũ and Mũmbi, and our clan, Anjirũ.

After we moved to the village and as I became aware of life around me, I noticed my father's wooden shrine, an oversized dollhouse look-alike. Besides noticing the gourds inside, I did not concern myself with the shrine or dwell on it because we did not mess with Baba's stuff.

As I grew older, I heard stories about Agĩkũyũ's old ways and practices, and by adulthood, I had listened to many Christian sermons, read parts of the Christian Bible's Old Testament, and learned other people's ways enough to realize that Agĩkũyũ worship practices differed little from the rest of humanity.

From the cave-dwelling time, humans have organized themselves into small or large clusters of communities, come up with therapies to help with the survival of their bloodline, devised and run social and legal systems to manage their communities, told stories, danced to educate and entertain themselves, and recorded their history in one form or another. To ground and harmonize their systems, each community came up with a story about their origin, belief system, and mode of worship.

*

Agĩkũyũ worshipped Ngai, the creator, the giver, and the Supreme Being. Ngai lived in the sky, but mountains, especially Kĩrĩnyaga, anglicized as Mt. Kenya by the colonizers, were Ngai's earthly resting places. Agĩkũyũ had deference and respect for mountains, built by an act of nature instead of by human hand, which was why they never built houses of worship.

To symbolize a mountain, people worshipped and performed their "religious" rites under a large tree while they faced Mt. Kenya. The trees included mũgumo, mũtamaiyũ, or mũkũyũ.

They believed Ngai created the first man, Gĩkũyũ, on Mt. Kenya, under a mũkũyũ (fig tree), and later his companion, Mũmbi, the first woman.

The Gĩkũyũ tribe derives its name from the first man, while they refer to their descendants as Chiana chia Gĩkũyũ na Mũmbi (the children of Gĩkũyũ and Mũmbi), or Chiana chia Mũmbi (the children of Mũmbi) or Agĩkũyũ.

Based on what I have heard throughout my life, and according to notes I got from Mũkũrwe wa Nyagathanga, the sacred place in Mũrang'a County, Ngai designated and described the boundaries of Kikuyuland to Gĩkũyũ and Mũmbi as follows:

Mt. Kenya (Kĩrĩnyaga) to the north; Ngong Hills (Kĩrĩmbirũirũ) to the south; Kĩanjahĩ or Kĩrĩma Mbogo to the east; and Nyandarwa Mountain Range or Aberdare Ranges (Mũtambũrũko wa Nyandarwa) to the west. ĩ

Ngai told Gĩkũyũ and Mũmbi to descend from Mt. Kenya and go between the four corners of their new land, the area occupied by a big mũkũrwe tree with nyagathanga birds perched on top. They ended up in the current Mũrang'a County and named the place Mũkũrwe wa Nyagathanga.

Figure 1: The text reads: The Home of Gĩkũyũ and Mũmbi

That spot remains Agĩkũyũ 's sacred ground, untouched—as of December 2015 when I visited the site—except for the fence and two gates (shown in Figures 1 and 2), and three shacks built after Kenya's independence (December 12, 1963) to explain to tourists and visiting school children the original Agĩkũyũ 's way of life.

Figure 2: The text reads: Origin of the Agĩkũyũ - Mũkũrwe wa Nyagathanga A Sacred Place

By the 1950s, the "original" mũkũrwe tree had fallen because of old age. Dr. Julius Gĩkonyo Kĩano (who later became the Minister of Commerce, among other posts) and his entourage planted a replacement tree in 1956 when he returned from the United States after his studies. He and the accompanying elders slaughtered a goat as an offering and poured a libation of beer on the sacred ground.

As before, they did not eat or drink the sacrificial meat or beer. They left them on the site for Ngai, although they knew Ngai's wild animals—or possibly other humans—would sneak in and eat the meat.

*

According to Agĩkũyũ mythology, Ngai has no gender or helpers like angels or enemies like the devil. Ngai has no form; no one can see or draw the phenomenon's likeness. Ngai does not punish wrongdoers; humans and other creatures do more than enough of that. And with the concept of *what goes around comes around*, there would be no need.

Like many other cultures' spiritual practices, Agĩkũyũ's worship intertwined with every part of their lives. To those born into it, like my parents, especially my father, the idea of converting others or converting to another belief system made no sense. And they did not indulge in regular prayers for things they could do for themselves.

Unintentionally, Dr. J.W. Arthur, in charge of the Kikuyu Language Committee (in London with British men as members) responsible for Kikuyu translations in the early and mid-20th century, [Bildad Kaggia 1975.48] who translated the Christian Bible into Gĩkũyũ, mistranslated many words and quotes that Christians relied on and still do. They translated "Pray," "prayers," "people who pray," and "let's pray" into hoya, mahoya, ahoi, reke tũhoe, which literally means beg, begs, people who beg, and let's beg. Ironically, those translators helped turn the tribe, if not most Kenyans, into ahoi, beggars, a term and practice my people scorned when I was growing up.

In this mindset, people not only beg God but also their relatives and others. Many seem to believe only God can help them directly or indirectly through others. (The corrupt system doesn't help.) It seems they have taken themselves out of the equation, and the answer for many of them is out there, not within—a very debilitating state of being.

If a person begs several times a day and even sings and listens to music about begging (implying lack or scarcity), it has to affect their psyche. I prefer gratitude affirmations and giving thanks.

Ngai dished out no favors for individuals, as highlighted in the Gĩkũyũ adage: Mbura yuraga ha mũthĩni na ha gĩtonga (it rains on the land of the poor and of the rich). A lazy farmer had no excuse for his paltry crop or small or non-existent herd of goats.

Worship was, therefore, event-based.

If it involved a family, the head of household conducted the ceremony. If it related to a clan, the head of that clan did the honors. But in matters of extreme importance to the entire community, such as lack of rain, an epidemic, or sending their warriors to war, the governing council, made of distinguished men, performed the prayers. That council also laid down laws on crime and punishment, general governance, interpreted traditions, customs, and the community's moral code.

Agĩkũyũ worship, a way of life that people may now term religion, did not comprise heaven, doomsday, or hell. People believed Ngai was satisfied with the creation and never intended to destroy the people or interfere in their daily lives.

But people still evoked Ngai's blessings and protection, rejoiced, and gave thanks during ceremonies, such as celebrating the birth of a child, rites of passage to adulthood, and for a community or a family's general welfare.

Without an imaginary utopia or misery-land after death, Agĩkũyũ believed people transitioned from the land of the living to the land of the dead, the spirit world. They named their children after their relatives, alive or departed, to keep a link between generations, a practice the tribe still upholds.

If people became concerned about the wrath of a departed, they combed their memories for what may have made the ancestor angry. For example, if a son or a daughter had mistreated a departed parent or elder, the ancestor returned as negative energy to haunt and inflict misfortune on the wrongdoer.

If this happened, people corrected the wrong (if the ancestor were alive) or performed a ritual and sacrificed a goat to appease the ancestor.

*

After the British invaded Kenya toward the end of the nineteenth century and turned it into a colony in 1920, they condemned the Agĩkũyũ's way of life and ceremonies. They called them primitive and pagans and wrongly labeled their belief system "ancestor worship."

The British conversion campaign through missionaries and schools trivialized or eliminated every part of the Agĩkũyũ and other tribes' cultures—worship, legal systems, music and dances, names, and languages—and indoctrinated them to reject or ignore the very essence of themselves. The campaign did not taper off until Kenya's independence on December 12, 1963. By then, as the saying goes, the die was cast.

Christianity and Western education had conditioned most Agĩkũyũ, even the university-educated, to scorn their own culture. The tribe's traditions and creativity became so diluted that people perfected the art of copying and enhancing European culture. The Agĩkũyũ and other Africans replaced their worship with Christianity or Islam, depending on what was available or prevalent where they grew up and in the schools they attended.

According to Wangari Maathai in "Unbowed," it took a mere two generations for the Agĩkũyũ to turn their backs on their religion and culture and embrace that of their colonizers. At best, they kept a hybrid of the two cultures.

As time went on, Agĩkũyũ and other Africans aspired to become, eat, and dress like their colonizers. Under the baptismal guise, they named their children after their colonizers, whom they considered superior, especially because of their economic and political muscle.

Today, because parents not born into it cannot grasp the nuances of the exalted European culture to teach it to their children, they have settled for a blend of European-African practices. Many children from affluent homes learn English only. Children of the working class speak pidgin Kiswahili, which has severed meaningful interactions with their older generations. This has further weakened, sidelined, or wiped out the richness of the Agĩkũyũ 's culture and literature.

But now, a cultural resurgence of small population segments is reclaiming and repackaging aspects of their culture. They spread their heritage and old practices through songs, radio, TV, YouTube videos, and other platforms.

Unfortunately, this may also promote tribalism, which has plagued Kenyans since the British invaded and wiped out micronations and their social and legal systems, and mixed different peoples like jellybeans, denying them a chance to assimilate organically—something the Agĩkũyũ and the Maasai were already practicing.

The cultural resurgence has also given ideologues a chance to promote heinous and outdated practices like female genital mutilation as if evolution (and progress) for Agĩkũyũ and others took a break for an entire century.

*

Although most Kenyans claim to be Christians, many do so with little or no thought besides fitting in socially. Some treat it as insurance in case the Christian apocalypse story turns out true. Sometimes, the practice extends only to using a Western name and the claim of a Christian title.

Some Kenyans convert to Islam—which has become more prevalent due to high birth rates and migration in recent years—and assume an Arabic name. But unlike during my generation, when people got their new names as young people or adults, most parents now give their children European or Arabic names at birth.

Sometimes, Kenyans resort to fading African traditions to help clarify gray areas left by their adopted religion. For example, if a series of unexplained misfortunes plague a family or a couple—say, a wife suffers multiple miscarriages—the husband and family might suspect he did not complete a vital stage in the marriage ritual, which may have angered the father-in-law. A ceremonial party or a quiet family visit to the in-laws, bearing gifts, usually follows.

Others may indulge in hush-hush consultations with shamans.

Nowadays, people pray in churches or mosques for peace, rain, or to end an epidemic. But when a Gĩkũyũ man (men still hold a monopoly on these matters) faces a calamity, he may fall back on tradition.

A distinguished group of respected elderly men, like the governing council of more than a century ago, may conduct a one-color goat-slaughter solemn ceremony. The location is not crucial. But calamities that affect the entire community or individuals at the top of the food chain may get solemnized at Mũkũrwe wa Nyagathanga, the sacred site.

When I toured the site in December 2015, an attendant told me that two months prior, one of the top officials in Kenya had held a ceremony there.

So, although Agĩkũyũ have copied or adopted European culture, myths, superstitions, and overwhelming religiosity, the fear of a curse—what goes around comes around—is embedded in their psyche. They have deference to the curse.

In the olden days, the curse played a critical role in governance because the micro-nation's legal structure had no police force. But today, the curse's usefulness as a deterrent gets diluted with every generation. It will likely be extinct in another generation or so.

Chapter 53

CHRISTIANITY VS BUSINESS

My siblings and I learned about Agĩkũyũ spirituality through stories or overheard conversations. After two years in the village, I heard women talk about "modern religion" or "worshiping the true God."

Although some farmworkers practiced Christianity even before villagization, they remained in the minority because they built their small homesteads scattered around the farm or lived in small clusters. Now grouped in a village, it became easier for them to recruit and convert new followers. There followed a wave of conversions throughout the village. I do not know how long Christianity took to reach our homestead, tucked at the back of the village, but when it did, for a period, it cast a dim shadow over my family.

It all started when, one morning, Mami claimed she had an "Awakening." According to her, Jesus appeared—she did not clarify in what form—in the wee hours of the night and told her to repent her sins, and all would be cleansed and forgiven. She could not wait to attend church that Sunday to share her epiphany and confess her sins. Her friends took notice, but the family paid her no attention, at least not yet.

Mami was a prime candidate for conversion. She lacked a religious background despite growing up during the height of the Christian missionaries' campaign against Agĩkũyũ culture, particularly religion, which they labeled "paganism" or "ancestor worship."

They concentrated all their conversion efforts in the more populated native reserves of Kikuyuland (Nyeri, Mũrang'a, and Kĩambuu). But Mami moved from Nyeri as a little girl. She grew up on a farm owned by a British farmer in Nanyuki and later, as a teenager, moved to Major Holman's, two farms away from Kamunge's. At the time, Christianity had not yet encroached on private European farms, and the farmworkers' living conditions were not conducive to cultural ceremonies and rituals.

With native practices stymied and no knowledge of European worship, Mami fell into a religious limbo. As a young woman, she immersed herself in the new cash economy, married, and focused on her work and her children.

At about forty years old and now living in a village, my mother was open and vulnerable to whatever perspective came her way. Amid social turmoil, Christianity stepped in and promised that if she believed and followed its dogmas, her toil would get rewarded in the afterlife.

By then, Kenya's colonization had reached its critical mass. The colonizers had stabilized the Three Cs of colonialism—Christianize, Civilize, and Commercialize.

Mami later liked to quote the Christian Bible verse:

It is easier for a camel to go through the eye of a needle than a rich man to enter the kingdom of God.

Did my mother understand this is a metaphor, which refers to an actual place in Jerusalem called the "Eye of the Needle Gate"? I doubt it. However, I hope she understood the fundamental message that a person's value is not measured by material wealth.

Mami liked to evoke another Christian religious benefit, a better equalizer than death. On the day of resurrection, the last—the peasants—shall be first, and the first—the British colonizers—shall be last.

With that "assurance," Mami's choice became obvious. She labeled the tobacco business she and Baba ran as "devil's business," revolted, and traded it for Jesus.

According to the converters and the converted, Christians did not touch or consume such substances as tobacco and alcohol or involve themselves with "pagan" cultural activities if they wanted to "inherit the Kingdom of God."

Next came Mami's wardrobe.

Like most women of her generation, she wore a plain or multi-colored skirt that reached an inch below her knees with a pocket on the right side. Over the skirt came a basic-color rectangular cloth doubled and clasped with pins on the right shoulder, leaving the left shoulder uncovered. She then attached the cloth with a line of safety pins from the armpit to below the waist, leaving the pocketed side of the skirt visible. She wore a belt over the ensemble.

After her Christian conversion, she discarded that style of dressing. (Before then, I never noticed that she wore different clothing from the dresses she made for my sister Tabitha and me.)

To update her wardrobe, she bought two "proper" dresses, one for weekdays and the other for Sunday church. She also bought two headscarves—symbols of a veil. She began wearing a scarf when she awoke in the morning until she retired at night, a practice she kept up for the rest of her life.

Instead of processing tobacco snuff and going to Sunday market twice a month to sell it, Mami went to church and returned home about the same time to cook our lunch.

I watched her transformation with little interest because whatever Mami wore, she looked the same to me.

It was, however, a different matter for my father, perhaps even traumatic. It had disrupted his business and his Sunday routine. But because he never overtly reacted, it never occurred to our family that Mami's alternative lifestyle had caused him such pain. But, as he showed us later, the biggest blow was that the change had undermined his authority.

For over ten years, my parents had gone to the market twice a month to sell their merchandise. On the Sundays they did not go, Mami did housekeeping while Baba puttered around the courtyard in the mornings. After lunch, he shared his homemade beer with a friend or two while our family remained at his beck and call. On the Sundays he had not brewed beer, he got it elsewhere and returned home drunk to find his homestead full of life.

Now that his wife had rebelled and attended church on Sundays and his goats were away in the pastures, his homestead had minimal activity most of Sunday, his one free day. He stayed in his thingira or idled around the courtyard, scavenging for scraps of chores, with only us little children around.

Unknown to us, he waited for a trigger to assert himself, put Mami in her place, and reinstate his authority.

Mami soon provided him with a reason he needed.

Before Mami's Christian awakening, although Baba drank his homemade beer from his prized shiny bull's horn, he served his acquaintances in our tea mugs. In her final remake, Mami spent her mbia chia ũtukũ mũũru (emergency money) to buy an assortment of new colored enamel tea mugs. She banished the old, "contaminated" mugs to thingira.

This may have seemed benign to an outsider, but to my father, it was an affront to his authority. It gave him the perfect opportunity to reassert himself and remind Mami who ruled the homestead.

Chapter 54

UNDISCIPLINED WIFE

One Sunday, Baba, the ruler of our homestead, decided without prior warning that this was the day to assert his authority. Oblivious to Baba's state of mind, Mami left for church while my three younger siblings and I played around in the courtyard. Midmorning, through thingira's doorway, I saw Baba drinking from his shiny beer bullhorn, which was uncharacteristic because I had never seen him drink alcohol that early in the day and never alone.

At about lunchtime, he ventured outdoors, his three-legged stool in one hand, his drink in the other, and his hat back on. He camped on the porch and propped his bullhorn against the wall. Every so often, he took a sip of beer.

Usually, when he relaxed on the porch in the late evenings, he removed and stepped on top of his sandals, placed his hat on his folded knee, and sat to watch his children and goats mingle and make merry. But today, he kept the sandals and hat on.

That afternoon, Mami rushed into the courtyard, her face shiny and brow sweaty with a trail down one temple. She changed from her church dress and washed her face. She hurried about, assembling ingredients to make lunch.

I noticed Baba mumble. He shifted, restless as if the stool had become uncomfortable to sit on. Tabitha and I, the oldest children in the group, looked at him, intrigued by his strange behavior. Soon, I realized he wanted to get Mami's attention because his mumbles got clearer and clearer whenever she came to the courtyard.

"No undisciplined woman will rule my homestead," he said. "You hear me? Never!"

Mami ignored him and continued with her chores, closed-lipped.

Baba fidgeted and shifted on his stool.

"A woman has taken over my homestead!" he said.

Mami remained quiet and returned indoors.

Baba arose. He ambled toward the center of the courtyard, stopped, turned to his right, and faced her house's open door. "I won't have it! Do you hear me? No undisciplined wife will ever rule over my family!"

My siblings and I abandoned our play. What made my father so angry? I asked myself. Baba was never vocal. A man of few words, he reacted to situations without fanfare. We children now gawked and waited for the suspenseful show to unravel.

Mami emerged from nyũmba, ignored Baba, veered away from him, and headed to the granary.

Baba quickened his steps toward her.

She stopped, turned and faced him, and squinted as if surprised. But before she took another step, Baba was onto her. He reached out, grabbed her arm, and raised his other arm to strike her. Mami yanked her arm free.

He reached again.

She freed herself and, this time, grabbed his wrists before any slap landed on her. Baba struggled to free himself while he swayed this way and that.

Mami took chances when she grabbed his arms. If he fell and the story leaked out, villagers would accuse her of beating her husband. No woman wanted such a reputation.

"Leave me alone," Mami said, released him, and stepped back.

Pure terror coursed through me. I had never seen Baba try to hit or insult Mami. He reserved his anger for my brothers, which he released through beatings.

I did not know yet what Christianity involved, but it had caused my parents to fight, and I wanted no part of it.

Baba closed in again and threw his drunken slaps. Every time he did so, his other arm flailed along with his body. In a cacophony of grabs and releases, he tried to throw Mami off balance. She dug in, and her feet stayed firm on the ground, which caused Baba to stagger and his hat to fly off. I feared he was the one who would end up on the ground. An old drunk was no match for a much younger, sober wife.

Baba stopped throwing slaps or trying to grab Mami. Instead, he retrieved his hat and stood, his head slightly hung, as if in deep thought.

Relief swept through me. But I wondered. How can Baba give up? I have never seen him falter in any decision or action he takes.

He now turned and strode toward his thingira.

"This homestead belongs to Warama son of Njerũ," he said. "No woman will ever rule over it!"

Those were the last words I heard him utter about the matter.

Mami remained where he left her, immobilized.

In a minute, true to form of finishing what he started, Baba emerged from his thingira. He clutched a hammer.

Oh! No! My heart sank. Does he want to clobber Mami?

Before he reached where she stood, he made a right turn and entered nyũmba. Dishes rattled and clanked. After the commotion died, he reappeared. He carried a white basin full of Mami's assortment of colorful new enamel mugs.

Her house now clear, Mami kept her distance, tiptoed to her porch, leaned on the doorjamb, and watched.

Everything went quiet—not even a chicken squawked. The stillness lasted for only seconds.

Baba set the basin by the granary and squatted. He picked up the first mug by the handle and hammered away. When he flattened half the mugs, Mami disappeared indoors. But we children continued to keep vigil.

After he smashed the last mug, hammer still in hand, Baba rose, paused, eyes on his handiwork, perhaps waiting for Mami to object. But she remained indoors, her fury restrained by her gender's low social status.

I was afraid of what my father was going to do next.

Our eyes followed him as he rambled toward his porch, dangling his hammer without uttering a single word since the first round. He gathered his bullhorn and stool on the porch and entered his thingira. He was done.

But we did not know it yet. We waited for about five minutes for him to reappear. When he did not, we gradually returned to our play, and Mami started where he left off. To her, Baba had crossed a red line, a deal-breaker.

She resumed her chores all right, but as one possessed. She belted Christian songs, cooked, swept the floor, and rattled dishes with stimulant-induced energy-like vigor.

I wondered whether my parents had gone mad. I never heard Mami sing unless she repeated a verse in a story or showed us how older women used to dance ndumo.

In between the singing, she made assertions.

"I'll remain a Christian whether one wants it or not!" she said.

Not a peep came from Baba's thingira throughout Mami's tantrum. With no opposition and needing to feed us, she ran out of steam.

Afterward, nobody mentioned the fight. It was as if we, the witnesses, were all ashamed; I know I was. The oldest children were spared. David was away at boarding school, and Simon and Joseph had gone goat herding. I doubt they ever learned of that fight.

Within a month, Mami replaced her destroyed mugs. Baba acted as if he did not notice the "infraction."

In the coming months, while my parents adjusted to the family's new rhythm, whenever one of Baba's acquaintances reached for a mug Baba had drunk tea in, Baba told on Mami. He stretched his hand and said, "No! No! Not that one! The woman in this homestead turned Christian. She doesn't want her mugs used for beer."

Meanwhile, Mami marched on as a born-again Christian, endured the church's discriminatory practices, and flourished.

But my father's business suffered irreparable damage.

He had no skill to grind and turn tobacco into snuff, his most lucrative product. Even if he did, grinding tobacco and scooping its powder like medicine at the market was a woman's job.

With no more free skilled labor, Baba's only product was dried tobacco bits, which he bundled into cylinders and sold wholesale at about a quarter of the profit he had gotten from snuff.

He also sold small amounts of loose bits to drop-in customers who, like him, balled and stuffed it under their lower lips. Younger men used newspapers to hand-roll the bits into homemade cigarettes called kīraikū. They smoked kīraikū down to tiny stubs pinched between their forefingers and thumbs, which left a body smell they could not clean off, an occasional cough, and yellowed finger and thumb tips.

"The wife has turned Christian and wants nothing to do with tobacco," Baba told occasional drop-in snuff customers before he referred them to the market.

In time, except for a small patch he nurtured for personal use, he left the rest of his tobacco plants unattended. When the plants died, Mami grew pigeon peas on that plot.

Baba also phased out his hides and skins business, even though Mami had never played a part in it. He never stepped into another market again and, except for his goats, never owned another business.

Chapter 55

CHRISTIANITY GROWING PAINS

After my parents settled their differences, and my mother marched along on her Christian regimen, I learned that becoming "born again" or converting to Christianity required people to confess their sins in front of the congregation at church.

Men's confessions were mostly about drinking alcohol and smoking cigarettes, the obvious sins. But women's confessions were another matter. Although most of them, like gossip or jealousy, turned out benign, others went rogue and wreaked havoc on families. I overheard my mother and her friends talk of women who confessed family "secrets" they should have kept to themselves.

One married woman confessed she had fallen into temptation; she had an eye for another man, she said. In her case, Christianity rescued her and cut out her desire.

A woman from another village claimed that because her husband beat her, a thought had occurred to her to stick a knife into him when he slept. According to rumors, from then on, despite her confession and repentance, her husband abandoned sexual intimacy and confined himself to his thingira.

The case of Kamunge's head milkman, Warũgũ, and his family turned out the worst.

Warũgũ and his first wife, Naomi, endured ten-plus years of childlessness, a big discontent because children were the centerpiece of Agĩkũyũ marriage and family. The couple agreed the husband should marry a second wife.

Warũgũ and Wanjeri, the second wife and Mami's best friend, had five children she and her co-wife, Naomi, raised together. Warũgũ had his thingira, but his two wives got along so well that they shared one big house for an entire decade. But after Christianity swept through our village, it left their household in tatters.

Wanjeri became nervous about her polygamous marriage. She referred to herself as an illegal wife, fornicating with another woman's husband, contrary to the Christian scriptures. That meant she would never see the kingdom of God unless she made changes.

She agonized for weeks about whether to leave her children with their father and his first wife, Naomi. Mami and the other women begged her not to abandon her children. They said Ngai would forgive her because she did not know the implications of polygamy when she married. Mami even offered herself as an example of a second wife.

Wanjeri rejected that claim, saying Baba divorced his first wife, which meant Mami became the first wife by default.

According to my mother, despite Wanjeri's usual quiet demeanor, she focused on religion so much that she became overly animated in church during singing and confessions.

Finding no acceptable way to resolve her marriage conflict, Wanjeri abandoned her family and joined a colony of Christians in Bahati Township.

Naomi, the "rightful" wife, could not cope. Mami said she was lazy and had only played a supporting role in raising the children before Wanjeri left.

The five children suffered the most. They gave up on life. None of them went far in school before they dropped out.

Wanjeri, whom Mami called "the sister I never had," never wavered in her faith or even returned to see her children or to visit her "sister."

Fifteen years later, I heard rumors she died destitute in a one-room shack but happy she would "inherit the kingdom of God."

Wanjeri's family was the only one in the village to fall apart. Otherwise, our village continued as before, with women the most enthusiastic about the new faith. This was likely because they did not commit the sins Mami and other women cited.

If this were the case, men were the only ones destined for hell. They snorted or chewed tobacco, smoked cigarettes, and drank beer. The know-it-alls among them claimed the Ten Commandments did not prohibit tobacco or beer. After all, some men said, Jesus served wine at his rallies.

Somehow, Christians deemed those activities sinful under different rules. Or perhaps with alcohol, the sin pertained to drinking African homemade beer, not store-bought or the wine that I heard Christians sipped during their communion sacrament. Despite their sinful ways, men went about their business without fretting or dwelling on sins as women did.

Others who ignored the changes were Mũgono and his wife, Mama Alan, our village matriarch and masseuse, who massaged ailing children of mothers who sought her free service. The two had worshipped Ngai way back in the late 1900s before the British conquered Kenya and imported Christian worship.

Their only son, Alan, like Warũgũ, ran a polygamous household. He converted to Christianity (hence the name Alan), but he and his two wives ignored their "sinful" state without a word, which, despite anemic gossip, made sense to most people.

*

Agĩkũyũ never practiced single parenthood or fragmented families. In the now-defunct custom, if a man died, his brother inherited his widow and children. (If the diseased had no brother, his widow married a widower or another man, mainly as a second wife.)

In the mid-1930s, when Alan's older brother died, he left a wife with three small children, including a set of twins. Although young and unprepared to marry, Alan married his widowed, much older sister-in-law, Alice (Elithi). The couple brought forth five more children.

Despite having that many children, Alan married Wanjikŭ, the woman he chose for himself.

Like Alan, Elithi converted to Christianity, attended church, and continued her life as usual. But Wanjikŭ, a woman of quiet demeanor, did not convert.

I overheard Mami and another woman say the Bible was silent about Alan's version of polygamy. The rest of the Christian women went along. Any judgments they may have harbored remained unspoken or relegated to whispers.

Mami lucked out on that score; polygamy was not an issue in her marriage. But a problem arose when the church leaders labeled her born and unborn children "sinners."

Chapter 56

BORN SINNERS

It is hard to quantify the effect of Christianity on my young mind because it came in spurts, and I focused only on the highlights: the buzz of a new faith and a wave of conversions, Mami's awakening, her fight with Baba, and Wanjeri's desertion of her family.

I blamed Christianity for my parents' fight. But they did not fight again. By then, although unaware, we, the people who lived on European farms (private properties), were experiencing the tail end of a religious renaissance that had swept through Kikuyuland and towns for at least two decades.

Not in school yet, I thought little about Christianity except what I overheard Mami and other women discuss. They talked about sins like drinking alcohol and smoking cigarettes and other sins I did not commit. Besides avoiding sins, for people to enter the kingdom of God—the chatter went—they had to study the catechism and assume Christian names. Years later, I realized they were Jewish or European names.

Despite her lack of reading and writing skills, my mother aced the catechism. It took her an entire year to memorize the required Bible verses in Gĩkũyũ. She practiced while at her plantation job, in our garden, or doing chores at home.

Because most of us children had not started school, no one in our household attended Mami's big event. But I loved to see her beam when she passed her baptismal test, especially the Sunday she got her new name—Mary. She talked to us with so much enthusiasm as if we were her best friends.

*

Through Mami, we learned the church would baptize infants born to Christians. For older children like us, parents could petition the church for a cleansing.

Excited that the church planned to cleanse children of their sins while still young, Mami was first in line to put in her petition.

The church people's reply devastated my poor mother. They ruled the church needed to cleanse each of us individually through our own efforts. Why? Because we, her children, were sinners born of her before she became a Christian. Mami pitied her sinful children and aired her disappointment.

The church officials said they were doing the Will of God.

Mami had no choice but to accept their ruling. As a Christian, at least her future unborn children would enjoy the anointment.

I was now about nine-and-a-half years old, and the ruling by church officials that my siblings and I were born sinners confused and disturbed me. This prompted me to look into my past and appraise my sins.

I had not lied or stolen (or did one fistful of sugar count?). I had not watched traditional dances or smoked cigarettes. Neither had I drunk alcohol, except for the homemade medicinal beer sips and rinses Mami treated my siblings and me with when we contracted measles and chickenpox.

During Mami's regimen of memorizing Bible verses and reciting the Ten Commandments, I realized those were the sins I needed to avoid. Not lying was no effort for me because I had become tired of Baba accusing us of lying whenever he asked who had done something, and no one came forward. I had promised myself I would never tell a lie or do another wrong until I grew up, when, I believed, adults became immune to lying. I do not recall a single lie I told before adulthood when I realized the adults deserved less credit than I had given them.

But I had committed two "major" sins by the church ruling. The first was when I accidentally struck Nyokabi's little sister with a rock. But that sin qualified as self-defense. The village elders' council had deliberated and passed a verdict of "not guilty."

I had sinned before that, at eight years old, when I sampled Baba's tobacco spillage. Before this writing, Ngai and I alone knew of that sin.

Back then, I was glad nobody caught me, although I understood Ngai saw everything. But as hard as I tried, I could not imagine Ngai, who supposedly lived in the heavens. I went along with what adults claimed. Whatever the case, I had sinned, and cleansing by the Anglican Church of England (now the Anglican Church of Kenya) sounded like a fitting penance.

*

When Mami's first petition for baptism failed, Waweru, her youngest child, was three years old. Meanwhile, I started school. The first week of that December, after I finished grade one, to my surprise, Mami gave birth to my little sister, Wairimu. I had noticed no changes in Mami's body.

Afterward, whenever church matters came up, I envied Wairimu for being the child of a born-again Christian. She would get a new name bestowed on her, and whatever sins the church officials thought she had committed during gestation and up to baptism would be cleansed without fuss.

The home church—that held services in my classroom— scheduled baptism twice a year. The pastor qualified to do the ritual came from Nakuru town.

Barely a month after Wairimu's birth, Mami resumed church service, not only to praise the Lord but also to ensure the church included Wairimu in the first baptism of the year before she got into any little children's sins.

Soon, the officials announced a baptismal date. Mami was among the first to register. To prepare for baptismal, she bought Wairimũ a new yellow dress and a beige cloth hat with lots of gathers and a drawstring that tied under her chin. Later, when it came time to wear it, Wairimũ hated that hat with a passion. She struggled to pull it off her head but failed dismally.

When the town pastor set the baptismal date, our pastor read the baptismal candidates' names during Sunday announcements before the sermon.

To Mami's surprise and discontent, she did not hear Wairimũ's name. How could that be? During the sermon, she replayed her life back to her awakening.

She had confessed her sins, become a devout Christian, followed all the church's tenets, and avoided sins like an infectious disease. She had even stopped eating those sausages whose stuffing Baba mixed with goat's blood. The church doctrine outlawed animal blood and fruits from the fig tree that Jesus allegedly cursed when he suffered from hunger and found the tree without fruit (Matthew 21:18–19).

And, of course, Mami did not eat meat from the animals that do not chew cud or without cloven hooves like the cursed pigs, which she could not eat anyway because nobody raised pigs or sold pork in Solai.

After the service, Mami cornered the pastor and pointed out the omission.

To her utter astonishment, the pastor said the church had ruled that Wairimũ was born a sinner, just like Mami's other children.

"How can that be?" Mami asked.

"Because your husband is a pagan," the pastor said.

To us, that meant an infidel, a nonbeliever, a primitive person. But to the church, baby Wairimũ came out a sinner because she fell under a bi-religion banner—half-pagan and half-Christian.

"Pagan" was a British construct, a term alien to Agĩkũyũ before their colonizers—ignorant of Agĩkũyũ ways—thrust it on them.

Mami lamented that no child of hers would get baptized in its purest state before the world contaminated its little mind. But she could do nothing about it. Church people, who did not know that they did not know, knew best. They alone knew the right pathway to the afterlife.

The esteemed officials included the pastor, Mr. Mbuthia, Alan's brother-in-law, who did odd jobs for Kamunge. His two helpers also worked as laborers. They knew as much as their grade four education allowed, backed by their literal application of the Bible and their commitment to the Anglican Church doctrine. The three men had no other qualifications to lead the "church" besides converting to Christianity, knowing how to read the bible, and being male.

*

Adults calling a baby a sinner confused me. Wairimũ could hardly sit up by herself. At work, Mami dug a hole in the ground, lined it with a towel, and placed Wairimũ in it so she would not tip over. How could she sin?

While Mami agonized about the rejection, Baba made fun of it when he was drunk.

"Go tell them my name is Enoch," he said. "That ought to settle it."

*

Contrary to Baba's fears, Mami's conversion to Christianity did not negatively affect our household, except for ending his business. He now viewed Christianity as a hobby, where believers went to squander their time. He dismissed it with a snicker or a flicker of his backhand or ignored it altogether. And he still hung on to his shrine.

"Why did he drag it here?" I heard Mami say once when she passed by the shrine

Another day, she said, "…like your father's shrine back there, supposed to ward off evil energy."

One day, while playing with other children behind the granary, I noticed the place where the shrine stood empty; it had mysteriously disappeared.

To discredit the shrine, Mami had made a point of retelling the story of when she took me as an infant to Nakuru General Hospital to prove she had abandoned traditional cures even before she assumed her new faith.

But that was not entirely true. Even after she became a Christian and adopted Christian myths, legends, and superstitions, Mami remained a staunch practitioner of home remedies and did not utter a negative word against Agĩkũyũ 's mythologies and traditions.

Chapter 57

RIGHT NAMES

A handful of fathers (and mothers) who practiced Christianity before we moved to the village already used Western names.

Because we children addressed our fathers as Baba (father), the few children of Christian fathers did not know their fathers' last names. When they started school, they used their fathers' Western names, the only ones they knew, as their last names.

For whatever reason, the teachers did not correct the children. Maybe that was how the fathers had registered their children. And it did not occur to the teacher to correct them, or they thought it did not matter.

For most of us in class, our fathers had no Western names. But I had a personal issue; my father's name—Warama—bothered me. His name, just like my mother's (Nyachuru), had embarrassed me since we moved to the fenced village. Children grimaced or said my parents' names sounded weird when they heard Warama or Nyachuru. From then on, I rarely used my parents' names.

Even after the children got used to the names and stopped teasing me, I never got over it. I wished my parents used common Gĩkũyũ names like Kamau or Njoki.

When I started school, I gave my last name as "Mwangi," a common name, supposedly Baba's first or second name, which appeared nowhere on his records, and nobody used it. From then on, I became Wanjirũ wa Mwangi, but the teacher addressed me as Wanjirū Mwangi, without the possessive "wa." Other than school, the possessive "wa" was used everywhere else.

Even the colonialists did not meddle with that format. They anglicized it by turning "wa" into son of (s/o), wife of (w/o), and daughter of (d/o). Thus, they wrote our names as Warama s/o Njerū, Nyachuru w/o Warama, and Wanjirū d/o Warama. The anglicized version stopped being used after Kenya's independence on December 12, 1963.

If I now give the Gīkūyū version of my name, I would use Wanjirū wa Warama. Non-Gīkūyū people would call me, as I see them do, Ms. WaWarama (equivalent to Ms. Daughter of Warama). But I did not concern myself with that back then because we became Christians by default when we started school.

We belonged to the Anglican Church of England. My cousins at the neighboring Major Stein's farm became Catholics, and so forth throughout Kenya, depending on which religion first lay claim to the area. Teachers then required us to immerse ourselves in Christianity and caned us if we missed Sunday school.

By the end of grade one, like the rest of my classmates, I learned my name was not quite right. To become Christians, however, Africans assumed Christian (European or Jewish) names).

Baba and many men in the village remained steadfast, quietly stuck to their names and traditions and their interpretation of God. They left Christianity to the school, the pastor and his two helpers, and their wives, the backbone of the faith (although, allegedly, God forbade women to lead).

Between my mother and our Sunday school teacher, my motivation heightened. I also wanted to study and get a new name without further delay.

Unlike Mami and other adults who studied their verses in Gīkūyū, we children studied in Kiswahili.

The desire to gain a new name crowded my heart. By then, we, at school and the village, were like debris in a torrent of a fast-moving river, ecstatic as the current swept us along. But in my case, it had nothing to do with religion; it was my pathway to a new name.

I pushed myself to recite the verses at home and learned them before our Sunday school teacher tested us. Reciting verses in chorus or individually and socializing with other children became one part of Sunday school I enjoyed and immersed myself in.

By the time I passed my baptismal test after a year's study, I had heard enough names mentioned—about five in my estimation—that I knew the name I wanted. But a village woman had beaten me to it.

Women gossiped that the woman was a busybody, a loudmouth who never kept secrets. The name sounded alluring; I wished I had discovered it first. I admired it so much that I discounted the gossip and adopted "Miriam" by the end of grade two.

When I finally met the woman, now my namesake, my mind already poisoned by village gossip, I thought of beauty and ugliness, which I doubt I had ever thought of before.

Besides her loudmouth, the woman walked unrestrained—one could say undignified—arms in motion, back arched, followed by her huge, quaky backside. If she scratched her hair, she never patted it back in place, and if she wore a headscarf, she left it raised on the side she scratched.

People called such a woman "calico," likely derived from the coarse, off-white, cheap cloth imported from India. For whatever reason, the term never applied to males. Instead, people referred to such men as "njaguti" or "ndigiri," rootless men who did casual grunt work for others.

I harbored misgivings about sharing a name, especially with such a woman. But because she was not in my mother's social circle, and she and I hardly ever saw each other, the name-sharing concern soon faded from my mind.

I changed my name to Miriam Mwangi. Like Warama, my real name, Wanjirū, disappeared from my school records. From then on, I insisted people address me as "Miriam." Whenever any of my siblings forgot and mentioned the "old" name, I did not answer them until they used the new name. If I had been older or had the ability, I would have entertained my siblings and others with tea and snacks, as some women did, to encourage them to adopt my new name.

Over the years, as my siblings and I earned our Christian symbols, we settled on the following names—picked on a whim, depending on when each of us stumbled onto the name:

Njerũ became David
Ndurumo = Simon
Machira = Joseph
Wanjirũ = Miriam
Nyandia = Tabitha
Gĩthũi = John
Macharia = Maurice "Morry"
Wawerũ = Fredrick
Wairimũ = Florence
Mũrĩithi = Stephen
Njomo = No extra name

After adopting new names, the church required the baptized to study for confirmation to qualify for the sacrament. But, to receive a sacrament, a candidate needed to reach age fourteen, the minimum age the clergy considered a person mature enough to appreciate the symbolism.

I doubted I could study for another two years. It had taken me an entire year of study for the baptismal, which meant I had no free time to speak of.

I went to school five days a week, did family chores all Saturday, attended Sunday school, and studied for the baptismal on

Sunday, which was like another school day. I thought of taking a break for a year. After all, I had met my goal of a new name.

Out of curiosity, I attended the introduction session. They defined confirmation as sharing the body and blood of Kristo. Then I understood why the converted said, "I'm washed with the blood of Jesus."

My mind conjured all kinds of negative images, something I habitually did if I encountered anything detestable, like eating locusts. I imagined the pastor and his helpers slaughtering a man. I felt queasy, like when I watched Baba slaughter a goat.

I could not bring myself to attend a single session. Besides the symbolism, it would have been another two years of a seven-day-week regimen. They held confirmation classes after the adults' service, a tough proposition for young people. It was a sacrifice for me to attend the orientation.

I drank porridge that morning and attended Sunday school and adult service back-to-back while I waited for confirmation orientation class after the service ended at about 1:00 p.m. All that time without a bite or a drink of water before I returned home at about 4:00.

Fortunately, the school did not require confirmation studies. Besides my mother, who put in another year's study for the church to confirm her, nobody else in my family continued with confirmation studies.

Without access to the sacrament, I convinced myself that to lead a sinless life, all I needed to know was the Lord's Prayer and The Ten Commandments.

I could not forget those two because, after baptism, teachers required us to attend the adult service. The pastor preached about the commandments often and warned the congregation not to break them, something I could not do because I did not get into the sins he highlighted.

And we closed with the Lord's Prayer after every service.

Chapter 58

NAME MISHMASH

Half of our household members' names stuck (including Mami's and mine). The other half, who did not push their new names, used them only in schools, later at work, or with people they met afterward.

Born at home and with no birth certificates, we adopted our new names with no drawback. Besides, most pupils stopped going to school after they failed the grade four standardized national exam, after which the name in their school records didn't matter. The few who passed received certificates, and as they continued to grade five and beyond, their new names gained permanence.

However, having a new name still presented no problem because most students did not get birth certificates until they became adults, after they completed their education. When they applied, they included their Western names that aligned with their school certificates.

People born in town hospitals experienced the greatest conflict when they took on new names. The hospitals issued them with birth certificates that showed African names only. Their parents had not become Westernized enough to know to give them European names at birth. Later, when these children got baptized, they ended up with different first names from the ones on their birth certificates.

In the twenty-first century, however, most parents have settled on Western names, which they give to their newborns at birth. For the not-so-enlightened, they give their children names like Washington, Jefferson, and Churchill. Some children are burdened with old English names they find hard to pronounce.

The magnetism of European names (or Arabic names for those who convert to Islam) and their connection to religion is embedded in the Kenyans' psyche. It has become what Ngũgĩ wa Thiong'o calls "normalized abnormality." People go about their lives oblivious to their reliance on foreign cultures. They may become indignant or laugh it off if one points it out. The people who stick to their African names are outliers.

But of late, there has been a cultural resurgence, with younger Kenyans using their African names only. Besides that, a small fraction, like myself, reclaims their original names.

Family and friends might resist using the restored names, claiming people who restore their original names are denouncing Christianity. The do-gooders may continue using a person's Western name behind their back. Gĩthũi

It is common for a relative or close friend to ask the name-restorer, "What do you believe in?" or "Do you believe in God?" as if their former colonizers' names have something to do with Godliness instead of oppression.

But I did not expect a person unknown to me to question my name until it happened in 2010 at Barclays Bank on Mama Ngina Street, Nairobi. As the teller ticked off the slip I completed, she looked at me through the counter guard's tiny cutout and said, "You left out some information."

"I did?" I asked and bent closer to see where she pointed with her pen.

"Yes," she said. "What is your first name?"

"Wanjirũ."

"I mean your real first name," she insisted, her voice impatient, as if I were wasting her time.

"You mean I must have a European name to cash a check?"

She threw me a long, offended look as she bent to process my check.

*

The surname issue remains sticky. With the dismantling of Agīkūyū 's *mbari* (family reference) and *riika* (age group—a yearly rite of passage) clan systems, which had been the way Agīkūyū kept track of their bloodline and age, we now have no family identifiers. People may only know their ancestry as far as their memory can take them.

And because Agīkūyū follow a patriarchal system, a father ends up with three names: European first name, African middle name—his actual Gīkūyū first name—and his father's name as surname. In a nuclear family, several scenarios may arise:

All family members use the man's surname, a very rare occurrence.

Or the man's middle name becomes his children's and his wife's surname, and the family ends up with two different surnames, the most common practice.

Or his middle name becomes his children's surname, and the wife keeps her maiden surname. In that case, the family ends up with three different surnames.

It gets even more muddled when some siblings omit their father's name and use their Western first name and their own Gīkūyū names as surnames.

Nowadays, I have noticed a trend where single or unmarried mothers give their children—boys and girls—their female Gīkūyū middle names as surnames. (Children born before marriage end up with different surnames from their siblings born in the marriage.). Maybe they are onto something. But this also announces to the world that the child's father went rogue, denied or abandoned the child, or the father was unknown.

The name muddle is complete when one incorporates cousins, nephews, nieces, and people living in different locales.

The current mishmash surname system shows a lack of feeling or pride in their names—like the olden days—and poses an enormous challenge when creating a family tree.

Prominent families like the Kenyattas, the Waiyakis, the Ogingas, the Koinanges, the Njonjos, and the Mois—just to name six—have used established uniform family names for decades.

Incidentally, the patriarchs of these families were all prominent politicians, which makes one wonder why they or the current politicians never saw the need to restructure the country's naming system for easier identity or to keep up with technology. If politicians and policymakers do not codify naming standards to match what they do themselves, it is only a matter of time before inbreeding—starting with cousins—becomes a big problem.

To get a head start a couple of decades ago, I put together a family tree that I hoped would streamline relationships and avoid possible inbreeding in my large family, spread all over Kenya and elsewhere. I believed, and still do, that it was a great legacy for my family.

Without disclosing my intention, I introduced our family's name to young relatives I could influence. It turned out to be a dismal failure.

The unfished Warama Family Tree collects dust somewhere in the tech cloud.

ON THE ROAD AGAIN

Chapter 59

GRADE THREE

When I was in grade one and attended school in the afternoons, if I mentioned something we did in class, Joseph never failed to point out that "mornings are when things happen." But when I started going to school in the mornings in grade two, except for the assembly, punishment, and checkups, we still attended school only half a day.

But grade three turned out different. We attended school the entire day. And because it was one year until we entered the senior class, big changes took place. In anticipation, I enjoyed another wave of euphoria similar to the one I felt when I first entered school.

Unlike in grades one and two, where we sat and wrote on benches, we sat two at a desk in grade three. We also did arithmetic calculations in our heads. Our teacher forbade us from using our fingers or the two-inch sticks we had used in lower grades.

It did not matter to me; I had mastered the multiplication tables up to 12 x 12. But, hunched over my writing, I could see a handful of laggards still counting fingers and toes under their desks. When the teacher caught any of them, he said they were no better than first-graders.

We learned new subjects and, because we already knew how to read, did not read in class anymore. Or perhaps there were no books because since we entered grade three, I never saw another reading book in my next two years in Tindaress Primary.

Besides arithmetic, writing, and Kiswahili, the teacher introduced civics, a trickle of European history and geography. On Fridays, we gardened and cleaned the school, and the intensity of punishment increased from ruler raps, hand knuckles, or shaved crosses through hair to sticks and slaps.

My fellow pupils and I became too careful in class in case we made mistakes that would result in a whack on the shoulders or verbal abuse. We curbed the free spirit we had enjoyed in the last two grades. Like my fellow pupils, I assumed an overtly docile, albeit subtly defiant, behavior while in class for the rest of elementary and middle school—if not for the rest of my life.

*

My anticipation of getting to grade three boiled down to two incentives: Learning English and writing with a fountain pen. Learned people—teachers and medics—spoke English and wrote with fountain pens.

I carried my ink bottle to school in case I needed a refill, even after I realized that after I filled my pen in the morning, it lasted for two days.

Then, one day, a classmate knocked over his bottle and messed up his exercise book and his neighbor's. I dreaded having such an accident, but not badly enough to leave my prized ink bottle at home. It announced to the world that I now belonged to a group of advanced ink writers. In time, however, hanging onto the bottle became cumbersome, and the likelihood of an accidental spill lingered in my mind. But my need to advertise my status still pestered me.

Since grade two, I had admired the prestigious dark-blue spots I noticed on the bottom corners of boys' shirt pockets. I envied the boys for having pockets. Girls had no pockets. It was not that the school's dress code forbade it, but perhaps it meant extra tailor costs for our parents or that no one thought pockets were necessary for girls.

I soon discovered a simpler way to get my evidence. On the days I refilled my pen in the morning, I put a dab of ink on my finger. I had to be discreet in case Baba or Mami saw me and ranted on the ills of waste.

Then I realized I could get the evidence I needed right from my pen while writing, away from our homestead's prying eyes. With a new pen that never leaked, I had to improvise. While writing, I held my fingers right up to the nib. My index finger or thumb got rewarded with a smudge every time.

Writing in ink meant I had learned a skill I could use outside school. It boosted my ego and gave me a sense of accomplishment.

Our teacher boosted my confidence even further when he said, "By the end of the year, you'll be able to read and write short letters for your parents."

But my parents were even more optimistic than our teacher. When I was in grade one, Mami thought Baba knew more than he did. And, now that I was in grade three, Baba thought I could read in Gĩkũyũ before the year-end, six months earlier than the teacher had told my class.

Both of my parents turned out grossly mistaken.

Chapter 60

TELL YOUR FATHER TO SHOW YOU

I shared my frustration with my mother when I struggled to decode horizontal arithmetic in grade one. She had a ready answer for me.

"Once upon a time," my dear mother said, "your father learned to write numbers. Ask him to show you."

Desperate for help, I kicked my shyness aside and rushed to thingira with a pencil and my exercise book folded inside out. As I handed them to my father, pointing at the numbers I needed help with, I said, "Mami said you can show me how to add numbers."

"Oh," escaped Baba's mouth as he took my exercise book without the pencil. He slightly clasped and pulled his nose, then rested his knuckles on his chin while he gazed at the spot I showed him. He squinted and held that pose for the longest time. I realized my father was embarrassed to say, "I do not know," a phrase I had never heard him use. The brief spell dragged on while I suffered embarrassment for both of us. Then, I gathered courage and took back my exercise book. I could not scuttle from thingira fast enough.

Much later, I learned that at one time, the area landowners ran adult education programs on their farms. With no schools, each landowner wanted to educate a handful of employees to help with simple record keeping, like tracking part-time employees' hours.

Kamunge started an adult school as well. The location could have been his huge storage shed near his colonial house because I saw no extra buildings on that farm. But, unlike other farmers' efforts, for whatever reason, his project failed.

With only a handful of evening classes he may have attended decades before, Baba had forgotten the little he had learned. I doubt he had learned basic arithmetic or knew how to read besides numbers and the alphabet.

*

Just as I had sought Baba's help in grade one, he unintentionally got back at me toward the end of my second term in grade three after we moved to our second village.

My older brothers had gone somewhere when Baba came from work with a letter. Eager to learn of its contents, he called me to his thingira. As soon as I crossed the threshold, he told me what he wanted. My first thought was: My father wants me to read him a letter like my older brothers do? Wow! A thrill coursed through me. Then, a sharp bolt of fear kicked out the thrill.

My class had studied in Kiswahili for two and a half years. Except for occasional peeks into the Gĩkũyũ Bible, I had read nothing written in Gĩkũyũ before then. Besides, Kiswahili and Gĩkũyũ did not share certain vowels and consonants. I could not muster enough courage to tell such details to my father as I braced myself to read the best I could.

I perched myself on a low stool and stretched my hand. When I received the letter, which he had already opened, I took a quick look and cursed my luck. The flowing writing, letters chained together in grownup cursive, came in blue ink like the one I hoped to write in when I got more education. I now ran my eyes through the letter to the end. The letter was from Aunt Julia, Baba's sister, who worked in Nairobi.

Trapped in my unease, I recalled when Simon told us how he read letters to Baba. "To avoid tripping on words," he had said, "I first read a letter to myself."

So, first, I will do a dry-run-read like Simon, I told myself. But I was unaware that my dear brother had forgotten to mention a crucial point.

Now, I swished saliva in my mouth to moisten it and swallowed.

I sounded the words phonically like one learning to read, making out a word here and another there. It never occurred to me to rehearse with my mouth shut like Simon, the point he forgot to mention in his tutelage.

I squinted, shoulders hunched, my nose buried in the letter.

In a moment, it crossed my mind to blame my poor performance on poor lighting. Before I verbalized the lie, Baba cut the charade and denied me the right to finish the dry-run-read of my first letter.

I doubt he waited for over a minute before he stretched his hand and asked for his blue aerogram letter back. He folded it and stashed it into his shirt pocket like a wad of shillings.

Embarrassed, I left thingira shrunk as a rained-on chicken.

He never asked me to read a letter to him again.

And it never occurred to me to wonder how my parents expected me, or my brothers, to write or read in Gĩkũyũ, especially at such an early age while we learned in Kiswahili. But because the school aged Simon out, and he never went away to boarding school, he was the one who read and wrote letters for Baba, and as a result, he became proficient in writing in Gĩkũyũ more than anyone else in the family.

To this day, I doubt most Agĩkũyũ can write in their own language, and some of them, shame on their parents' short-sightedness, cannot even speak in it.

Chapter 61

LANGUAGE OF THE LEARNED

In grade three, my big thing was to write with a fountain pen, and I went into much trouble to get noticed. Several months in, when I could not read a letter for my father, although I got embarrassed, it did not bother me that I could not read in my own language, let alone write in it. Besides writing with a pen, I craved to learn English, the language of the learned, the mysterious language nobody in my world spoke.

Before I entered school, I had heard English spoken once— by medics when Baba and I took my little brother Waweru to Nakuru General Hospital.

In my mind, no matter what other lessons teachers introduced, none equaled English.

I took Gĩkũyũ and Kiswahili for granted. One did not need to attend school to speak those two languages, I believed.

Most people who lived and worked on British-owned farms in the then Rift Valley Province (divided into fourteen counties in 2013) spoke at least two languages—their native language and Kiswahili. People who spoke one language only, like Mama Alan and her husband Mũgono, too old to have use for a second language, mostly had grown up before the British invasion, before people left Kikuyuland to seek jobs elsewhere or got evicted from their ancestral lands.

Wherever job seekers went to towns or European farms, they mixed with other tribes who spoke different languages. The tribes soon learned Kiswahili and interacted with each other.

My grade-three class started learning English in our first week. Our teacher walked around the classroom while our eager eyes followed him. He touched and named items at random while we repeated after him. He started with common items: pencil, rubber (eraser), paper, pen, chalk, blackboard, duster (blackboard eraser), desk, wall, and on to body parts.

Because I knew how to read and write in Kiswahili, I expected to learn English without too much effort.

In Kiswahili (and in Gĩkũyũ), the sound of vowels remains the same no matter which consonant you join them with. This means one can write words even without knowing their meaning.

I listened to how the teacher pronounced the English words. I then joined consonants and vowels in my mind and guessed the spelling based on how they sounded—pencil = pensŭ; paper = pĩpa; pen = pen; chalk = chok, and so forth.

It baffled me when the teacher wrote those words on the blackboard, and the spelling looked different from how he pronounced them. To my disappointment, I soon realized the Kiswahili rule did not apply to English.

To complicate English even more, unlike in Kiswahili, we came across English words that ended with consonants. To this day, most Kenyans have trouble pronouncing the letter "r" unless a vowel follows it. Work becomes wok; third becomes thud; first becomes fast, and sir becomes Sah.

And English included eight extra letters—F, L, P, Q, S, V, X, and Z, which are not in the Gĩkũyũ language.

The letter "L" caused a challenge for the few pupils who joined us from Kikuyuland, where they studied in Gĩkũyũ. They rolled L like an R.

But for those of us born and raised outside Kikuyuland, we had studied in Kiswahili, which has an L, so we did not have that issue. We could roll the "R" in Gĩkũyũ and easily pronounce "L" when we switched to Kiswahili.

Today, because of mobility and diverse teachers, most Gĩkũyũ, Embu, and Meru who speak their native language roll their "Ls," no matter where they are born and raised in Kenya.

*

After we learned the English names of the items in our classroom, our teacher used each item's name in a sentence and then translated it into Kiswahili. If we still did not get it, he translated it into Gĩkũyũ.

The teacher disregarded Sikukuu, the one non-Gĩkũyũ boy in our class. I doubt Sikukuu missed out, although he may tell a different story today.

Sikukuu, a Luhyia boy, started with us in grade one, and because ninety-nine percent of farmworkers in Solai and adjacent farms were Gĩkũyũ, he understood the language. An occasional boy chided him when he mispronounced Gĩkũyũ words. Otherwise, nobody paid attention that he was non-Gĩkũyũ.

Within months, he spoke in Gĩkũyũ as well as we did; no one could differentiate him from the other boys when they romped around the schoolyard.

*

When we advanced to grade four, we started learning how to write longer English sentences. Sometimes, the teacher gave us sentences with a scatter of words I could not make out. "Gibberish," my mother said, at least before her children learned the language, and she considered English respectable.

Other times, the teacher tricked us. He wrote a sentence in English on the blackboard and asked us to translate it or write its meaning. For our homework one Friday, he wrote, "Do you live to eat, or do you eat to live?" and told us to write what the two clauses meant and return our answers that Monday.

What an easy homework, I thought, happy I knew all the words.

Without enough vocabulary, I wrote in my exercise book, "It is one," meaning the clauses meant the same.

Our entire class flunked.

If he were alive today, I can imagine Teacher Kĩmani sighing with satisfaction to learn his homework question still serves me on my life's dietary journey.

*

Although we never heard English spoken during that period, besides the single rudimentary lesson we did each day, we understood that Europeans and educated Africans spoke the language. Africans learned the language (besides the bits of transactional English that cooks and gardeners spoke with their employers) only if they continued further than grade four. Hence, English was the language of the learned. The ones who reached grade eight and above spoke at least three languages—their native languages, Kiswahili, and English.

Like religion, none of us pupils or the adults—except for an enlightened few—realized we were in the midst of a major societal transformation and a burgeoning class set up in Kenya. Many of the "learned" turned into a tribe who thumbed their noses at their ancestors' good or bad ways, their lives ruled by the Western education they received and the financial freedom that education availed them.

In their official capacity, they insisted on speaking in English, even when they spoke to a person from their own tribe, especially when they deemed that person below their station in life.

When these so-called learned individuals started their own families, many taught their children English only, a practice that continues. This has created a language barrier and severed the link between generations. It has also robbed the younger generation of the nuances and richness of their culture, and society is poorer for it.

As Ngũgĩ wa Thiong'o says:

> "If you know all the languages of the world…but not your mother tongue or the language of the community [in which] you were born, that is enslavement. But if you know your language and you add to it all the languages of the world, that's empowerment."

*

Nowadays, every Kenyan speaks Kiswahili, the national language. But the most popular Kiswahili spoken is sheng, a pidgin Kiswahili mixed with English, made-up words, and words from the speaker's native language or other dominant languages.

(I first heard of "Sheng" in the 1970s, started by disadvantaged children in towns, particularly Nairobi: Sandwiched between parents who spoke native languages and rich children who spoke in English, these children created their own language that neither the parents nor the rich could understand. From my observation, Sheng has now become mainstream)

Little passes from older generations to younger ones except for basic transactional communication.

This has muddled languages because many people, if not the majority, hardly speak one language fluently. It is frustrating if one watches a political rally on TV (or an interview). The speaker may jump from Kiswahili to English and their native language throughout the speech. At its worst, a fraction of listeners understand only a third of the speaker's speech.

But not all is lost. Language consolidation or extinction is a part of evolution, a phase with which African languages are wrangling. Many of the languages will become extinct or cannibalized and absorbed by others. But languages with developed or developing literature like Kiswahili, Yoruba, Hausa, Lingala, Gĩkũyũ, Kizulu, Igbo, Kiganda (Luganda), and many others, will live on, thanks to writers determined to produce literature in these languages.

Chapter 62

A PEEK AT CONDITIONED MINDS

Kenya's excessive religiosity, which does not seem to curb the ills of society, and the brutalization of our languages and culture started before my time.

By the time I started school in 1957, I had learned bits of the Gĩkũyũ history. But, by then, we were at the cusp of obliteration of our indigenous ways, from our languages to our names.

We pupils learned in rote, with zero critical thinking. We accepted and embraced most of the changes as a matter of course. Soon, we fell in sync and changed our learning focus from wanting to know to just passing tests.

(Nowadays, students and teachers focusing on tests is part of the establishment; hence, it is much worse. Many schools inundate their students with homework on several subjects—evenings, weekends, and on school holidays.)

But in my time, before I settled in school and before my childish quizzical mind got damped down, I was confused when we called a mountain or a river by one name in Gĩkũyũ at home, and we called it by another name in school.

The Nyandarua Mountain Range—so named because it's shaped like a dry, wavy cowhide—became the Aberdare Mountains when Lord Aberdare, the head of the Royal Geographical Society, named the mountain range after himself in 1884. The Cania [Chania] River, which flows from Nyandarua Mountain to the Indian Ocean and which my father and his ancestors had crisscrossed, became Tana River; Kĩrĩnyaga became Mt. Kenya, and on it went.

To this day, we, at least the older generation, still use most of the original names when speaking in Gĩkũyũ.

The renaming or anglicizing of Kĩrĩnyaga to Mt. Kenya is of note. Over the years, I have heard and read accounts of how the name "Kenya" came about. These accounts are by educated people, some of them university professors. The accounts are likely recycled from early European explorers' writings, full of faulty conclusions, ignorant of the people they encountered, or highly embellished.

The following is one such account from *Unbowed* by Wangari Maathai, PhD, a Nobel Peace Prize recipient and a woman worthy of great respect. She states:

"The story goes that the explorers Johann Ludwig Krapf and Johannes Rebmann, upon encountering the mountain [Mt. Kenya,] in 1849, asked their guide, a member of the Kamba community, who was carrying a gourd, "'What do you call that?'" Thinking the two Germans were referring to the gourd, he replied, "'It's called kĩĩ-nyaa'" but pronounced "Kenya" by the British. This became the name of the mountain and later the country."

This story strikes me as highly implausible. The simple question I ask myself is: Is it logical for the two Germans to have pointed or raised their quizzical eyes toward a snowy mountain, and their porter/guide thought they were referring to a small water gourd he carried?

From the colonizer's records, the British East Africa Protectorate was established in 1895, forty-six years after the alleged gourd incident. And it was not until 1920 that it morphed into the Kenya Colony under the British.

It's improbable that the British looked for notes made by two German explorers seventy years earlier to help them create a name for their new colony.

As mentioned before, according to Gĩkũyũ mythology, Kĩrĩnyaga (Mt. Kenya) is a focal point in Agĩkũyũ 's creation story—where Ngai created Gĩkũyũ and Mũmbi, their primordial parents. They prayed and made sacrifices for Ngai (which some still do) while they faced Mt. Kenya.

When I was growing up in Solai in the fifties and sixties, my family moved several times. In each homestead we lived, my father's thingira faced Kĩrĩnyaga. To this day, when a Gĩkũyũ person dies, people bury them with their head facing Kĩrĩnyaga. Nobody talks about it, though they will correct a pallbearer if he gets mixed up.

Kĩrĩnyaga came up in my father's accounts about his life in Nyeri. Sometimes, he mentioned how, on clear days, one could see the mountain's snow-topped peak, a sight people always treated with reverence because the community called it kĩhumo—the origin, the beginning, the source.

At one time, one of my younger brothers asked Baba, "What does Kĩrĩ-nyaga, [it has ostrich] mean?"

Baba said, as a matter of course, "Nĩta nyaga yambĩte mathagu," it's shaped like an ostrich spreading its wings.

My great-grandparents never met a white person. But they held Kĩrĩnyaga in high regard and considered it a holy mountain. It would amaze my ancestors that the British mangled Kĩrĩnyaga to "Kenya," but it came out sounding so right.

It takes intentional or unintentional dismissive or indulgent minds of non-Africans and lazy or indoctrinated minds of Africans to believe that Agĩkũyũ people had a name for everything in their homeland, from the tiniest insect to the biggest mammal, from a water drop to the biggest river, from a grain of sand to the stars in the heavens, from a molehill to the Nyandarua wavy mountains, yet did not have a name for their highest mountain, their "origin," their one sacred place.

Despite Kenya's growing pains, unlike South Africa, which endured a much longer occupation and foreign entrenchment, the Kenyan administration has taken pains to reinstate most of the country's original names.

As an aside, perhaps, while Kenyans and other Africans consider mangled historical accounts, African-Americans might rethink the line they have been fed that their ancestors back in Africa sold them to slavery—a storyline I doubt the captured or the captors thought to come up with.

It's likely the slaveholders made claims to spread the blame for that despicable era, and historians assisted the doctored claims set foot into the annals of history.

Chapter 63

MUSIC AND DANCE

Like my fellow pupils, I fell into a gap. The songs and stories in class and Sunday school stopped in grade three.

After baptism at the end of grade two, the school required us to attend either Sunday school or the adults' church service. Having already gone through Sunday school Bible lessons and stories with pupils in my age group, I did not want to repeat the same material with younger children. So, I opted for the adult service.

Unlike In Sunday school, where we sat wherever we wanted, in adult service, men and women, and even small boys and girls, sat on opposite sides of the aisle. The service was in Gĩkũyũ only. The readings and the Bible metaphors the pastor told were too advanced for me. Even in telling the Bible stories, Joshua Mbuthia, the pastor, a quiet man in the best of times, spoke too softly. His service turned out to be the dullest I had ever attended. I just went through the motions, bored half the time, and dozed off the other half.

Teachers required grades three and four pupils to join the school choir as a non-academic lesson. Besides practicing, the choir sang nowhere else. I looked forward to joining the choir because I knew nothing about singing as a lesson other than our no-rules songs in grades one and two and in the mind-numbing adult service and the allegedly "sinful" but popular melodious songs Tugen migrant workers sang on weekends.

We practiced in the back double classroom. Mr. Kĩmani, the headmaster, taught the choir. He acted as strict and punished pupils as he did when he taught other lessons. As in church, we could not tap a foot in rhythm or nod a head during the choir. We remained erect, with only our mouths moving. We sang in Kiswahili songs that pertained only to religion—nothing, as I had hoped, about tradition, love, riches, or other life landscapes.

Mr. Kimani arranged the choir into soprano, alto, tenor, and bass. He started us with DO-RE-ME-FA-SO-LA-TI-DO! We sang them over and over—forward and backward—until they stuck in my memory.

I could sing those, but they did not sound like Kiswahili, the language we learned and sang in.

During each singing lesson, Mr. Kĩmani sang while we repeated after him. He stood still and listened from different angles—front, back, and sides. Without fail, he could tell what section the off-key voice came from. Solemn, ears perked, he bent and tiptoed toward that section, pausing at intervals.

Sometimes, he asked a row to sing repeatedly while he listened. Other times, he shut his eyes and waited like a hunter. When he zeroed in on his prey, he asked the person to sing alone. The verdict came fast, followed by a swift ruler rap on the pupil's head. Then, Mr. Kimani repeated the note and asked the pupil to repeat after him several times.

Not once did we sing an entire verse without interruption.

I believe my voice sounded average. But whenever Mr. Kĩmani approached my section, I tensed, and fear gripped me. My voice stumbled. When he reached where I stood, my voice croaked like a two-pack-a-day smoker's.

I received several ruler swats before he concluded my voice was untrainable. To my relief and loss, he dropped me from the choir.

Even if I did not sing, I could still enjoy what the colonizers called "primitive" and the religious crowd called "sinful" or "devil's workshops"—the traditional songs and dances performed by Tugen migrant workers one or two Sundays a month, in a spacious vacant plot outside our only gate.

As non-Gĩkũyũs, the Tugen lived outside the fenced-in village.

Teachers forbade us to watch those dances; they appointed our fellow pupils to spy on us and report on Monday morning assembly. Besides the duty master caning untidy students and latecomers on their bottoms or palms in front of the assembly, he caned pupils who had committed sins over the weekend. Sins included missing Sunday school or adult service or getting caught watching those sinful dances.

Whatever the punishment, I took my chances and watched the devil's workshops. The ones on Sunday afternoons after payday, or Christmas Day, were the best because dancers from neighboring farms joined the performances.

If the spies hung around close by, I found a way to enjoy the dances, no matter how briefly. I volunteered to draw water from the hydrant, located fifty feet past the main gate and the dancers. I made several stops and watched. When I got to the hydrant, I opened the spigot to a trickle so I could watch before my container filled. On such days, to Mami's surprise, I made more trips to the hydrant than usual.

But I could not enjoy it much because acting disinterested stressed me, worrying a spy might catch me and call me on it.

To help out, boys had formed a network that kept track of the spies' movements. Word spread if they went to Njeki's or their parents sent them to Patel's or anywhere else. I then enjoyed the devil's workshop in the open without worry, especially on celebratory days when other dancers came from different farms.

Men and women, tall and skinny, wore plain or checkered orange or red colorful wrappers across their midriffs and over their shoulders. Many wore tight bangles made of beads on their wrists. Some men wore clips of beaded earrings and thin bead bandanas around their heads, while the women wore dangling earrings and adorned their necks with large multi-colored beaded garlands.

The group sang and performed in an arc of about twenty dancers and singers—women on one side and men on the other—and the spectators at the periphery.

A man and a woman led the singing while the group sang alternate lines. Sometimes, the two leaders sang the chorus, while the women danced and ululated during the highlights, or the men synchronized bass humming sounds.

In another style, the dancers maintained the same formation, with women on one side and men on the other. Women crossed the center and tapped their partner of choice. Men outnumbered women, but the dancers rotated until every person danced with a partner.

One of the best routines was where dancers made a similar formation. The women cascaded their bodies from their heads to their haunches and rolled back up, garlands in motion like a wave while they sang. The men punctuated the women's dance with their jumping routines as if in a chorus.

Sometimes, I got so absorbed I forgot myself. When I realized my folly and snapped back to reality, I looked around for the spies. More times than not, I did not spot them.

Even without knowing the Tugen lyrics, I shut my eyes to let the music flow in. The lovely melodies reached the deepest recesses of my heart and touched my emotional center, and I experienced a euphoric love of music for the first time. I enjoyed a bonanza and socialized with my fellow spectators during the spy-less school holidays.

Until I turned eighteen, Tugen men and women were the only people I saw dancing, although I had heard farmworkers at Stein's farm danced on Sunday afternoons.

Otherwise, Gĩkũyũ people had undergone much turmoil and destabilization since the British landed on their borders. The ones who lived and worked on farms wore no jewelry and practiced no entertainment or art form. Elongated earlobes—signs that a person had previously worn ornaments—remained the only evidence of their old ways, when hard work and no play were not the norm.

Sometimes, Mami told us stories of her younger days when the Gĩkũyũ people danced ndumo, mũchũng'wa, mũthĩrĩgũ, and others. She showed us how women danced ndumo. Bent forward, knees folded as she dipped her body while her shoulder-width hands, palms open, scooped the air. She synchronized the up-and-back-and-forth movements, turning left-center-right, with intermittent, deep, guttural sounds. But a minute of a one-woman show in her sitting room tickled nothing within me. It only called for a crack of a smile and an amused glance at my mother.

Nowadays, many sections of Kenyan communities have revived their traditional dances and songs. Ironically, Christian songs and performances now dominate the arena.

Chapter 64

THE DIRTY WAR

Tindaress River divided Kamunge's farm into two parcels. We lived on the southern piece while a sprawl of virgin savanna dominated the northern side, with Kamunge's colonial house nestled at the foot of Jumatatu Mountain to the east.

My half-brother Waigwa and his family were still living with us after their return from Kikuyuland. For months, Kamunge had not allocated them a plot to set up their homestead.

While they waited, Kamunge's workers started building houses on the vacant land across the river to the north. The circular cottages measured about 450 square feet, built of stone blocks and reed roofs.

Rumors swirled through the villagers that Kamunge wanted his employees to live in better houses. Because he, as usual, gave instructions at the last minute, nobody could tell his intentions. We received our news through rumors sprinkled with morsels of truth. Many times, though, the morsels turned into truths.

After building about ten cottages, the construction stopped. People claimed the project became time-consuming or too expensive, an argument that made little sense. The materials came from the farm, including the stone blocks that the farm's three part-time stonecutters chiseled at the quarry.

Other rumors said Kamunge was tired of owning the farm. They said he planned to split it, transfer the northern piece to his son, Kang'oro, and sell the southern side where we lived in the fenced village.

Meanwhile, workers resumed building. But now they built with sticks, mud, and thatch.

Except for the goat herders, children like me had never gone across the river. But we eavesdropped on adults' conversations and complaints or pieced things together from what Mami told us.

We heard about the instructions adults received from Kamunge, the sad letters from relatives in Kikuyuland, and the restrictions they had to abide by. But we all remained ignorant of the state of the war or the discomfort that the Mau Mau freedom fighters, their supporters, and the civil society had caused the colonizers.

As we learned later, the colonial government's bombings had devastated the Mau Mau. But England had become weary of the "dirty war," British citizens running around, flexing their muscles on Kenyan native freedom fighters, who, despite using inferior weapons—and being captured and dying in great numbers—hung on like ticks on an animal's back.

Things had been different two generations earlier when the British descended on Kenya. The invaders had then rained terror on the natives with impunity. Without the press to document the atrocities, their crimes against humanity went unreported—besides the invaders' personal diaries—save for the natives' complaints, with no listeners but the wind.

Over the years, the Colonial Office in England had relied on the invaders' diaries, months-old skewed reports, or occasional personal letters sent to relatives and friends in England to tell the story of what was happening on the ground.

But things had changed by the late 1950s in Kenya; the foreign press had appeared on the scene. The colonizers' brutality toward the natives during the Mau Mau revolt had not only to contend with a nosy and noisy press (the journalists who dug deeper instead of listening to the colonizers' lies or embellished accounts) and the civil society in England but also with the British Parliament. Too many "eyes" stared at the colonizers' mischief and criminality.

Meanwhile, other colonized countries in Africa also strived to gain their independence. And in the United States, advocacy against atrocious Jim Crow laws and the fight for civil rights had gathered momentum.

Unknown to the villagers, because of these external pressures and internal agitation, the colonial government had loosened its grip on Kenya. The country had become a liability, more trouble than it was worth. But many British landowners still hung on; they had too much vested in the country. They may have expected the English do-gooders who hovered above such matters to exhaust themselves.

But Kamunge preferred to make changes when he could predict which way the political wind would blow—during the British rule and in his favor.

Chapter 65

THE WHITE CARD

Kamunge finished the houses he required, per the unwritten rule that he would build one house per employee. He allocated one concrete cottage each to Waigwa and the other families. He left it to them to partition the inside. The recipients erected timber walls or hung cloth sheets around beds for privacy. The men started building whatever other cottages their families needed.

While they built, this time with mud and thatch, rumors said Kamunge might have needed only those families to work for him. The entire village became restless, worried about their fate.

People stayed alert for any scraps of news, especially when Kamunge categorized employees into three groups. The first group of concrete houses was now building and moving. He assigned the second group, which included Njaga, the village drunk, to remain in our current fenced village.

He asked the final and the smallest group to reapply for jobs or leave the farm.

At least he did not fire them, people said in subdued, unsure tones.

Things had changed since the time of European settlements. Back then, the new landowners were desperate for workers. To help them, the colonial government levied taxes to force men, who had always worked for themselves, to leave their homelands in search of work.

But in the late 1950s, landowners could afford to choose.

Unfamiliar with references, fired workers wondered how potential employers knew of past trespasses, laziness, stubbornness, and other infractions. Because of this, farmworkers believed all Europeans in Kenya knew one another.

However, references were not the primary concern of most Africans. They contended that Europeans did not apply the same standards to their own. A white person who came off the boat, criminal or otherwise, could start life afresh. Such a person found a job waiting or found one soon after. Retired military personnel received land and seed money to start them off.

For the Europeans to get whatever they needed, their "white card" surpassed qualifications, referrals, or networking.

But if an African was convicted of a misdemeanor because of curfew or trespassing, he got fined. With no ability to pay the fine, he served a jail term.

Besides the court records, his employer recorded the crime. At worst, the man got fired. With a criminal record, he had a minimal chance of getting another job. Consequently, he farmed out his family to relatives on the farm or elsewhere. Homeless, he left in search of a job that needed little scrutiny. People never called it homelessness; they instead labeled the man a drifter or a loser, especially because, without an employer to issue current travel papers, the man had to watch his movements.

On Europeans knowing each other, farmworkers did not know how close they came to the truth. I confirmed it decades later when I read "I Dreamed of Africa," where author Kuki Gallmann, who owned a farm in Nanyuki, Kenya, details how she and other Europeans kept in touch.

They used a radio-call phone network that connected European farmers' households. The network authority assigned an ID number to every European farm. Even farm owners who had never met each other knew of one another by phone number, name, and voice. They kept in touch on business and personal matters, on the Kenyan local news, and with those from England. And, of course, friendships flourished.

This ability to communicate for business and with friends affected Kenya in ways the British colonizers may not have envisioned or intended.

During the sixty-plus years they occupied the country, with their needs met, they did minimal development, except the institutions like hospitals that catered to them or the railway line to haul exports from inland to Mombasa for shipment to England and elsewhere.

In towns and surrounding areas, landowners constructed only narrow tarmacked roads, the width of one car, to get to their residences. In rural areas, Europeans rode on horses and traveled in Range Rovers, Land Rovers, or other vehicles suitable for rugged or hilly untamed landscapes, as well as private planes.

As a result, the colonizers remained unmotivated to improve roads or other communication.

Meanwhile, dispersed away from their former homelands, natives trekked on pathways for miles. They walked or rode on rickety buses—hours apart—that traveled on narrow, unkempt dirt roads. They often took an entire day or days to arrive at their destinations. Africans also lacked an independent method to communicate. Their occasional mail or telegrams had to go through their employers.

*

I learned of our precarious state a year before workers started building the concrete houses when Kamunge fired a man and instructed his tractor driver to haul the man, his family, and their meager belongings away on a tractor-trailer. The driver dumped them on the public Nakuru-Solai dirt road, where only one daily bus left early in the morning. People claimed the family spent the night by the roadside. I never learned what happened to them.

At twelve and a half years old, I felt afraid when families started moving to the new village while my family remained in the old one. Kamunge had not assigned our family to any group. I feared he might fire Baba, eject my family from the farm, and drop us by the roadside. My father then looked so old that, even with no criminal record, I doubted any landowner would employ him.

I remained in occasional gnawing panic until my family learned of its fate.

Chapter 66

END OF AN ERA

My worry that my family could end up by the roadside turned out baseless. From the beginning, unknown to us children, Kamunge had put Baba in the first group. But our family had to wait until the sorting ended because, during the transition, Kamunge needed to consult with my father about which employees were best suited for which farm.

When my family finally moved to our second low-security village in mid-1959, we settled in a homestead of all-mud houses, one built by Kamunge's workers (Kamunge provided one cottage per permanent employee) and the rest built by Baba with the help of other village men. Mami and her friends helped with the building, too. They joined young men during the wall muddying—Baba did not do such work. They also cut and carried bales of grass and did the thatching.

Like in our earlier homesteads, Baba's thingira faced north, but Mami's nyũmba faced west. The builders who eyeballed the building plot and used a sisal string to map the plan lacked experience dealing with a pear-shaped plot. We ended up with an elongated courtyard with a big backyard garden behind Mami's nyũmba.

It disappointed me that Kamunge did not offer my father one of the stone-block houses. But perhaps that was not suitable for him and Mami. In those houses, men shared the houses with their wives. My parents preferred a traditional setup—Baba in his thingira and Mami in her nyūmba. Because of children, wives always occupied the compound's biggest, most imposing house. Would Baba have yielded the stone house, the main house, to Mami and instead lived in a mud one? I don't know.

Those "better" stone houses fronted Kamunge's private road that ran for about a mile to the dirt public road, which he, unlike most landowners, had never tarmacked. When his family, friends, and farm equipment driver drove by, they left clouds of dust in their wake, which settled on the sides of the road, and, in time, the wind spread it to nearby houses and backyard vegetable gardens.

And to leave the village, people at the back, and those from Stein's farm, walked on footpaths that wove through the village past the stone houses. Baba did not like that; he craved privacy. Kamunge likely offered him a stone house, and he refused.

Like in our previous village, we ended up at the back of the village, next to a chain-link fence that hugged the village on two sides with a gateless pedestrian entrance near our homestead. To prevent people who entered the village from the back from crossing our courtyard, Baba erected a fence between our homestead and the village. We ended up with our main entrance facing the back of our neighbor's house; they had also erected their own fence. We had now to walk between their house and fence.

We children felt cut off from the village because other children never came to play in our courtyard; they preferred to play in open areas. Sometimes, we skipped our chores and went out to seek playmates. Mami called the slackers even when they were a football field away. She even shouted out our skipped chores, from babysitting to washing dishes. Her behavior shamed me to silence as I rushed home so she would shut up.

About sixty feet behind our homestead's back fence was another dirt road, wide enough for an occasional tractor-trailer, plow, or Kamunge's Land Rover. The road started from the pen where cows spent their nights, then stretched along scrubland before it weaved through lush virgin land to end by a coffee plantation.

By the end of the year, Kamunge split the farm into two parcels along the Tindaress River. He then sold the southern farm. Whoever bought it sold it several years later to Mr. Patel of the Patel General Store, whose family still owns it.

Over the next fifteen years, as European landowners sold their farms, Mr. Patel and his sons bought several more farms in Solai and elsewhere and other businesses. The family (like others with a similar background) is now equivalent to a conglomerate that rubs shoulders with the country's politically connected and wealthy.

The family still owns the old general store, but they have now added accessories like a gas station, the only one for miles.

About Kamunge's northern parcel—where we now lived—gossip claimed he had transferred it to his son, Kang'oro. Another rumor surfaced that the colonial government had bought and awarded the farm to a World War II veteran.

In 1959, except for Kamunge's farm, World War I retired British military majors owned all the farms in the surrounding area.

That did not matter to villagers. After all, we came with the farm. Adults said one white man was no better or worse than the next. Others quipped, "What's new?"

Chapter 67

LIFE CHANGER

We moved to our second low-security village six months after I entered grade three. There were So many changes. Our parents had to go to their jobs, build new houses, move, farms changing hands, rumors on politics, and we children had to deal with our own school changes.

Although I listened to rumors, curious to know what was going on, I did not dwell on what happened outside our homestead. I focused only on the changes that affected my family and me directly.

For starters, my siblings and I now had to walk through our new village, jump on jagged stones to cross Tindaress River, and circumvent our former fortified village. This added an extra half a mile to get to school. But it mattered little to me. Having advanced to grade three, I focused on writing in ink, learning English, and attending school all day.

What got to me were the home changes.

Before Baba built enough houses for our now bigger family, my two sisters, two younger brothers, Mami, the baby, and I all slept crowded in Mami's house. My other brothers shared the much smaller one-room thingira with Baba.

Our two previous moves back-to-back had not disturbed me much. Besides being much younger, at only six years and five months old, my parents insulated me from feeling the effect of the chaos that surrounded our move, especially because they kept the same schedule. But now, at almost double that age, I had heard and seen enough onerous restrictions and changes that Kamunge had subjected to my family and others.

By then, I had no illusion about my parents and other adults' powerlessness. Although I looked up to them outside their homes, they were just like us children. They followed orders and remained in the dark about changes that affected their lives and those of their families.

At that age, a few months before I turned thirteen, my two life goals became clear.

My first goal sprouted from deep within me after the school bug bit me, and I offered to give up meat if my father registered me in school. I had wondered whether he lacked the money to pay for my school fees and supplies. I then promised myself that when I grew up, I would earn my own money so I did not have to kowtow to people begging for it.

My second goal came about because Kamunge kicked my parents around like football without their say-so. I had watched them build new houses three separate times amid commotion and complaints. Property ownership, therefore, became the second life quest to get branded into my psyche. When I grow up, I vowed, I would buy a house where nobody would order me to move.

Those two intentions—money and home—and later the escape from the life-sapping manual labor became my guiding star and more than motivated me to stick with school no matter what.

*

About three months later, when my family settled enough and ceased complaining about having to build houses yet again, good news fell upon us. As a parting gift to Baba for over thirty years of loyal service, Kamunge offered him twenty-five acres, almost a third of which grew robust coffee bushes. The wide dirt road behind our homestead ended at an area called Gĩtũra, part of the neighboring Steins farm, with twenty-five acres to the right.

Because Jumatatu Mountain's shadow enveloped the land in the early mornings, the land enjoyed a temperate climate and produced moist coffee the size of fruit cherries. My siblings and I, many times, had picked coffee cherries for pay on that very land. Those coffee cherries filled our containers faster than the ones grown just a mile away. Sometimes I could not resist sucking on the juicy sweet cherries.

Mami and we children could not contain ourselves when we heard the life-changing news. We all became giddy with anticipation.

"My mother said your family will have their own land," a girl told me two days later.

"Maybe," I said.

Baba had mentioned the offer to Mami in passing, but they had not discussed it yet. It never occurred to us to wait until our parents talked or wonder how Baba, the ultimate authority in our family, took the great news and how he would plan to go about it.

All we knew and banked on was that Baba had only two words to tell Kamunge if he had not done so already.

"Thank you."

I expected my father to build a spacious concrete stone house with several bedrooms and a veranda that hugged the entire front, where he and Mami could sit and savor tea. People said Kamunge's house had many rooms and his family and friends drank tea on their veranda.

I smiled when I tried to imagine the furniture Baba would buy. None came to mind because I had not seen dining chairs or couches yet. The only furniture I had seen were hospital chairs, which I had seen three years prior, and the folding, homemade wooden chair we owned.

But I knew my father would replace the little benches and stools we sat on with beautiful, cushy white-people-type furniture, and he would buy us new clothes and a second school uniform for each of us. We would even wear shoes!

The thought alone made my heart swell with pride and my body fill with a sense of well-being.

With our money troubles gone, without a doubt, my family would belong to a rich class, not like the British colonizers' class, who owned miles and miles of farmland and vehicles, with peasants at their beck-and-call, but a rich class, nonetheless.

And that sounded wonderful to me.

End of Book 2

Afterword

I wrote *The British vs Kenya's Mau Mau* to record life events that would otherwise go unrecorded and, in the process, enlighten, entertain, and inspire.

I hope you learned something new or enjoyed a chuckle now and then. Or perhaps you got inspired to share your own story with your family, friends, or the world in whatever form you choose—verbal, diary, memoir, or voice-recorded.

Until the next book, thank you for spending your precious time with my words.

Wanjirũ Warama
Wanjirũwarama.com

Acknowledgments

I believe this book may be the most important in THE COLONIZED series. But it might not have been so without the support of the following people, who I thank sincerely:

Mary Thorne Kelley, my cheerleader and proofreader, has been with me from the beginning of my writing journey. After reading the advance copy of this book, she emailed me and said, "It's a fine book; it should be on history bookshelves in libraries, & should be required reading at least in college history classes."

My Editor, Isabella Furth, with her keen eye and expertise, this book would not be the same without her.

My family, whose lives I have paraded in the book at will, and especially Simon Ndurumo Warama, my late brother, for clarifying and updating me on our family's peaks and valleys (he never lived long enough to see the book in print), my half-sister, Nancy Wairimũ Warama Mũriũki (Wairimũ-big), for clarifying my father's rocky relationship with his children; my nephew Duncan Karũthũ Machira and his daughter Nduta for providing the cover image, and also the authors whose books I used for references.

And thanks to you for spending time with my words. Words are meaningless if no one reads or hears them.

Wanjirũ Warama
Wanjirũwarama.com

Reference Books

I read many books that helped me clarify and widen my knowledge of historical facts for the period the book covers. Below are some of the names of the authors and the titles of their books:

Kuki Gallmann: I Dreamed of Africa

Maina wa Kĩnyattĩ: *Agĩkũyũ: 1890–1965, Waiyaki-Kenyatta-Kĩmaathi*

Maina wa Kĩnyattĩ: History of Resistance in Kenya 1884–2002

David Anderson: *The History of the Hanged, The Dirty War in Kenya and the End of Empire*

Ngũgĩ wa Thiong'o: *Weep no Child*

Ngũgĩ wa Thiong'o: A Grain of Wheat

Dennis Holman: THE HISTORY OF THE MAN THEY CALLED…BWANA DRUM

Jomo Kenyatta: *Facing Mt. Kenya*

Caroline Elkins: *Imperial Reckoning: The Untold Story of Britain's Gulag in Kenya*

Bildad Kaggia: *Roots of Freedom 1921-1963*

Wangari Maathai: *Unbowed*

Gakaara wa Wanjaũ: *Mwandĩki wa Mau Mau Ithaamĩrio-ini* [a detention diary from 1952–1960]

Mathew Njoroge Kabetũ: *Kĩrĩra kĩa Ũgĩkũyũ*

Peter Godwin: Mukiwa, *A White Boy in Africa*